ATTRACTING
BIRDS
to your
GARDEN
IN SOUTHERN AFRICA

ATTRACTING BIRDS *to your* GARDEN

IN SOUTHERN AFRICA

STRUIK

PHOTOGRAPHIC CREDITS

L.Hes – 12 (left, right), 13 (top), 14 (left), 15 (left), 17 (left, top right), 18, 19 (right), 21 (left), 24 (right), 27, 28 (top, bot. right), 29 (centre, right) 30, 31, 32, 33, 34, 35 (top), 36 (left), 37, 39, 40 (top, right), 41 (top right), 42 (top left), 47 (bot. right), 51 (right), 53, 54, 55 (right), 56 (top left), 57, 63 (right), 65, 67, 69, 72 (left, right), 76 (right), 82 (right), 83 (left), 84 (top), 85 (left), 93 (bot. right), 94 (right), 97 (right), 98 (top right), 99 (right), 100 (bot. right), 102 (left), 103 (top left, bot. right), 106 (top right), 107 (left), 110 (bot. right), 114 (left), 115 (bot. left, right), 119 (left, bot. right), 122 (bot. right), 125 (right), 126 (right), 129 (bot. right), 130 (top right), 132 (left), 134 (bot. right), 135 (top right), 137, 139 (bot. right), 140 (left), 142 (bot. right), 143 (right), 145 (right), 146 (right), 149 (right), 154 (bot. right), 164 (right), 166 (right), 167 (right), 169, 171 (right), 174 (right), 175 (top right), 176 (right), 180 (right), 181, 182 (right), 184 (top right), 187 (bot. right) • ABPL/N.J.Dennis – 10, 45 (bot.), 70, 86 (left), 106 (left), 109 (left, top right), 130 (left), 139 (left), 142 (left), 161 (left), 178 (left), 183 (left) • ABPL/B.Ryan – 29 (top left), 91 (left), 104 (bot. right), 135 (left), 141 (left), 151 (left) • ABPL/J.van Jaarsveld – 35 (right), 172 (right), 188 (left) • ABPL/C.Haagner – 55 (top left), 91 (right), 92 (top right), 110 (top right), 124 (left), 125 (left), 127 (bot. right), 134 (top right), 136 (left), 138 (right), 140 (top right), 158 (left) • ABPL/P.Donaldson – 95 (right) • ABPL/H.von Horsten – 99 (left), 107 (top right), 173 (left) • ABPL/A.Bannister – 156 (left) • ABPL/R.de la Harpe – 164 (left) • ABPL/M.P.Kahl – 178 (right) • ABPL/A.Frankental – title page (left) • L.von Horsten – 11, 12 (top), 45 (bot. right), 48/49, 50 (top), 51 (bot. left), 52 (bot. left), 62 (left), 103 (bot. left), 115 (top left), 123 (left), 134 (left), 138 (left), 143 (left), 149 (left), 155 (left), 157 (right), 158 (right), 163 (left), 165 (top right), 173 (right) • H.von Horsten – contents page, 9 (bot.), 50 (left), 58 (right), 59 (bot.), 82 (left), 87 (top left), 88 (top), 89, 93 (left), 112 (top right), 116 (left), 123 (top right), 152 (right), 166 (left), 167 (left), 179 (left), 180 (left) • T.Carew/Photo Access – 13 (bot.), 78 (left), 84 (bot.), 106 (bot. right), 175 (left) • HPH Photography/Photo Access – 14 (right), 26, 52 (right), 80, 90 (bot. right), 95 (left), 101 (bot.), 122 (top right), 131 (left), 144 (right), 147 (right), 154 (left), 159 (bot. right) • J.Laurie/Photo Access – 45 (top right) • J.J.Brooks/Photo Access – 52 (top left), 176 (left), 111 (right), 122 (left), 133 (right), 152 (left) • V.Loxton/Photo Access – 61, 62 (top) • J&B Photographers/Photo Access – 93 (top right) • P.Steyn/Photo Access – 100 (top right), 101 (top right), 147 (left), 153 (right), 168 (right) • L.Hes/Photo Access – 114 (top right) • G.P.L.du Plessis/Photo Access – 127 (top right) • D.Steele/Photo Access – 123 (bot. right), 139 (top right), 163 (right) • N.J.Dennis – half-title page, 15 (right), 19 (left), 21 (right), 24 (right), 28 (left, top right), 38, 40 (left), 41 (left), 42 (top left), 47 (top right), 60, 81, 82 (top), 86 (top), 88 (bot.), 92 (left), 98 (right), 100 (left), 110 (left), 121 (left), 127 (left), 153 (left), 157 (left), 165 (left), 182 (left), back cover (bot. left) • SIL/L.Hoffman – 8 (left), 17 (bot. right), 25 (left), 43 (top right), 47 (top right), 71, 72 (top), 73 (right), 77 (left, bot. right, 2nd from top right), 78 (top left), 92 (bot.), 131 (bot. right), 132 (bot. right), 140 (bot. right) • SIL/R.Bock – 36 (left) • SIL/P.Pickford – 56 (bot. left), 77 (top), 90 (top right), 94 (left), 102 (right), 130 (bot. right) • SIL/A.Johnson – 75 (left), 79 (bot. left) • M.Alexander – 20 (left), 46 (right), 58 (left), 103 (top right), 156 (right) • S.Brandt – 9 (top), 20 (right), 25 (bot. left), 46 (centre left, bot. left), 66 (right), 78 (bot.), 121 (right), 124 (right), 136 (right), 184 (bot. left) • K.Pienaar – 25 (bot. right), 68 (centre), 188 (right), 189 (right) • J.Szymanowski – 42 (right), 66 (left), 107 (bot. right), 117 (bot. right) • Albany Museum – 44 (bot.) • C.Paterson-Jones – 44 (top), 45 (top left), 97 (left), 98 (left), 109 (bot. right), 120 (left), 133 (top right), 135 (bot. right), 170 (right) • R.de la Harpe – 45 (centre right) • Z.Wahl – 46 (top left), 47 (left), 51 (top left), 74 (right), 108 (right), 55 (right), 85 (right), 104 (top right), 105 (top right), 120 (right), 133 (top), 148 (top right), 150 (right) • R.Trendler – 50 (left), imprint page • Percy FitzPatrick Institute of African Ornithology – 59 (top), 105 (bot. right), 116 (right), 151 (right), 155 (right), 160 (left, bot. right), 168 (right) • W.Mangold/World of Birds – 8 (top), 62 (right), 79 (right), 83 (bot.), 105 (right), 128 (right), 90 (right), 96 (right), 104 (right), 132 (top right), 165 (bot. right) • K.Zari Roberts – 63 (left), 118 (top right) • Landmarks/Matthews – 68 (left) • P.van Wyk – 83 (bot. right), 112 (bot. right) • S.Adey – 87 (right) • P.Steyn – 96 (left), 111 (left), 117 (top right), 118 (bot. right), 131 (top right), 141 (right), 145 (left), 160 (top right), 174 (left) • G.Cubitt – 101 (bot. right) • Natal Parks Board – 108 (left) • Natal Parks Board/R.de la Harpe – 179 (right), 190 • Natal Parks Board/P.Craig-Cooper – 183 (right) • R.Johannesson – 119 (top right) • J.van Jaarsveld – 128 (left) • H.G.Robertson/S.A.M. – 74 (right), 76 (right), 113 (top right), 114 (left), 128 (left), 129 (top right), 148 (top right), 161 (right) • A.Weaving – 128 (left), 129 (left), 154 (top right) • R.Wright – 142 (right) • C.Urquhart – 148 (top right) • R.Bloomfield – 150 (left), 162 (right) • N.Larson – 73 (left), 77 (2nd from bot. right), 78 (top right), 159 (top right) • N.Myburgh – 170 (left), 172 (right) • K.Young – 175 (bot. right) • N.Brickell – 177 (left), 185 (left), 187 (left), title page (right) • C.Velasquez – 113 (left) • P.Craig-Cooper – 184 (left), 185 (left), 186, 187 (left), 189 (left), 144 (left), 146 (left), 159 (left), 162 (left), 171 (left), 177 (right) • W.R.Tarboton – 126 (left) • Cape Bird Club – 87 (bot. right) • Deciduous Fruit Board – 75 (right) • N.Gardiner – 79 (top left) • M.van Aardt – 43 (bot. right) • T.Helm – 113 (left).

Illustrations on pages 22 and 23 by Dave Snook; illustration on page 117 (left) by K.Newman © The Trustees of the John Voelcker Bird Book Fund.

Struik Publishers (Pty) Ltd
(a member of the Struik Publishing Group (Pty) Ltd)
Cornelis Struik House, 80 McKenzie Street
Cape Town 8001

Reg. no.: 54/00965/07

First published in 1994
Second impression 1995
Third impression 1995

Text © Roy Trendler and Lex Hes 1994
Photographs © individual photographers (see left) 1994
Illustrations © Struik Publishers 1994

Editor and co-ordinator: Pippa Parker
Designer: Alix Gracie; Assistant: Rob House
Picture editor: Jackie Murray
Editorial assistants: Ann Stapleton and Tracey Hawthorne
Illustrator: Clarence Clark
Indexer: Sandie Vahl
Consultant: P.A.R. Hockey
Typesetting: Struik DTP

Reproduction: Hirt & Carter (Pty) Ltd, Cape Town
Printing and binding: Tien Wah Press (Pte) Ltd, Singapore

All rights reserved. No part of this publication may be reproduced, stored in a retrieval system or transmitted in any form or by any means, electronic, mechanical, photocopying, recording or otherwise, without the prior written permission of the copyright owners.

ISBN 1 86825 515 8

Front Cover: (clockwise from top left) *Paradise Flycatcher, Dusky Flycatcher, Black Sunbird, Lesser Doublecollared Sunbird*; (centre) *Spottedbacked Weaver.*
Back Cover: (clockwise from top left) *Crane Flower; Plumcoloured Starling, Hoopoe, Cape Weaver, Grey Heron, Red Bishop*; (centre) *Malachite Kingfisher*
Above: *Masked Weaver*
Half Title Page: *Red Bishop*
Title Page: (left) *Glossy Starling*; (right) *Natal Robin*
Contents Page: *Dusky Flycatcher*

Foreword

In a world where the natural environment is being reduced and exploited at such an alarming rate, city gardens and parks have come to represent valuable habitats for birds. In southern Africa, where the effects of environmental degradation are sometimes further compounded by droughts, private gardens have become even more important in supporting birds and other life. Here, gardens represent little sanctuaries which, with their areas of woodland, scrub and water, collectively offer a variety of habitats for birds. And yet, for all this, few of us have any real knowledge of the fascinating little creatures to which we play host.

It is therefore especially heartwarming that two such knowledgeable and accomplished conservationists have taken the initiative to bring gardeners this comprehensive body of information on attracting birds to the garden. Although there are many local gardening books and a number of excellent bird books available, this is the first publication to combine these subjects in a way that enables all gardeners – be they beginners or experts, urban or rural dwellers – to plan their gardens for birds and, through this, to gain a greater understanding of them while at the same time playing an active role in environmental conservation.

There is no doubt in my mind that all people need to be educated in nature and environmental conservation in order for this planet and its inhabitants to survive. With their informative text, many magnificent photographs and explanatory illustrations, Roy Trendler and Lex Hes have made a most worthy contribution in meeting this need. By following the practical advice and the many exciting and imaginative ideas offered in this book, both the conservation-minded layman and the gardening expert really can make a difference. Conservation, after all, begins right in our own backyards.

KEITH KIRSTEN

Acknowledgments

I would like to thank my wife, Karen, and son, Jason, for their patience and understanding while I was bent over the keyboard for what seemed to be years. I am also grateful to my partner, Peter Mullins, who never questioned the time and effort spent on the book. I am indebted to all the conservationists that I have come to know over the years and who have, through their enthusiasm and imparting of knowledge, contributed to the contents of this book. The nurserymen of South Africa who have shown a willingness to promote the use of indigenous plants and have supported the concepts of 'bird gardening' have motivated me to put pen to paper.

A very special thanks has to go to Pippa Parker of Struik who went far beyond the call of duty and shaped the contents of the book through intense research and commitment. Also, many thanks to Jackie Murray who researched and edited photographs, and to Alix Gracie who designed the book under considerable pressure. Grateful thanks to Phil Hockey for consulting on the 'Directory of Garden Birds'. Last, but not least, to Lex Hes, who invited me to write without ever having met me: your honesty, support and friendship are greatly appreciated.

Roy Trendler

Many people contributed to this book. First, grateful thanks to David and Janet Cruse for their all-round help. The hospitality shown by birding people all around the country was overwhelming, and I would especially like to thank the following individuals for allowing me to intrude on their lives and for sharing their birds and gardens with me: Antonio D'Almeida and Jonathan Selzan, Michael and Rita Meyer, Sheila and Gordon Cunningham and Jill and Bo Attwell, Biddy and Sandy Lawther, Jo and the late Bill Onderstall, Guy and Jacky Arkell, Julie Strehl and Dorothy and Hugh Hall, Denise and Brian Gould, Lesley and Athol Marchant, Sally and David Johnson and Rudolf Schmidt.

I am indebted to Ivor Ginsberg and John Wileman of Pro Warehouse in Johannesburg and to Jonty Peters and David Cruse. Grateful thanks also to Carol Bridgeford and Helen Cartwright of Bushwillow, Nigel Fernsby of Hennops Bird Creations, Nico Myburgh, Alete Whyte, Raymond Bezuidenhout for his help, Colin and Val Lazenby, Hilary Mauve, Otto Schmidt, Jan Hofmeyr and Peter Steyn and Mick and Joan Melle, Colin Hall, Olga von Freytag-Drabbe, Duncan Butchart, Peter Lawson and my father, Jimmy, who each contributed in some way.

Foto First provided excellent service. Pam Steinbrucker, John McAllister, Michael Pope and Rupert Horley supplied us with bird lists for the Johannesburg area. I would like to thank Roy Trendler for his wonderful enthusiasm and support, and also his wife Karen for her assistance.

To those people I may have overlooked, please forgive me and accept my grateful thanks. Last, but not least, a very big thank you to my wife, Lynn, and children, Tammy and Dale, for putting up with many difficult days on their own.

Lex Hes

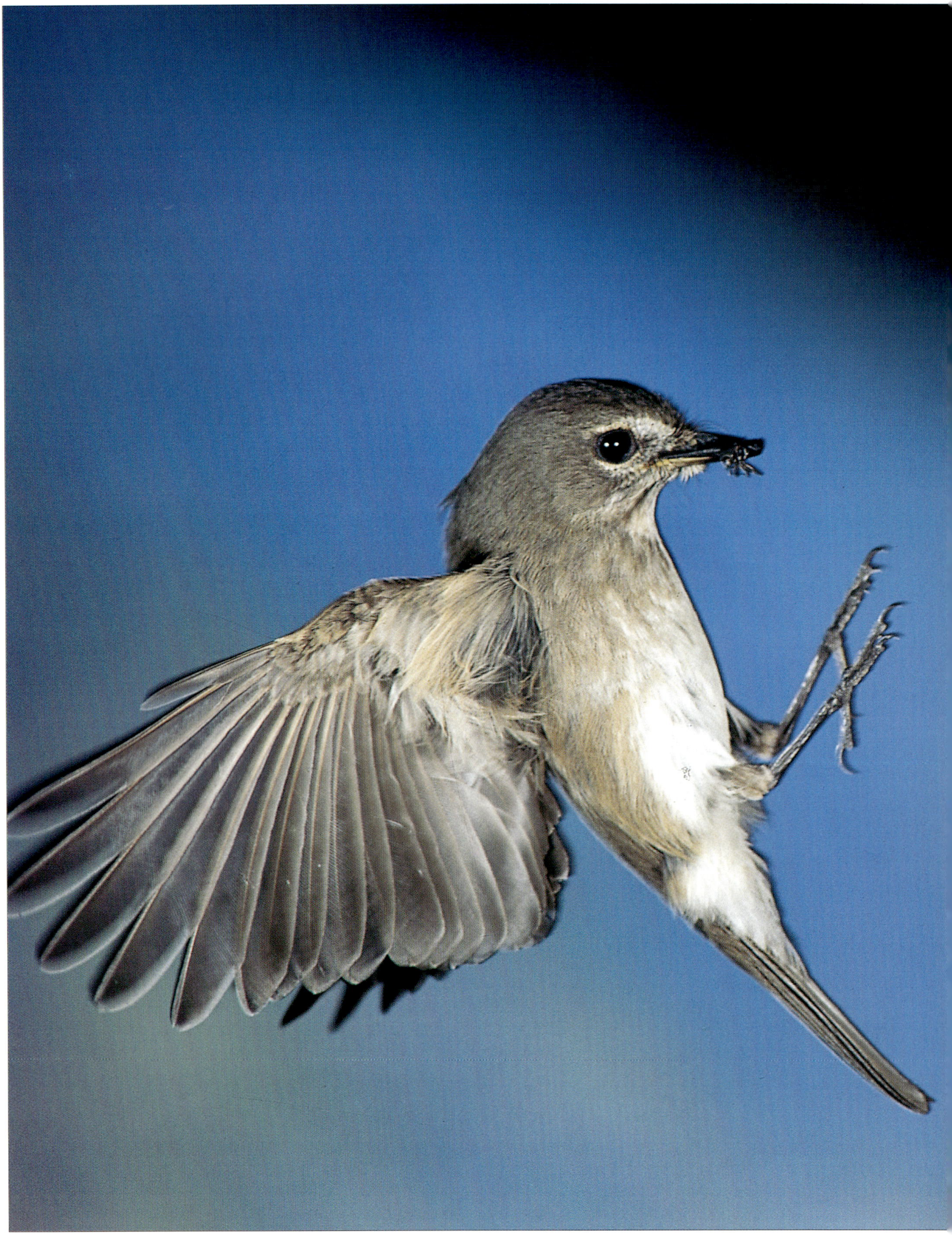

CONTENTS

Introduction 8

1
Planning the Garden 10

2
Feeding and Bird Fare 26

3
Water in the Garden 38

4
Nesting 48

5
Maintaining the Indigenous Garden 60

6
Pest Control 70

7
Birds on Smallholdings 80

8
Directory of Garden Birds 88

Table of Indigenous Plants 192

Useful Addresses 204

Further Reading 205

Index 206

INTRODUCTION

Some people consider gardening to be therapeutic, a view which many modern psychologists would support; and bird-watching is generally regarded as an enjoyable pastime, as long as it does not involve hanging off a cliff to examine some unidentifiable LBJ (little brown job) nesting halfway between heaven and earth. This book attempts to combine all the positive elements of gardening with the most entertaining aspects of bird-watching.

Planning and nurturing a garden in order to make it a place that birds will want to visit adds new purpose to gardening and brings many rewards. Here is an opportunity to carry out some serious birding without the bundu-bashing that is often associated with more avid 'twitching'.

Creating a suitable environment for birds will ensure many hours of pleasure for you and your family, but embodies another very serious concern – that of conservation within the urban and suburban context. The destruction of the countryside to make way for settlement areas has placed enormous pressure on birdlife, and city gardens, parks and open areas have become more and more important in supporting it. The use of indigenous plants within these areas goes a long way towards improving the situation, providing birds with a natural source of food, refuge and protection. It also assists in the preservation of the environment, which becomes increasingly important as our cities stretch forever outwards.

Attracting Birds to your Garden in Southern Africa will serve as a manual to help in the planning or adapting of your garden to best suit birdlife, and the managing of it once you have achieved this. Such a venture may be tackled in moderation, by retaining but elaborating on existing features, or more dramatically, by restructuring the entire area to create a 'bird garden'.

Contained in the book are discussions on feeding birds, both naturally and artificially, providing natural and artificial nesting sites and creating water features, all of this aimed at capturing the interest of birds and ensuring that they become regular visitors, even residents in your garden. There are guidelines to maintaining and caring for indigenous plants and, at the back of the book, there is an extensive list of indigenous plants (provided in tabular form), selected for their usefulness to birds. A directory of garden birds provides short but informative profiles of 100 bird species, including a guide to providing for each species according to its need for habitat, food and nesting.

The joys of attracting birds into your garden are many; at all times you are the manager and can determine variety and numbers by the extent to which you plan and provide. You may become a fanatic and create a garden wetland boasting numerous bird species or you may merely choose to erect a platform on a window-sill from which to feed Rock Pigeons and doves. Should you decide to follow the guidelines in this book, one thing is sure: you will wake each morning to the sound of birds feeding, bathing, singing and generally welcoming in the new day, and you can safely throw away your alarm clock!

URBAN DEVELOPMENT AND THE NATURAL ENVIRONMENT

Human encroachment on the natural environment is today a fact of life, and we are continually reminded of the destruction of habitat in the name of development. Concrete replaces soil, houses stand in place of natural habitats, and rivers have mostly been converted to concrete channels which either flood or trickle but seldom sustain any life. Where rivers have been left, exotic poplars and Spanish Reed choke the indigenous plantlife.

Even in the countryside, exotic forests have come to replace natural grasslands and indigenous forests. The effects of population growth and expansion on the environment are notable, and it is now urgent that we should begin to acknowledge the problems and address them.

Within the urban context, open areas – which include road reserves, parks, green belts and gardens – constitute as much as 40 per cent of the land. These areas provide an essential link with nature, and have enormous potential in terms of attracting birds by offering them a suitable environment. Our region is fortunate to have one of the most extensive plant collections in the world, but these have been sadly underutilized in city areas, and are still poorly represented in most city gardens. Nurseries are often poorly stocked with indigenous species and must carry some of the blame, but the general public, and gardeners in particular, need to be made aware of the value of indigenous plants and the role that they have to play in preserving our environment.

Upgrading your garden to 'bird readiness' does not mean replanting the entire area with indigenous plants. What it entails is planning your garden to create a variety of bird habitats, and incorporating a few indigenous plants as part of the plan. The addition of two or three native species to a garden dominated by exotics will give a pleasing blend of vegetation, and will certainly make the birds happier.

The majority of plant species mentioned in this book are indigenous and are commercially available; there is nothing more frustrating than rushing into the nursery with your book under your arm, only to face the blank look of a salesman as you reel off the list of plants you must have for a successful bird garden. Refer to the 'Table of Indigenous Plants' at the back of the book for help in selecting plants that fit in with the plan for your garden.

For those of you who think that gardening is 'for the birds', you are quite right! Hopefully, this book will guide you in this challenge and help uncover a world that you thought existed only in the local bird sanctuary or nature reserve. It *is* possible to bring back the many bird species that have been driven away by urbanization, and for people and birds to co-exist in areas to the benefit of both.

Above: *Urban gardens have become very important in supporting birdlife.*
Right: *Birds will become regular visitors to bird-friendly gardens and may even breed there.*

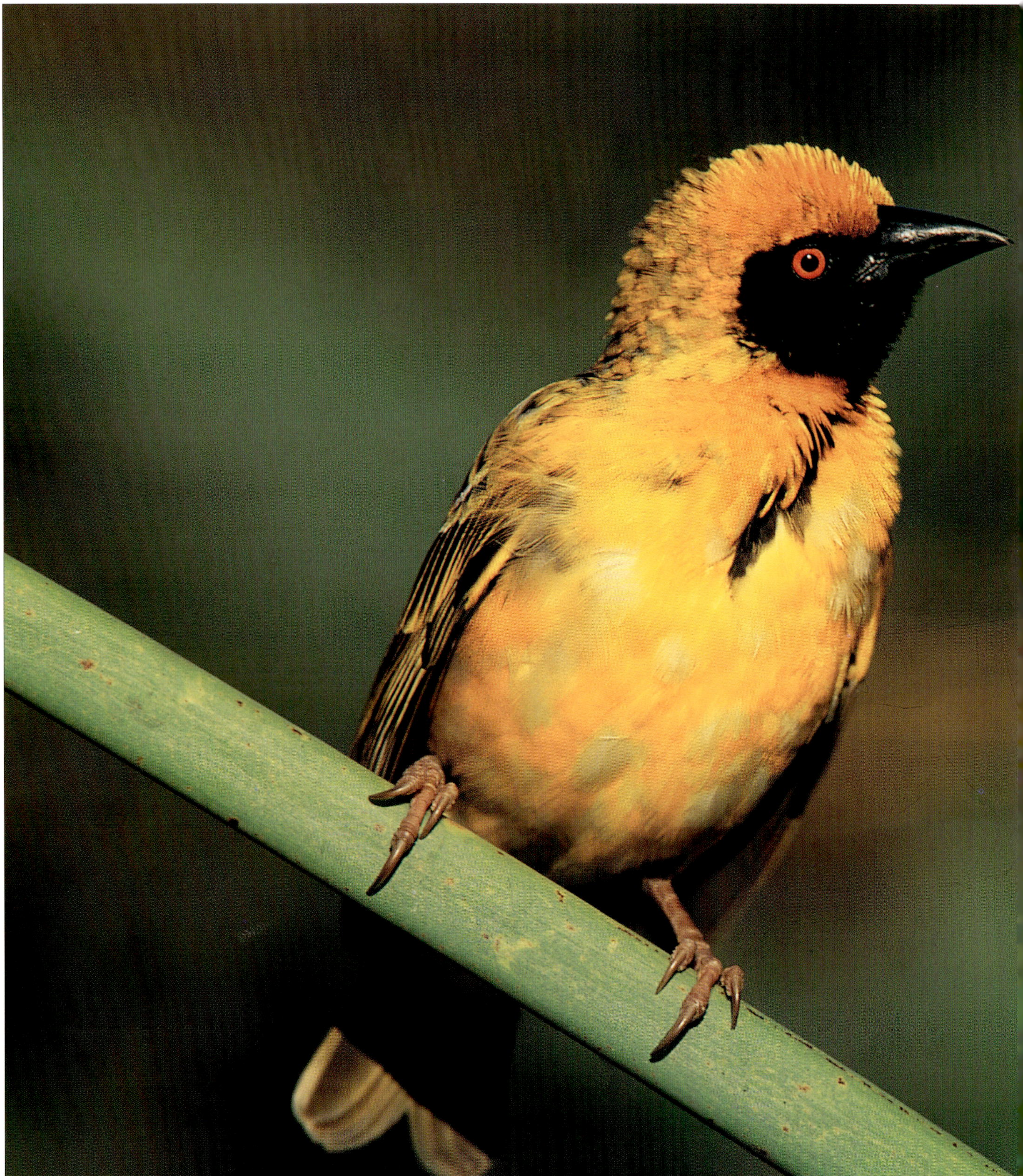

1
Planning the Garden

Creating a bird-friendly garden begins with a garden plan. The design of the garden and the choice of plants play a crucial role in satisfying the basic needs of birds for food, shelter and nesting. The provision of suitable habitat in town and city gardens is imperative for the conservation of indigenous birds within the urban context.

Spottedbacked Weaver (Ploceus cucullatus)

PLANNING THE GARDEN

Planning the Garden

Planning your garden for birds does not mean uprooting the entire area and redesigning it from scratch. However, the greater your effort to plant for birds, the greater your reward will be in attracting diverse bird species.

Before setting about planning your garden, imagine a bird flying up and down the block viewing all the urban properties in search of a new home. An aerial view will probably show each garden to be fairly similar, with a patio, swimming pool and several islands of shrubs and annuals. An Australian Acacia may provide shade in the patio area and there is probably a traditional rose garden. If it is lucky, the bird might be offered an asbestos bird-bath, or food from a plastic seed-feeder. It might have to do battle with many scores of sparrows and doves to be able to view the food on offer, but that has become an occupational hazard. A closer inspection of the garden will reveal the compost heap, generally situated between the tool shed and the neighbour's wall, and this may provide a quick meal if it has not been laced with poisons to control the flies, rats, mice and other unwanted pests.

Is this a basic picture of your garden? Good news: you have a truly representative garden which blends well with the rest of the city. The downside is that your garden is not a bird-friendly one and is merely serving the most resilient of bird species that are prepared to make do in the absence of anything better.

A Southern Boubou, one of many species adapted to urban conditions.

Most of us 'inherit' gardens which are the product of previous occupants, their decisions and choices. As the owner of an already established garden you may be reluctant to start from scratch in planning a bird garden. Clearly, the greater your efforts to meet the needs of the birds, the more birds you will attract. However, even subtle changes – the introduction of a few indigenous plant species, or the creation of a small water feature – can have a dramatic effect on the number of birds that will visit.

Even the inclusion of a simple bird-bath will provide incentive for birds to visit the garden regularly.

PLANNING THE GARDEN

A well-established suburb seen from a bird's perspective shows patches of greenery and dense lines of vegetation. Birds seek out the green belts within these areas for food and shelter.

If you are fortunate enough to be starting a new garden, you will not be limited by any existing style or design and can actually plan your garden from scratch. This will present an exciting challenge and also the opportunity to plan specifically for birds. To get ideas, visit a natural bird sanctuary. Observe the various habitats and the species using each one, and take note of the way in which the plant material occurs, whether it is in dense stands or sparse in areas. Also note the height of trees and shrubs, the types of groundcover that occur, and the use of open areas.

For those lucky people who have properties bordering onto a green belt, sanctuary or open bush, the opportunity to blend your garden with the natural environment will make gardening for birds even more interesting. Very often the garden can provide a more inviting home than the adjoining bush, but the trick is to send out the right invitations for each bird species so that they are aware of what you have to offer.

Enlisting the Neighbours

One of the most successful ways of making the environment attractive to birds is to work together with the larger community. Begin by approaching your immediate neighbours to inform them of your intentions, and encourage them to join you in your venture. Or get the ball rolling by sending a circular to all surrounding properties, explaining your new purpose. You may wish to recommend the use of 'safe' insecticides or invite people to send you their bird lists. Working with friends and neighbours can generate enormous enthusiasm and commitment, and may cause a chain reaction which in time could see a whole community working together to support a successful ecosystem. In fact, some urban communities have become involved in the protection and management of their local green belts and bird sanctuaries. This principle is also being applied in game-farm management, where huge conservancies have been established and the fences dividing properties

Sand Baths

Incorporate a sand patch as part of the open area (*see page 14*) in your garden. This is essential for the well-being of all bird species, which use the sand to keep their feathers in peak condition and reduce the number of parasites. The section you choose for this patch must be well-drained or it may become a wallow. The sand should be powdery so that it always remains loose and light. If your soil has a high clay content, it may be necessary to bring in some suitable sand from another area. Dig out the existing soil to about a half a metre. Place a layer of river sand at the bottom to allow for drainage, and fill in the hole with loose sand. Birds will spend a great deal of time here, scooping up the sand with their wings and shaking them to allow for maximum penetration.

Guineafowl, in particular, enjoy a sand bath.

PLANNING THE GARDEN

taken down in an effort to provide a less restrictive environment for the animals that inhabit these parts.

As we all know, birds fly and because of this wonder of nature are not restricted by property boundaries. This means that from a bird's perspective no garden is viewed in isolation. Thus, a concerted effort to collaborate with surrounding home owners in developing a 'greater' bird garden makes a lot of sense.

GARDEN HABITATS

In planning or adapting your garden, remember that the bird-friendly environment should consist of a variety of habitats. Some of these you may have to create; others are attainable through simple modifications to what already exists. These areas can be created or adapted to varying degrees, and include:

- OPEN AREA
- EXCLUSION AREA
- CANOPY HABITAT
- WETLAND AREA

OPEN AREA

There is not usually a shortage of open areas in the standard urban garden, so you won't need to worry about creating one. The wide grass lawns constitute open areas and are probably the most common of these, but any area that is free of trees, tall shrubs or other features that might interfere with some birds' need for 'space' could be similarly classified. Open areas are an important part of the bird garden and will be well used by:

Birds like the Hadeda favour open areas where danger is quickly detected and there is room for a speedy take-off.

SUGGESTED GRASSES AND GROUNDCOVERS FOR OPEN AREAS

BOTANICAL NAME	COMMON NAME
Aptenia cordifolia	Aptenia
Arctotheca calendula	Cape Weed
Arctotis 'Silver Lining'	Silver Arctotis
Carpobrotus deliciosus	Purple Sour Fig
Drosanthemum speciosum	Red Ice-plant
Dymondia margaretae	Silver Carpet
Eragrostis spp.	Love Grass
Gazania hybrids	Gazania
Geranium incanum	Carpet Geranium
Lampranthus spp.	Vygie
Monopsis lutea	Yellow Lobelia
Othonna carnosa	Othonna
Panicum maximum	Guinea Grass
Phyla nodiflora	Daisy Lawn
Sutera pauciflora	Trailing Phlox

- large birds, such as the Grey Heron, which require a 'runway' to take-off;
- nervous species that like to have a clear view around them, for example, the Hadeda;
- ground-loving birds that feed and nest at this level, like guineafowl and francolins.

In many established gardens the open areas are planted with Kikuyu. Although lush and fast-growing, this grass requires vast quantities of water to flourish – a luxury which we in our region can ill afford. It is also an invasive species in southern Africa. The fine grasses (*Cynodon* species), such as Florida and Bayview, are better equipped for frequent drought conditions and require far less maintenance generally. Once established, they can be left without water and will rapidly 'green-up' with rain.

Wild grasses can also be used in an open area. Try sowing Guinea Grass (*Panicum maximum*) and Love Grass (*Eragrostis* species), both of which are used as fodder grasses by farmers. A strip of wild grass adjacent to a lawn can be very attractive and when seeding will be used by many seed-eating birds. Wild grasses are often difficult to grow due to the specialized structure

PLANNING THE GARDEN

of the seed, which can be damaged in collecting. It is easier, therefore, to dig out clumps of the grass (without damaging the ecology) and to plant these in the garden. Look for varieties that carry attractive and full seed heads, and you are sure to enjoy many entertaining hours watching the finches, weavers, canaries and other seed-eaters hanging onto the stalks to feed.

An open area need not consist of grass only; low-growing groundcovers and shrubs will also do the trick. And if you live in a dry part of the country, try using the wealth of succulent plants – such as those found in the Karoo – as a basis for groundcover. These plants are unmatched in their potential to flower under less than ideal conditions, and will serve to attract insects which feed the birds. Vygie plants (Mesembryanthemaceae family), with their vibrantly coloured flowers, are also a good option as many varieties grow close to the ground and, moreover, are a valuable source of nectar to sunbirds.

An open area should ideally comprise two elements: a section which is truly low-growing, as in a lawn, and areas of groundcover or wild grass which blend with it.

EXCLUSION AREA

Ideally situated in a remote section of the property, the exclusion area is probably the most important part of a bird garden. This is an area where the least disturbance is likely to take place: the children do not play here, the dog is not happy about the number of thorns found here, and gardeners, much to their delight, must leave this part of the garden entirely alone.

The exclusion area should not be an island, but should rather consist of a generous bed along the perimeter of the

An exclusion area in a remote part of the garden is planted to create levels of vegetation, with tall trees at the back, shorter shrubs in front of this, and groundcovers at the lowest level.

Burchell's Coucal will keep to the more protected parts of the garden and will utilize trees in the exclusion area for nesting.

property. It is an area designed to accommodate and serve all the shy and more furtive bird species that will be active in densely planted bush but which will not compete with the bolder birds that flock to your feeding table. Here you will find the Olive Thrush foraging in the mulch, along with the robins, babblers and francolins, while other birds such as Burchell's Coucal might well choose this undisturbed area for nesting.

In designing the exclusion area, avoid reaching for the standard garden manual that instructs you to space trees six metres apart to prevent their crowns from overlapping. Here you can plant the trees and shrubs as close together as your pocket allows; this is the way nature works and your aim here is to emulate nature as closely as possible.

By planting a number of trees next to each other you will find that, in the competition for sunlight and nutrients, some will grow tall and strong, while others will remain 'shrubby' and help to fill in gaps lower down, all the way to the ground. Together the plants will create *levels* of vegetation, each of which will appeal to different birds. Indigenous thorn trees are ideal for the back of the exclusion area, where fallen thorns will be safe from bare feet. Plant a number of them together and watch how quickly the birds begin to nest there. Select shorter shrubs with a dense growth habit for the area in front of the trees, and plant these close together to ensure a wild, bush-type growth that will protect more introverted visitors. Shrubs such as the Tree Fuchsia (*Halleria lucida*), Orange Thorn (*Cassinopsis ilicifolia*), Natal Plum (*Carissa macrocarpa*),

PLANNING THE GARDEN

SUGGESTED PLANTS FOR THE EXCLUSION AREA

	BOTANICAL NAME	COMMON NAME	HEIGHT x SPREAD
TREES	*Acacia albida*	Ana Tree	15 m x 10 m
	Acacia caffra	Hook-thorn	9 m x 6 m
	Acacia erioloba	Camel Thorn	9 m x 7 m
	Acacia galpinii	Monkey Thorn	18 m x 16 m
	Acacia karroo	Sweet Thorn	8 m x 8 m
	Acacia sieberiana var. *woodii*	Paperbark Thorn	12 m x 14 m
	Acacia tortilis subsp. *heteracantha*	Umbrella Thorn	9 m x 7 m
	Acacia xanthophloea	Fever Tree	12 m x 10 m
	Ziziphus mucronata	Buffalo-thorn	9 m x 9 m
SHRUBS	*Barleria obtusa*	Bush Violet	1 m x 1 m
	Carissa bispinosa	Num-num	2 m x 2 m
	Carissa macrocarpa	Natal Plum	3 m x 2 m
	Cassinopsis ilicifolia	Orange Thorn	4 m x 4 m
	Duvernoia aconitiflora	Lemon Pistol Bush	3 m x 3 m
	Halleria lucida	Tree Fuchsia	4 m x 2 m
	Hypoestes aristata	Ribbon Bush	1,5 m x 1 m
	Mackaya bella	Forest Bell Bush	3 m x 2 m
	Orthosiphon labiatus	Pink Sage	1,5 m x 1,5 m
	Pavetta lanceolata	Forest Bride's Bush	5 m x 4 m
	Phoenix reclinata	Wild Date Palm	6 m x 4 m
	Plectranthus ecklonii	Plectranthus	1,5 m x 1,5 m
	Plumbago auriculata	Cape Leadwort	3 m x 3 m
	Rhamnus prinoides	Dogwood	4 m x 4 m
	Tecomaria capensis	Cape Honeysuckle	3 m x 3 m
GROUNDCOVERS	*Agapanthus africanus*	Dwarf Agapanthus	50 cm x 50 cm
	Agapanthus praecox subsp. *orientalis*	Common Agapanthus	1 m x 0,75 m
	Aloe striatula var. *caesia*	Basuto Kraal Aloe	1 m x 1 m
	Aptenia cordifolia	Aptenia	15 cm x 60 cm
	Asystasia gangetica	Creeping Foxglove	30 cm x 60 cm
	Bulbine frutescens	Stalked Bulbine	30 cm x 40 cm
	Chlorophytum comosum 'Vittatum'	Variegated Hen & Chickens	30 cm x 30 cm
	Cineraria saxifraga	Wild Cineraria	15 cm x 40 cm
	Crassula multicava	Fairy Crassula	20 cm x 30 cm
	Felicia amelloides	Blue Felicia	50 cm x 50 cm
	Gazania krebsiana	Gazania	25 cm x 30 cm
	Plectranthus verticillatus	Gossip Plant	10 cm x 50 cm
	Protasparagus densiflorus 'Sprengeri'	Emerald Fern	40 cm x 90 cm
	Stachys aethiopica	Stachys	30 cm x 50 cm
	Sutera pauciflora	Trailing Phlox	10 cm x 40 cm
	Tulbaghia violacea	Wild Garlic	40 cm x 25 cm
	Veltheimia bracteata	Bush Lily	45 cm x 45 cm

PLANNING THE GARDEN

Stratified vegetation should characterize the exclusion area, the different levels serving different bird species.

and the Cape Leadwort (*Plumbago auriculata*) are ideal for this section. To complete the exclusion area, plant groundcovers in front of the shrubs. If you like colour in the garden, reserve a strip in the very front of the bed for annuals or colourful, low-growing perennials.

Add interest to the exclusion area by distributing logs, rocks and piles of stones between the plants. So often it is these very objects that we first rid our gardens of, particularly if they are not presentable enough to be built into attractive features. Scattered through the exclusion area, however, they will help to support a great many life forms, which in turn will provide birds visiting this area

Top: *Compost as nature intended it, in the form of mulch.*
Bottom: *This common garden pest, the fruit beetle* (Pachnoda sinuata), *breeds in compost heaps – another good reason to get rid of these unsightly mounds.*

Compost Heaps, a Rotten Idea

Most gardeners have a compost heap tucked away somewhere on the property, an element of the garden which we are all brought up to believe is essential. Well, not all traditions are valid or well founded, and this is one of them. Compost heaps are unsightly, often smelly, and mostly house a number of rodents.

Mother Nature provides us with a picture of what should be happening when we take a walk through a forest. The forest floor is a carpet of springy mulch, which derives from leaves, dead grass and branches. Similarly, in your garden, grass cuttings and leaves can simply be emptied onto the garden beds and spread out to form a thick mulch layer. Even organic kitchen refuse can be placed between plants, the more unsightly peels and egg-shells out of sight in the exclusion area. Don't be tempted to dig any of this material into the soil as this will rob the ground of nitrogen, and defeat the object. Surface material will be carried underground by nature's ploughs, the earthworms. The worms aerate the soil and ensure that organic material is incorporated into it.

The mulch layer is an invaluable part of your soil. It keeps the moisture content of the soil in your garden high; it makes it more difficult for weeds to germinate; it houses numerous insects which provide a tasty meal for many birds; it forms valuable compost needed by plants; and earthworms depend on it for a source of food: remove the mulch and you will be without a healthy and valuable population of worms.

For those who remain sceptical: try to break the habit of dumping *everything* on the heap, and place at least some of your organic waste directly on the soil around your plants.

PLANNING THE GARDEN

SUGGESTED TREES FOR THE CANOPY HABITAT

Botanical Name	Common Name	Height x Spread
Acacia albida	Ana Tree	15 m x 10 m
Acacia caffra	Hook-thorn	9 m x 6 m
Acacia galpinii	Monkey Thorn	18 m x 16 m
Acacia karroo	Sweet Thorn	8 m x 8 m
Acacia sieberiana var. *woodii*	Paperbark Thorn	12 m x 14 m
Acacia tortilis subsp. *heteracantha*	Umbrella Thorn	9 m x 7 m
Acacia xanthophloea	Fever Tree	12 m x 10 m
Bolusanthus speciosus	Tree Wisteria	7 m x 4 m
Brachylaena discolor subsp. *discolor*	Coast Silver Oak	7 m x 10 m
Calodendrum capense	Cape Chestnut	10 m x 4 m
Calpurnia aurea subsp. *aurea*	Natal Laburnum	4 m x 3 m
Cassia abbreviata subsp. *beareana*	Sjambok Pod	6 m x 4 m
Celtis africana	White Stinkwood	10 m x 4 m
Combretum erythrophyllum	River Bushwillow	12 m x 10 m
Cussonia paniculata	Highveld Cabbage Tree	5 m x 2 m
Dais cotinifolia	Pompon Tree	6 m x 4 m
Diospyros whyteana	Bladder-nut	5 m x 3 m
Dodonaea angustifolia	Cape Sand Olive	4 m x 3 m
Dombeya rotundifolia	Wild Pear	6 m x 3 m
Ekebergia capensis	Cape Ash	12 m x 12 m
Ficus sycomorus	Sycamore Fig	12 m x 14 m
Grewia occidentalis	Cross-berry	5 m x 3 m
Harpephyllum caffrum	Wild Plum	10 m x 8 m
Heteropyxis natalensis	Lavender Tree	6 m x 4 m
Kiggelaria africana	Wild Peach	12 m x 11 m
Loxostylis alata	Tigerwood	6 m x 4 m
Olea europaea subsp. *africana*	Wild Olive	8 m x 6 m
Pappea capensis	Jacket Plum	7 m x 6 m
Peltophorum africanum	Weeping Wattle	9 m x 8 m
Phoenix reclinata	Wild Date Palm	5 m x 4 m
Podocarpus henkelii	Henkel's Yellowwood	10 m x 4 m
Rhamnus prinoides	Dogwood	4 m x 4 m
Rhus chirindensis	Red Currant	6 m x 5 m
Rhus lancea	Karee	7 m x 7 m
Rhus leptodictya	Mountain Karee	5 m x 5 m
Rhus pendulina	White Karee	8 m x 7 m
Schotia brachypetala	Weeping Boer-bean	12 m x 8 m
Syzygium cordatum	Water Berry	9 m x 7 m
Trichilia emetica	Natal Mahogany	10 m x 10 m
Ziziphus mucronata	Buffalo-thorn	9 m x 9 m

with a tasty meal. Insects, in particular, appreciate the facilities provided by rotting wood, and many will congregate beneath rocks and stones. Several bird species will also appreciate the inclusion of logs here. The Spotted Eagle Owl and Helmeted Guineafowl, for example, will happily nest between rocks and logs in an area where there is minimal disturbance.

PLANNING THE GARDEN

The Blackeyed Bulbul, a common garden bird, will use all parts of the garden, moving freely between the open area, exclusion area, canopy habitat and wetland area.

The canopy habitat is utilized by furtive birds which prefer to keep to areas of cover.

CANOPY HABITAT

The canopy habitat, as the term suggests, is the area occupied by the tree tops and, to a lesser extent, the tops of tall shrubs. This is a vital habitat for birds, providing food, nesting facilities, a resting spot, as well as a place for territorial vocalizing and display. This habitat can be divided into two areas relative to activities on the ground: high-traffic areas and low-traffic areas.

HIGH-TRAFFIC AREAS

These are the areas in the garden where human presence and activity are at their greatest. The patio and braaiing area, the swimming pool, swings and any other facilities which attract people are certain to exclude birds. The only way of accommodating them in such areas is higher up, at a safe distance from the ground. A tall tree, such as the White Karee (*Rhus pendulina*), an indigenous evergreen, is ideal for the entertainment area where it will provide ample shade. This species is also fast-growing and long-lived, unlike many of the Australian Acacias which tend to fall over after a few years, causing expensive damage to walls or fences. The berries and flowers which the White Karee produces are additional advantages; the berries attracting birds such as barbets and bulbuls, and the flowers drawing many insects which in turn attract insectivorous birds such as shrikes and warblers.

Your choice of trees for the high-traffic areas must be well thought-out and should aim to accommodate your

Most birds will restrict themselves to the tree canopies in high-traffic areas of the garden.

own needs and objectives as well as those of the birds. Although an evergreen tree will provide year-round protection for bird species, it is also going to rob you of valuable sunlight in winter and so should not be planted too near the house. Thorn trees are not a good idea because of the menace factor they pose to people and animals once their thorns drop; they should therefore be planted only in the exclusion area. Trees that support insect life are ideal for insectivorous birds, as are the berry- and fruit-producing varieties for the fruit-eaters. Indigenous fig trees (*Ficus* species) are a good choice, supplying birds with fruit and also a wealth of insect life. Olive trees (*Olea* species) grow well in most parts of the region, and will appeal to berry-eating louries, mousebirds and thrushes.

PLANNING THE GARDEN

SUGGESTED PLANTS FOR THE WETLAND AREA

Botanical Name	Common Name	Height x Spread
Aponogeton distachyos	Cape Pondweed	spread 1 m
Aristea major	Aristea	1,5 m x 1 m
Chondropetalum tectorum	Thatch Reed	1,5 m x 1,5 m
Crinum bulbispermum	Orange River Lily	1 m x 1 m
Crinum macowanii	River Crinum	1 m x 1 m
Crinum moorei	Moore's Crinum	1 m x 1 m
Cyperus papyrus	Papyrus	2 m x 1 m
Dierama pendulum	Harebell	1 m x 1 m
Dietes bicolor	Yellow Wild Iris	1 m x 1 m
Dietes grandiflora	Wild Iris	1 m x 1 m
Elegia capensis	Broom Reed	2,5 m x 1,5 m
Nymphaea capensis	Blue Water Lily	40 cm x 80 cm
Typha capensis	Bulrush	2 m x 0,5 m
Wachendorfia thyrsiflora	Bloodroot	2 m x 0,5 m
Zantedeschia aethiopica	White Arum Lily	1,5 m x 1 m

In low-traffic areas, where human activity is more limited or absent, birds will utilize all levels of the vegetation for nesting, roosting and feeding.

For obvious reasons, the exclusion area should be as far away as possible from high-traffic areas.

Low-Traffic Areas

Most parts of the garden fall into this category, the traffic under most trees being fairly limited, except for small pockets here and there. The canopy habitat throughout the garden plays an important role, and with a bit of extra planning can assume even greater significance. You can plant trees in a way that ensures that their canopies interlink and form a corridor of greenery along which birds

A pond is a valuable addition to the bird garden and will meet the needs of all visiting birds to bath and drink.

PLANNING THE GARDEN

can move. Furtive birds, like Burchell's Coucal, will then use these corridors as 'highways'. By planting your trees along the perimeter of the property you can ensure that the canopies eventually link with those of the neighbours, and it may, in time, be possible to form a green belt of tree canopies which continues out of the urban environment into nearby wilderness areas.

Perimeter planting of trees has further advantages in that it helps to reduce traffic noise levels and wind. Also, by creating a barrier of trees, you might even be able to manipulate the micro-climate of your garden. For example, in frost-susceptible areas you may succeed in growing more tender plant varieties than would otherwise be possible. Trees can also be used to improve the security status of the garden. A barrier of thorn trees will certainly make a burglar think twice before climbing your wall.

WETLAND AREA

Any bird-lover will tell you that a wetland is the richest and most rewarding birding spot, not only for the waterbirds it attracts but also for the wealth of other species that associate with this productive biome. A miniature wetland is really simple to create and need not cost a lot of money.

Details on how to construct a wetland area (and other water features) are dealt with more fully in Chapter 3, but before you embark upon this scheme, make sure that the area has been well thought-out and fits in with the greater plan you have devised for the garden.

A wetland area needs to combine aspects of the exclusion area with those of an open area. Thus, it should incorporate dense vegetation – reeds and bulrushes, for instance – and also uncluttered areas with low-growing groundcovers and grass. Try to locate the wetland in an area which allows for an open approach, but backs onto a well-planted section like the exclusion area. If you are incorporating a pond or water feature, this can be carried through into the exclusion area for maximum effect.

A wetland area could consist only of a swamp or bog-type system. It is, however, worthwhile to integrate open water. This need not be a dominant or intricate feature; even the simplest of structures will be effective. As humans we often try to make our creations as grand as possible and frequently fail in our efforts to please. It is important to remember that birds do not make use of deep water unless they have webbed feet, and are much happier to drink and bath in a shallow pool. All bird species will utilize the water. Shy species will tend towards the densely planted and protected areas; others will prefer an open approach before they will stop to drink.

The creation of a wetland will introduce you to a wealth of plants that thrive in damp conditions. Some, such as Bloodroot (*Wachendorfia thyrsiflora*), will grow with their roots in water and are ideal for planting in ponds or wetlands. Many Cape species of the Restionaceae family are also excellent wetland plants. This group includes the Broom Reed (*Elegia capensis*) and Thatch Reed (*Chondropetalum tectorum*). The *Crinum* species are also happy to stand in water and their magnificent flowers provide a spectacle in any wetland.

Aside from the birds you will attract, your wetland will draw and support a bounty of other life forms, and these in turn will provide food for many of the avian residents: frogs' legs for the Hamerkop, fish for the kingfishers and snails for the coucals.

Above: *A garden water feature incorporates many of the elements needed to satisfy birds.*
Right: *A Cape Weaver at its nest.*

PLANNING THE GARDEN

THE BIRD-UNFRIENDLY GARDEN

A typical urban property, its garden planned without regard for birdlife, offers little encouragement and no incentive for birds to visit.

A Expansive lawn with token bird-bath in exposed position.
B Entertainment area with pergola and shade tree.
C Compost heap located between tool shed and garden wall.
D Garden path bordered by neatly manicured beds of annuals, and flanked on either side by islands of exotic plants.
E Neat garden bed planted with a variety of annuals.
F Boundary beds planted with various low-growing plants.

The elements of this garden make for a barren environment from a bird's perspective and, aside from a single shade tree, offer few opportunities to feed, roost or breed. Indigenous plant material is lacking and there is a marked absence of any significant protection or cover for birds. As such, the garden fails to offer any viable bird habitats.

PLANNING THE GARDEN

THE BIRD-FRIENDLY GARDEN

Planned with the needs of birds in mind, the same urban property is transformed into a haven for birds.

A Lawn area is encroached on to a greater extent by garden beds.

B Entertainment area incorporates indigenous leafy creeper over the pergola, which will attract nesting birds.

C Compost heap has no place here; organic garden and kitchen refuse is placed directly on the garden beds to form mulch.

D Garden path is bordered by the same neatly manicured beds, but flanked by beds of indigenous plants which flow into *corridors* of vegetation alongside the house.

E A continuous green corridor of mostly indigenous shrubs and tall trees (canopy habitat) replaces the garden bed.

F An exclusion area has been created by extending a boundary bed. Vegetation is planted to create different strata – thorn trees at the back, shrubs at a lower level, and groundcovers below this. Logs and rocks scattered around this area serve ground-nesting birds.

G A small wetland area has been created in front of the exclusion area and adjacent to a shallow, natural-looking pond. The wetland is planted with bulrushes and indigenous reeds.

These areas (F and G) are the focal point of the bird-friendly garden.

PLANNING THE GARDEN

Attracting Birds to Small Gardens

Being the owner of a small garden does not preclude you from attracting birds to it, nor does it mean that you will be robbed of the pleasure of observing bird behaviour at close range, or learning about breeding habits and feeding patterns in your own garden. It does mean that there probably won't be area enough to contemplate a wetland or exclusion area, but with a little careful planning, creative thinking and co-operation with your neighbours, a great deal can be achieved.

Neighbourhood Watch

One of the best ways of overcoming the size restriction of your garden is to involve the neighbours in your attempt to make your area bird-friendly. Birds do not respect property boundaries as we do, particularly if the vegetation in an area is continuous. Trees planted along boundary walls can interlink with those of surrounding properties if neighbours are prepared to co-operate. Thorn trees, the Sweet Thorn (*Acacia karroo*) and Hook-thorn (*Acacia caffra*) for instance, can be trained to have a fairly upright growth, and once established will be utilized by nesting birds. Shrubs such as the Natal Plum (*Carissa macrocarpa*), Cape Leadwort (*Plumbago auriculata*) and Cape Honeysuckle (*Tecomaria capensis*) can also be used along a boundary to create dense lines of vegetation or a hedge effect. These plants are also useful as filler plants because of their bush-type growth.

If you are able to generate sufficient enthusiasm and involve several neighbours in your plan, you might be able to simulate a large garden, if not on the ground, then certainly from a bird's perspective in the air. This can be achieved by each of you agreeing to devote your own garden to a different function in terms of satisfying birds. For instance, one garden might be planned largely for the birds' watering needs. An adjoining garden might be planned with the birds' nesting or feeding requirements in mind, while another gardener might devote a large section of the garden to open lawn and a patch of wild grass. You may even convince one gardener to create a type of exclusion area. In this way the birds' needs will be met on every level, just in different gardens, and you can all enjoy and share in the experience of watching birds carry out their various daily and seasonal routines.

Water in the Garden

Although a wetland area is an unlikely element of a small garden, a water feature is not. A pond need not be large to satisfy the birds, and should easily be accommodated adjacent to a boundary or wall of a building. Small fibreglass ponds are readily available from garden centres and are not difficult to install, or you can build your own small feature (*see* Chapter 3). Even the smallest water-holder, however, will satisfy most birds' need to drink and bath.

Nesting Opportunities

Because the small garden is not able to offer a variety of nesting sites, nest-boxes and nesting logs certainly have a place here. A nest-box (*see* page 54) can be fixed beneath the eaves of the roof or to a branch, even to a wall if there are no trees available. It is important that the box is not exposed to full sun throughout the day and is in an area

Above: *A Cape White-eye visits a small, stone bird-bath.*
Left: *A Red Bishop on a Bulrush.*

PLANNING THE GARDEN

Bulbuls are among many birds that may nest in a small garden. Here, chicks impatient for food await their parent's return.

that offers relative privacy. Barbets and starlings may breed in nesting logs provided for them, and these need only be fixed about two metres above the ground.

Dense tree canopies, creepers and thorny bushes will all support natural nesting, even in a small garden.

Feeding

There are many shrubs and flowers that can be planted in a small garden to attract birds to feed (*see* box opposite and the table at the back of this book). However, a feeding table is a feature worth including in a garden where space is limited. Many birds will respond immediately to a new source of food, especially if it is offered on a regular basis; and in winter, when natural sources are in short supply, birds rely more heavily on other supplies.

A feeding table occupies very little area at ground level, but can easily be attached to a garden wall with brackets if space is very tight. Food items can range from over-ripe fruit to seed and meat scraps, depending on which species you hope to attract. (*See* Chapter 2 for a more detailed discussion of feeding and bird foods.)

First-time visitors to the garden will be a bit wary of entering a confined space so it is important to build their confidence progressively. It may be a good idea to offer food items high up in a tree until the birds become regular visitors, and then gradually bring the food closer to the ground. Birds are quick to catch on if food is involved and will soon realize the benefits of entering a garden that caters for them, even if it is small. Eventually they will become accustomed to the area, and you will have the

Choosing Plants for the Bird-Friendly Small Garden

The same principles for selecting plants for larger gardens apply here, and again indigenous species are the best ones to choose. As space is at a premium in your garden, your selection of plants must be carefully thought-out. It will be impossible to satisfy the birds in *all* their needs in a fairly small area, and it may be better to make your garden a focus of one activity, say feeding or nesting – even if you are not working in conjunction with the neighbours.

Ideal 'feeder' shrubs for a small garden include the Wild Fuchsia (*Halleria elliptica*), Dune Crow-berry (*Rhus crenata*), Natal Plum and the Cape Myrtle (*Myrsine africana*). These can be complemented by a bed of nectar-producing flowers such as the various erica and protea species, Red-hot Pokers (*Kniphofia praecox*) and Cape Honeysuckle. Sunflowers and wild grasses, even in a small patch, will provide food for seed-eaters like sparrows, weavers and bishops.

Thorn trees (*Acacia* species) make ideal nesting sites, but any dense vegetation cover will provide nesting opportunities. A creeper trained up a wall is an invaluable addition to a small garden and will easily house a wagtail or robin nest. You can increase nesting space here by nailing strips of wood onto the wall behind the creeper.

Above: *Canary Creeper* (Senecio tamoides).
Right: *Red-hot Pokers.*

pleasure of watching birds, and learning more about their various habits, in the comfort of your own backyard.

Remember, predatory cats, noisy dogs and rowdy children are not conducive to attracting birds into the garden, particularly the small one.

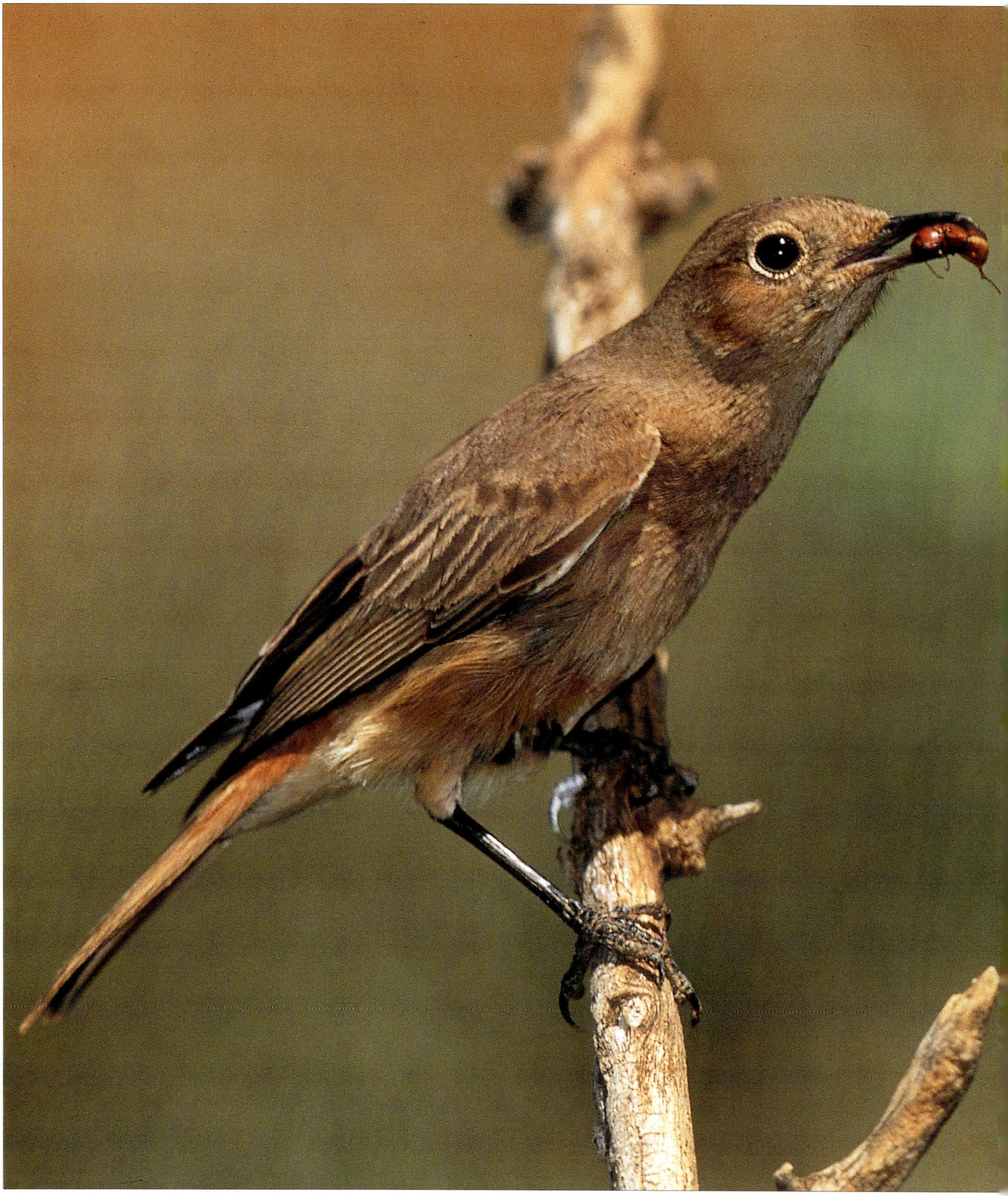

2
Feeding and Bird Fare

Feeding the birds will be one of the greatest pleasures of your new gardening strategy, and the reward of seeing so many happy clients at the best 'fast food' outlet in the suburb will be satisfying to say the least. Feeding offers the opportunity to observe birds at close quarters, study their behaviour, and understand their role in the garden more fully. You will be able to improve your knowledge of each species' diet and the 'food' plants they are attracted to, and gain insight into how they interact with other bird species competing for a meal.

Familiar Chat (Cercomela familiaris)

FEEDING AND BIRD FARE

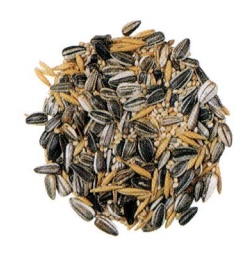

Feeding and Bird Fare

The number and variety of birds you attract to feeding spots will depend on how regularly you provide food and how varied the menu is. Random feeding will prevent the birds becoming totally dependent on you, but the carrying capacity of your garden will be lowered. Like a roadhouse, the better the food and service, the more customers you will attract.

If you choose to offer food on a regular basis in your garden, you will be taking on a fair responsibility. It is much like having children who expect a regular meal, and as soon as their tummies rumble appear at the kitchen in anticipation. The birds will become dependent on your charity, and if you stop making donations you can expect a fair amount of disruption in the garden. The birds will have to work harder to satisfy their appetites and to do this they will generally move farther afield. So if you do decide to feed regularly, establish a routine and try not to deviate from it.

You will find that birds' food requirements fluctuate with the seasons. There will be a greater demand on your cuisine during winter when berries, seed and fruit are scarce, and you can increase the amount and variety of food you offer at this time. Winter is also a leaner period for the insect-eaters, which will appreciate a steady supply of protein until spring heralds a new generation of 'creepy-crawlies'. The bounty of blossoms and fruit brought by spring and summer, particularly with well-chosen plants, will mean that much of what you offer goes untouched, and you can reduce the extent of artificial feeding at this time.

Top: *A Green Pigeon feeds on the flowers of a* Maytenus *plant.*
Bottom: *This Thickbilled Weaver is attracted to seed scattered over a rock surface in a garden.*
Left: *A Black Sunbird on a Red-hot Poker* (Kniphofia *species*).

FEEDING AND BIRD FARE

Summer heralds a rich natural source of food for birds, and artificial feeding can be reduced at this time. Here, a Plumcoloured Starling takes advantage of nature's offerings.

WHERE TO FEED

Birds feed naturally at all the different strata in your garden, from the berries at the top of the trees to the mulch layer on the ground, and artificial feeding can be carried out at each of these levels. Where you decide to feed birds will depend on your interest and involvement, however. You may choose to sprinkle a few bread crumbs on your window-sill to feed the doves, or you may wish to go all the way and place a variety of food and feeders in different areas, so catering for the diverse diets of several bird species.

Before identifying the best areas in which to feed, first eliminate the parts of the garden to avoid. Food offered in high traffic areas (*see* page 19) or in areas frequented by the local cat will not encourage birds. If you own a cat, try feeding it in the morning rather than the evening. A full stomach during the day will ensure that any hunting is done at night on the nocturnal rats and mice. Collars with bells are also useful to warn birds of impending danger.

Rodents are quick to learn where food is provided on a daily basis and may become a problem once you begin feeding. You can discourage these pests by raising the level of the food, using either a hanging or a standing feeder. Standing feeders can be further rat-proofed by placing a funnel-shaped collar made of thin sheet metal around the pole. Alternatively, a plastic bowl with a hole cut through the base can be slipped up a pole and secured below the level of the table.

When erecting or hanging a feeder, bear in mind that you will want to watch the activity and select a spot that is within view of a window. A shaded or partially shaded location is preferable to one in full sun. If you feed from one point only, however, be prepared for the arrival and dominance of bolder species, such as sparrows, doves and starlings.

To cater for a greater variety of birds, it is necessary to provide food in several places. The exclusion area is a good spot for birds that don't enjoy the jostling at more open feeding sites. Place the food at ground level under the shrubs and you will be amazed to see how much is devoured in a day by thrushes, robins and other birds with similar habits. Make use of all the different habitats in the garden, if possible, and offer food at different heights within these. A number of bird-feeders spread around the garden will help to keep all the visitors happy, particularly if you offer different food at each feeding point.

FEEDERS: SHAPES AND SIZES

As humans, we tend to be very conservative in our approach; our first instinct is to buy rather than create, and even what we buy must be designed for the job, packaged and correctly labelled. Commercial products may satisfy our need to please, but don't necessarily impress the birds. Where feeders are concerned, if it holds food the birds will be there.

COMMERCIAL FEEDERS

There is a wide variety of hanging bird-feeders available commercially. Of these, the gravity-fed, plastic birdseed holder has certain advantages: it is easy to fill, it is rain- and wind-proof, it hangs out of the way of cats, and rodents will have difficulty reaching it. However, because seed is concentrated in a small area, there is always a great deal of bickering among birds competing for food, and only those bold enough will participate.

MESH BAGS

A plastic mesh bag, which can be filled with fruit or nuts, is just one of many hanging feeders that you can make at home. This type of feeder will limit the number of bird

FEEDING AND BIRD FARE

Natural Feeders

By using your imagination and skill, you can create your own bird-feeders which can be built to meet the needs of particular species. Home-made feeders can be made to blend naturally with the garden and may be as simple or as intricate as you please.

Pieces of driftwood make excellent natural food holders, and can be suspended from a branch with sisal rope, a thin chain or, for a more natural look, treated leather thongs. Fill the holes in the driftwood with bird puddings (*see* page 35), and wedge fruit onto any protruding branches; nails driven into the wood can also be used to hold food. Remember that all feeding containers must incorporate drainage holes so that rainwater does not accumulate and cause the food to rot.

Feeding logs can be made easily if you have access to a saw and a drill. Simply cut off a section of a log or branch, about 500 mm long. A rough bark is ideal as it enables the birds to perch, but you can always secure perches below the holes on smooth bark logs. Drill a number of holes into the log, approximately 20-30 mm in diameter and about the same depth. Insert a strong cup hook in the top of the log and use rope to hang it from a branch. The holes can be filled with all sorts of appetizers such as suet pudding, fruit, and mealie meal.

Mature pine cones also make useful bird-feeders and generate much excitement among children, who love to paste delicacies such as peanut butter, mince, fruit or suet between the scales; the cones can be hung in trees or secured to a feeding platform.

A feeding log made from a section of a Syringa branch.

FEEDING PLATFORMS

A feeding platform is the most conventional way of providing food for birds, and can easily be constructed (*see* pages 32-33) or purchased, ready-made and in various degrees of sophistication, from most nurseries. Simple, home-built platforms may be suspended from a tree, erected on a pole in the lawn, or secured to a kitchen window-sill, and can incorporate a variety of features, as desired: nails to hold fruit items; a narrow border to prevent crumbs from being scattered; and a roof to keep the rain off.

More elaborate feeding tables can also be made at home, particularly if you are a competent woodworker. A five-star feeder would include a variety of feeding options: a flat platform for grain, breadcrumbs and fruit; a mesh holder, for kitchen scraps, fruit and peanuts, which will encourage birds to stay and eat rather than carry the food off; a tin can to hold suet puddings; and a seed-holder. A good meal should be rounded off with a drink: water could be provided in a drinking fountain such as those used in bird cages, or simply in a shallow dish.

When introducing a platform to the garden, start off by hanging it among foliage in a tree to allow the birds to become accustomed to it, and move it closer to the house until you can safely place it on or near a kitchen window-sill. Here it will be easy to keep clean and fully stocked. Adult birds may be a little shy to use the facility while you are around, but their offspring will be fearless. Miss a feed, and the chances are you will have them pecking on the window, 'shouting' to remind you of your chore.

One of the more elaborate feeding platforms available commercially allows for a variety of food types to be offered at once. A roof helps to protect the food items from the elements.

species congregating at this point because certain birds, like doves, will not hang upside down to feed. It will be interesting, however, to see how quickly they adapt so as to get a bite to eat. Weld-mesh can also be used to make a similar structure, and one that will be more durable.

FEEDING AND BIRD FARE

What to Feed

Deciding what to feed the various birds visiting the garden can be a problem, particularly if you want to satisfy all the different tastes and attract a large variety of bird species. Generally, any organic scraps that come out of the kitchen can be fed to birds, and what they don't eat will be cleaned up by the ants. Bread, cake, cooked or raw meat, and other food scraps will all be enjoyed by 'urban' birds, which have adapted to a western lifestyle and diet, with its associated excesses of fat and cholesterol.

However, the less discerning you are in what you offer, the less select a group of birds you will attract. Birds have differing food requirements, and although many have adapted to a 'bird-table diet' there are numerous others with particular needs. Ready-packaged bird foods, in the form of mixed seed, generally suit the seed-eaters, such as finches, sparrows, weavers and canaries, but exclude many other fine bird species.

Fruit of any kind will be met with enthusiasm by both seed- and fruit-eating birds. Place the fruit in mesh bags, weld-mesh containers, or on spikes, not forgetting to lay some on the ground in the exclusion area. Soft fruit can be squashed into cracks and holes in branches so that the birds have to peck it out rather than fly away with large pieces. Barbets are often first on the scene when fruit is offered, and will defend the area until they have eaten their fill. Mousebirds are also partial to fruit, and if fed on a regular basis will be discouraged from wreaking havoc in any fruit trees you might have in the garden. Coconuts are also popular, and can be cut in half and hung from a branch for the birds to peck out the flesh.

Insectivorous birds are more difficult but not impossible to cater for. Large bones with meat still attached, chopped bacon rinds, and meat scraps from a braai will be relished by these birds. Bone-meal is also a favourite, and can be obtained fairly cheaply from any butcher. Place it loosely on the feeding table or squash it into pine cones, and watch the birds celebrate. Bone-meal is an excellent source of calcium and protein, and is ideal for feeding young birds. Mealworms (*see* page 34) will also be taken to feed nestlings. Avoid offering hard foods (bacon rinds, peanuts, etc.) during the breeding season as these can cause chicks to choke.

Feeding the Seed-eaters

Seed is popular bird fare and is the food most commonly offered to garden birds in feeders of various shapes and sizes. It can also be scattered on the ground in open areas to limit competition at the feeding table. Grains and seeds, in their various forms, contain important fats, minerals and carbohydrates, and will be enjoyed by a great many birds.

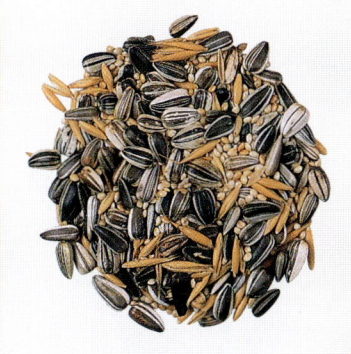

A commercial seed mix, available from pet shops for cage birds, is readily consumed by wild seed-eaters too.

Popcorn will be enjoyed by larger seed-eating birds such as doves and Rock Pigeons.

A finer seed mix harvested from wild grasses is a favourite food of finches, canaries and weavers.

Mixed poultry grain can also be fed to garden birds, the doves and pigeons in particular.

31

FEEDING AND BIRD FARE

FAT FOODS AND TUMMY FILLERS

Foods such as stale cheese, meat scraps and bacon rinds are valuable sources of fat for birds, especially during winter when natural supplies are scarce. Carbohydrate foods are less nutritious but will readily satisfy a hungry tummy in the absence of anything else.

Bacon rinds are relished by many insect-eating birds, but may choke their chicks.

Bread, both white and brown, will be taken by most seed-eating birds.

A left-over baked potato will not go amiss on the feeding table, especially if barbets and robins are about.

Suet is an ideal winter food, providing a much-needed source of energy.

Cheese, offered in small pieces or grated, is known to attract robins, Heuglin's Robin in particular.

HOW TO BUILD A SIMPLE FEEDING PLATFORM

The simplest feeding platform takes the form of a pole sunk into the ground with a flat piece of wood secured to it.

Materials:
1 x 1736 mm x 36 mm x 36 mm length of pine
1 x 1500 mm x 70 mm x 46 mm length of pine
1 x 305 mm x 460 mm x 18 mm pine plank
18 x 40 mm nails
4 x 60 mm brass screws
yacht varnish

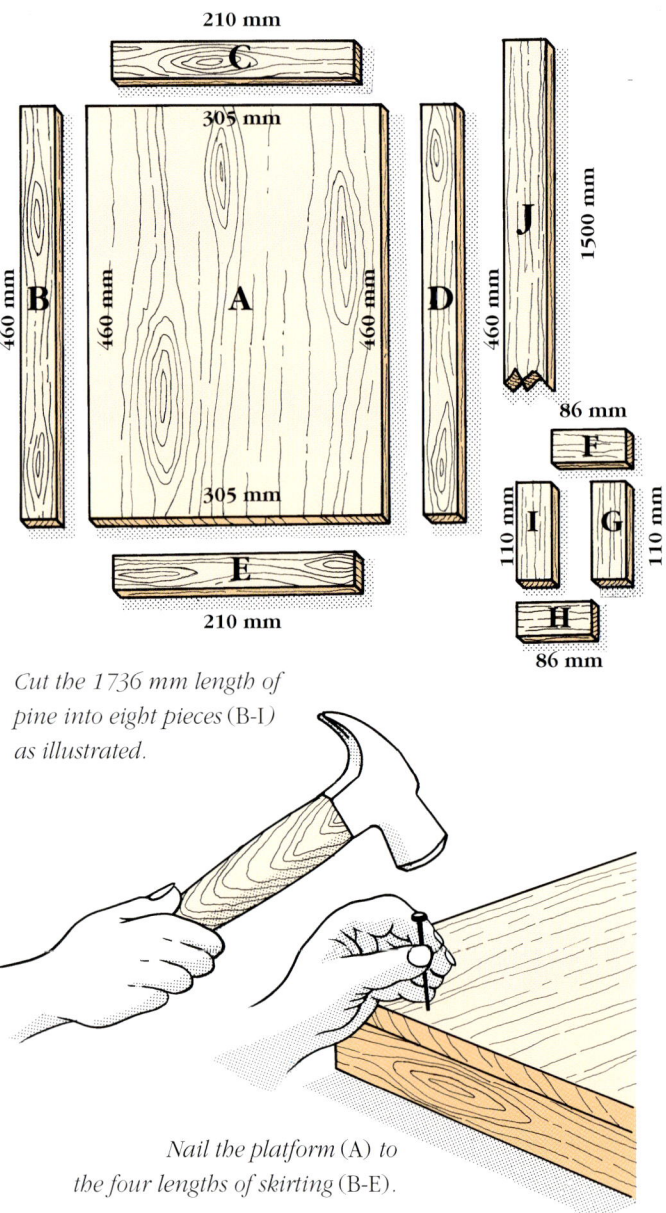

Cut the 1736 mm length of pine into eight pieces (B-I) as illustrated.

Nail the platform (A) to the four lengths of skirting (B-E).

FEEDING AND BIRD FARE

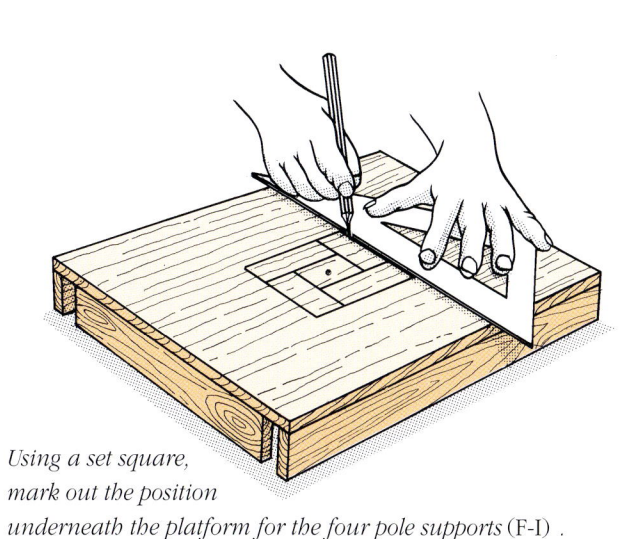

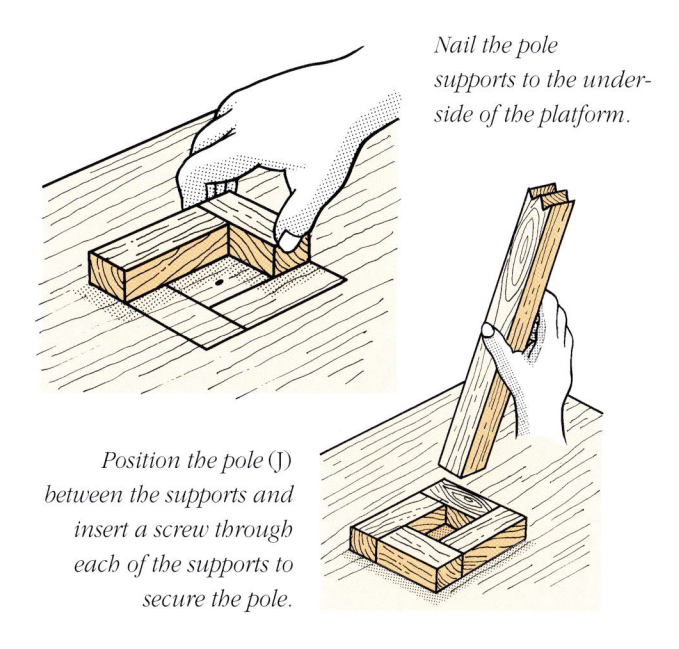

Using a set square, mark out the position underneath the platform for the four pole supports (F-I).

Nail the pole supports to the underside of the platform.

Position the pole (J) between the supports and insert a screw through each of the supports to secure the pole.

Apply three coats of varnish, sanding lightly between each coat.

The finished product. An inverted plastic bowl is secured to the pole to discourage rodents.

To create a hanging feeder, use the platform section only and suspend it from each corner using cup hooks and four even lengths of rope.

FRUIT FEASTS

Fruit is a great temptation to a host of birds, including barbets, bulbuls, white-eyes and mousebirds, and can be offered in various parts of the garden. Fresh apples, oranges, grapes, guavas and bananas will be relished, especially if over-ripe, and dried fruit can also be offered but should be softened in water first.

Orange halves or slices are a good source of juice for nectar-eating birds.

Dried fruit provides an alternative when your fresh supplies have run out.

Apples that are over-ripe are a better option than crisper ones, which tend to dry out in the sun.

The juicy flesh of pears will appeal to mousebirds, bulbuls and barbets.

The soft fruit filling of bananas is ideal for squashing into holes and cracks.

FEEDING AND BIRD FARE

> ## A MEAL OF WORMS
>
> Insect-eating birds can be catered for specifically by offering them mealworms, that is, the larvae of various beetles of the genus *Tenebrio*. Mealworms are not always easy to obtain, but some friendly words to a local bird-breeder or zoo may get you enough to start your own breeding colony.
>
> Keep the worms in a plastic bucket, and cover them with a tight-fitting lid with a hole cut out and covered with fine gauze. This will keep out competitors which may kill off the worms. Half fill the bucket with bran and place sliced potatoes or apple on top of this for the worms to feed on. Ensure that the bran is always moist, but not wet, and keep the container at room temperature. Soon you will have a thriving population of mealworms and will be able to harvest these tasty treats on a regular basis for the birds.
>
> Offer the worms in a shallow glass bowl rather than directly on the feeding table, to prevent them from crawling away. If you feed the birds at the same time each day, however, they will soon be waiting in anticipation and the worms will be snapped up before they have had a chance to escape.

Broken-off pieces of termite mounds – complete with the inhabitants – will prove popular with birds such as bulbuls and shrikes. If you place the termites (in the mound) in the fridge for a short spell, you will slow down their metabolisms and therefore the rate at which they evacuate the feeding table. You need not worry about them colonizing the garden, unless you have gathered the winged termites which are programmed to start a new family wherever they land!

Nectar-feeding birds, such as sunbirds and sugarbirds, will depend on flowers in the garden for their food. However, with a bit of determined coaxing, they can be enticed to take sugar water from a bird drinking-fountain. A hamster's drinking-bottle can also be used; the birds quickly learn to stick their long tongues into the tube to extract the sweet water. Place the feeder among nectar plants at first, to allow the birds to become accustomed to it. In time they will accept the mixture as a free meal, and you can move the feeder to more visible sites in the garden.

Make up the sugar water using one part sugar to four parts boiling water, and allow it to cool. The mixture will spoil after three or four days and should be replaced. You may also find that fungus growth occurs on the sides of the container; this can be cleaned by soaking the feeder in bleach for a few hours.

THE GARDEN LARDER

Although artificial feeding can be great fun and will call on your imagination to concoct new meals and find suitable containers in which to offer them, do not forget what Mother Nature has to offer as nourishment for birds.

The mulch layer (*see* page 17), which should be present between all your trees and shrubs, provides an abundance of insects which will be eaten by many bird species. Earthworms, crickets, wood lice and numerous other invertebrates thriving on the composting material will be relished by the thrushes, robins, guineafowl and francolins, which will spend hours scratching away to find the choicest morsels.

Rocks and logs in the exclusion area will also house various insect species which the wrynecks and woodpeckers will happily dig out. This untended section of the garden is where lizards and geckos will breed and hibernate, and with some luck may be discovered by small birds of prey, such as the Little Sparrowhawk and Lizard Buzzard. Indigenous rodents living in this area will also attract birds of prey, and in particular the Barn Owl.

Worker termites, here seen building their tunnels in the mulch layer of a garden bed, will soon be discovered by thrushes, robins or guineafowl.

FEEDING AND BIRD FARE

BIRD PUDDINGS

Much enjoyment can be had from creating your own pudding recipes for birds. The base of the puddings is suet (animal fat), which is available from most butchers. Melt the fat in a pot on the stove and then add the secret ingredients. Input from the family, especially the amateur cordon bleu chef, will be useful. A variety of seeds, bread, cake crumbs, nuts, and any other kitchen scraps may be added to the melted fat, but avoid using uncooked vegetables as they tend to decompose rapidly. Pour the mixture into moulds (tin cans are ideal) and store these in the freezer, taking out small quantities on a daily or weekly basis, as required. A bird pudding can be fixed to a tree by inserting a bolt through the bottom of the tin can and into a base board before you fill the container; when the pudding has set, attach the base board to a branch. Alternatively, remove the mould once the suet sets and offer the pudding on a feeding table to enable birds to peck at it from all sides. A dowel placed through the centre of the mixture just before it is set also makes a useful holder from which to suspend the meal.

Birds can also derive nourishment from other areas in the garden, but just how much depends on what you plant. Selecting the 'right' plants is integral to creating a bird garden, not only in terms of their food value but also for nesting (see pages 50-52) and protection from predators and the elements. In choosing plants, gardeners tend naturally towards the most colourful and attractive varieties, which in many cases are the exotic plants. Although not worthless in a bird garden, imported plants will not appeal to birds in as many ways as will indigenous ones. Flowering plants, whether indigenous or exotic, play an important role in feeding birds, but it stands to reason that native birds will be better adapted to native plants. This, of course, is how nature intended it, and by increasing the number of indigenous plants in the garden, you can be assured of increasing the birdlife.

TREES AS A FOOD SOURCE

Indigenous trees and shrubs are hard to come by, and for the avid bird gardener weekend trips to nurseries and botanical gardens will become the norm. Try to find a nursery with a dedicated staff who will find the right products for you and share your enthusiasm for the hobby.

Only a fraction of the worthwhile indigenous 'food' trees are commercially available, so it is pointless to mention the many excellent varieties that might one day be stocked by nurseries (see page 36 for suggested 'feeding' trees). It is safe to say that the vast majority of indigenous fruit-producing trees will attract birds, but be careful to select varieties that are suited to the local conditions of your area.

Fruit trees, both indigenous and exotic, will attract a wide variety of bird species to the garden. Here, a Redwinged Starling enjoys a free fruit meal.

By planting all the *Rhus* species in the garden, you would be assured of enough fruit to feed birds all year round. There are over 70 of these species in southern Africa, but only a few of them are stocked by nurseries. One of the most popular is the White Karee (*Rhus pendulina*), which grows to a height of about seven metres and has a six-metre-diameter crown. This fast-growing evergreen grows well in most parts of the region, and is ideally suited to a patio area as a shade tree. The berries it produces will encourage birds to feed, even in the busiest part of the garden. A smaller variety, the Dune Crow-berry (*Rhus crenata*), is found naturally along the southern Cape coast but does equally well under Highveld conditions, and provides a feast of berries for fruit-eating birds.

FEEDING AND BIRD FARE

'FEEDING' TREES FOR THE BIRD GARDEN

Botanical Name	Common Name	Height x Spread
Celtis africana	White Stinkwood	10 m x 4 m
Ekebergia capensis	Cape Ash	12 m x 12 m
Ficus ingens	Red-leaved Rock Fig	12 m x 12 m
Ficus sycomorus	Sycamore Fig	12 m x 14 m
Grewia occidentalis	Cross-berry	5 m x 3 m
Harpephyllum caffrum	Wild Plum	10 m x 8 m
Kiggelaria africana	Wild Peach	12 m x 11 m
Olea europaea subsp. *africana*	Wild Olive	8 m x 6 m
Pappea capensis	Jacket Plum	7 m x 6 m
Phoenix reclinata	Wild Date Palm	5 m x 4 m
Podocarpus henkelii	Henkel's Yellowwood	10 m x 4 m
Rhamnus prinoides	Dogwood	4 m x 4 m
Rhus lancea	Karee	7 m x 7 m
Rhus leptodictya	Mountain Karee	5 m x 5 m
Rhus pendulina	White Karee	8 m x 7 m
Schotia brachypetala	Weeping Boer-bean	12 m x 8 m
Syzygium cordatum	Water Berry	9 m x 7 m
Trichilia emetica	Natal Mahogany	10 m x 10 m

Some of the most attractive fruiting trees, like the Cape Ash (*Ekebergia capensis*) and Natal Mahogany (*Trichilia emetica*), are sensitive to frost, particularly in their young stages, and need to be well protected in the colder regions. If the trees survive the frost, birds will discover and gorge themselves on the juicy fruit produced.

SHRUBS AS A FOOD SOURCE

Flowering shrubs are an integral part of the bird garden. The bright colours of the blooms attract many insects, which in turn feed birds such as flycatchers and shrikes, while plants like the Wild Dagga (*Leonotis leonurus*), the Tree Fuchsia (*Halleria lucida*), ericas, and even the exotic Bottlebrush (*Callistemon* species) and *Russelia* species are a rich source of nectar and attract a host of sunbird species. The sight of sunbirds hovering at the flowers, their long tongues soaking up the sweet juices, is a picture that every bird gardener will relish. If your garden is well stocked with nectar-producing plants, these birds

The Dogwood (Rhamnus prinoides) *produces an abundance of berries, which ripen to a rich black colour.*

The Crane Flower (Strelitzia reginae) *is a rich source of nectar for the Cape White-eye and many sunbird species. It is also an attractive ornamental plant.*

will take up residence here and their nests, lined with carefully collected spider webs, will come to form part of the character of your garden. Fynbos varieties (see page 64), which are so popular with nectar-eating birds, are best suited to the south-western and southern Cape, but the Cape Honeysuckle (*Tecomaria capensis*), another rich source of nectar, can be used in most parts of the country. Some of the indigenous shrubs, like the Kei Apple (*Dovyalis caffra*), the Num-num (*Carissa bispinosa*) and

FEEDING AND BIRD FARE

'FEEDING' SHRUBS FOR THE BIRD GARDEN

Botanical Name	Common Name	Height x Spread
Aloe arborescens	Krantz Aloe	3 m x 3 m
Aloe striatula var. *caesia*	Basuto Kraal Aloe	1 m x 1 m
Carissa bispinosa	Num-num	2,5 m x 1,5 m
Carissa macrocarpa	Natal Plum	3 m x 2 m
Cassinopsis ilicifolia	Orange Thorn	4 m x 4 m
Chrysanthemoides monilifera	Bush-tick Berry	2 m x 2,5 m
Dovyalis caffra	Kei Apple	4 m x 3 m
Duvernoia aconitiflora	Lemon Pistol Bush	3 m x 3 m
Ehretia rigida	Puzzle Bush	4 m x 4 m
Halleria elliptica	Wild Fuchsia	2,5 m x 2,5 m
Leonotis leonurus	Wild Dagga	2 m x 1,5 m
Myrsine africana	Cape Myrtle	1,5 m x 2 m
Ochna serrulata	Mickey Mouse Bush	2,5 m x 2,5 m
Phygelius capensis	Cape Fuchsia	1 m x 0,5 m
Rhamnus prinoides	Dogwood	4 m x 4 m
Rhus crenata	Dune Crow-berry	3 m x 2 m
Strelitzia nicolai	Natal Wild Banana	8 m x 4 m
Strelitzia reginae	Crane Flower	1,5 m x 1,5 m
Tecomaria capensis	Cape Honeysuckle	3 m x 3 m
Vepris lanceolata	White Ironwood	6 m x 5 m

the Puzzle Bush (*Ehretia rigida*), produce large, delicious fruits which can be used to make tasty jams. It is unlikely that you will be given the chance to harvest the fruit, however, as the 'early bird' is usually first on the scene.

Birds and the Fruit and Vegetable Garden

If your gardening interests lie in fruit and vegetable production, you may find this pursuit difficult to reconcile with an interest in 'bird gardening'. Many birds have a predilection for fruit and vegetables and will eagerly await the first signs of budding fruit to satisfy their appetites. There are ways of accommodating both of these gardening interests, but compromises must be made along the way.

Fruit trees can be covered with bird netting to protect them from birds, and to permit you to enjoy fully the products of your labour. Alternatively, you can protect individual fruits with plastic mesh bags, so leaving some of the fruit and the rest of the tree for the birds to utilize.

Generally, fruit and vegetable production is a worthwhile undertaking if you wish to attract birds, and you can always protect your share to avoid any conflict of interests.

Nightwatching

Bird-watching can be extended into the night by hanging a light in a tree in the garden. The light must be about 1,5 metres above the ground and should be suspended from a branch which ensures free flying space all around the bulb. Insects will be attracted to the light, especially in the summer months, and this in turn will attract nocturnal birds such as dikkops and owls. You may even be lucky enough to encourage some diurnal species of insectivorous birds. Drongos and swifts are among those that might fly around a lamp, congregating as if in broad daylight for a free meal. The light will also attract toads, which form part of the Spotted Eagle Owl's diet, and may help to encourage these wonderful birds of prey to take up residence in your garden.

The Spotted Eagle Owl

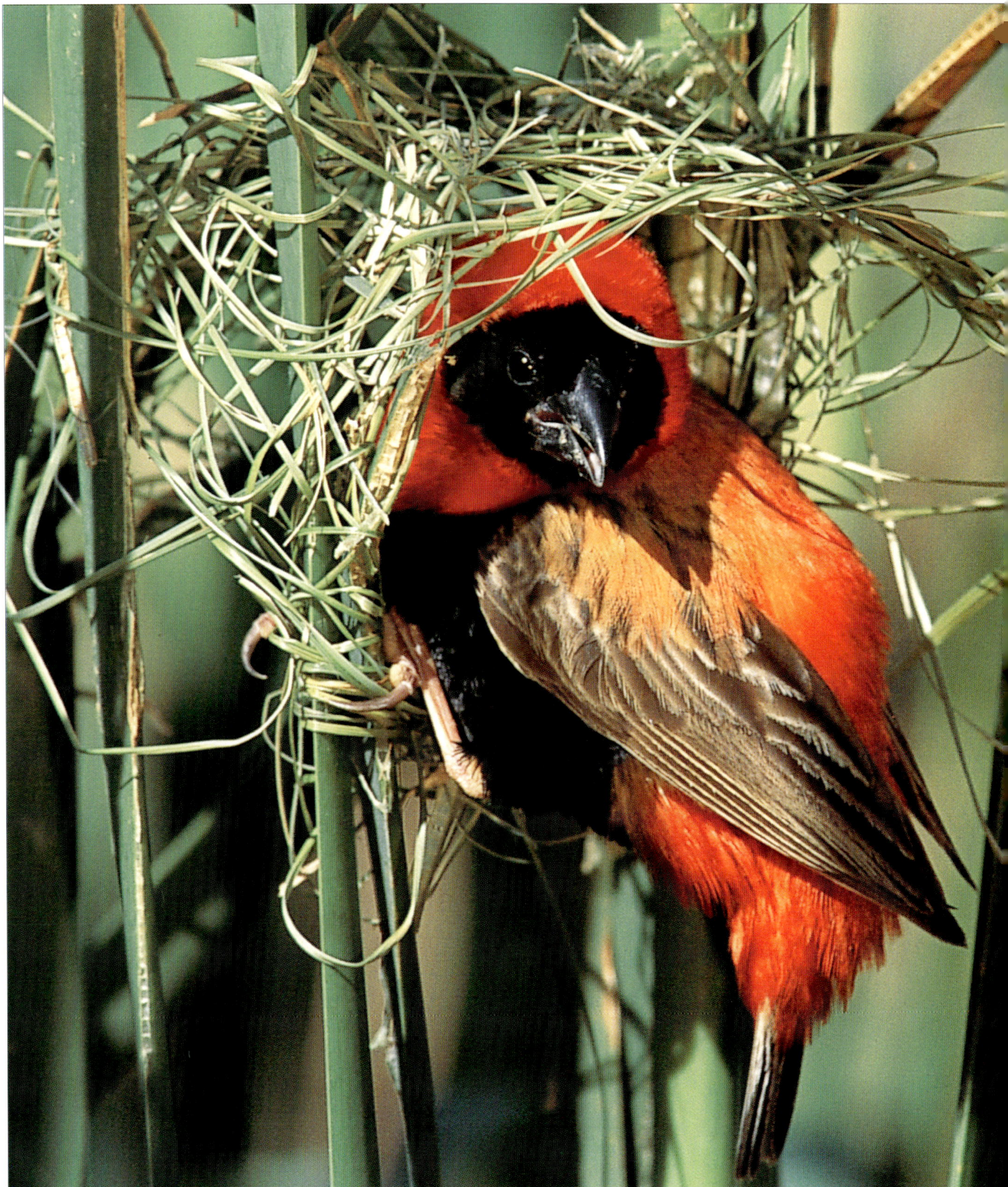

3
Water in the Garden

One of nature's most valuable commodities to the bird community is water, and no garden planned for birds is complete without it, even in the most elementary form. Aside from the numerous birds which naturally occur on water, the waders which feed in the shallows, and the many species that use reedbeds for nesting or roosting, most birds rely on water for drinking and bathing, a need for which even the smallest garden can provide.

Red Bishop (Euplectes orix)

WATER IN THE GARDEN

Water in the Garden

All birds will value an accessible source of fresh water when visiting the garden. This may be purely functional, serving only their needs, or may be of a grander nature and a focal feature in the garden. Upturned dustbin lids, car hubcaps, modest ponds, or elaborate water features with cascading waterfalls will all satisfy the bird visitors to a greater or lesser extent.

Creating a water feature will provide ample opportunity for the inventive gardener to design and build, or to modify an existing pond so as to make it more bird-friendly. But before contemplating such a venture, take a trip to a natural area and see how water is provided in nature. Compare the design of areas where small birds bath and wade to those frequented by larger birds, and observe the surrounding vegetation and its role in satisfying the needs of different bird species.

Where in the Garden

Many gardens feature a traditional bird-bath which stands on a pedestal in the middle of the mown lawn. Although this facility means that the bathing ritual is visible to the gardener, and that its users are fairly safe from predation, an exposed bird-bath generally only attracts species such as sparrows and doves, which are bold enough take a bath in the open. The many shyer birds attracted to the garden, however, will avoid a watering spot such as this, or will only make fleeting visits.

A Pied Kingfisher will visit larger water features.

A Cape Turtle Dove settles contentedly on an open bird-bath. Only bolder birds, such as doves, sparrows and weavers, will make regular use of an exposed watering point in the garden.

A bird-bath can always be placed in a more protected part of the garden to overcome this problem, but it is preferable to provide water at ground level to cater for the diversity of bird species visiting. Water should ideally be channelled from the open area, through the exclusion area, to the wetland (*see* Chapter 1 for garden habitats). The more water you provide, and the more areas you provide it in, the greater the range of birdlife you will attract.

If your budget allows, try to create a water feature that is ecologically balanced (*see* page 44) with fish, microbes and other essential elements. This feature will be self-sustaining and will allow for more permanent breeding cycles of the life it supports.

WATER IN THE GARDEN

How to Modify an Existing Water Feature

Many of the water features that are bought or constructed are based on formal Victorian designs with steep sides and uniform depth; usually there are no shallow areas. These typify the features chosen for recreational parks and formal landscapes, and although perhaps appealing to the human eye, do little to attract birds. Most commercial pond builders do not take the needs of birds into consideration when designing their ponds. A little time spent watching birds in a natural wetland area will reveal that steep-sided ponds with water levels out of reach of all but flamingos, are not what birds are used to, or need.

Birds require a gentle slope into the water so that they can determine a safe level at which to bath and drink. If you have a pond which does not have any shallow areas, you can modify it to suit birds by using flat rocks to build up a platform. An attractive log can serve the same purpose; leading from the side of a pond into the water, a log will provide a perch, enabling the birds to walk slowly into the water rather than fall in.

An existing cement pond can be modified structurally to make it more bird-friendly. This is done by reconstructing one side of the pond to incorporate a gentle slope. The slope should be nearest to the open area of the garden to allow the longer-legged wading birds easy access to the water. Start by draining the pond, then break away the cement and brickwork on one side, and redesign this section to include a gentle ramp leading down into the pond. Use a non-toxic bonding liquid to join the old to the new cement so as to prevent leaks. Incorporate a shallow shelf at the point at which the slope falls steeply away. This shelf, which need only be 3-5 cm below the surface of the water, is the most important part of the pond as it enables birds to bath and drink without fear of drowning. Keep the cement work along this section fairly rough, so that once algae start growing, the birds will be able to stand securely while bathing. Another option is to lay river sand on top of the cement work. This will result in a more natural look and will limit the fancy footwork needed to balance on an algae-covered surface.

A Cape Weaver on a Bulrush flower.

The gardener took advantage of a natural stream to create this small garden pond, bordered by indigenous water-loving plants and surrounded by a variety of fynbos vegetation.

Flat rocks used within a pond serve as useful platforms for many waterbirds. Here, a Hamerkop perches on a large rock in the shallower reaches of a water feature.

Building a Water Feature

Generally, the average garden does not include a pond, and this is often because of the high cost of installing one. Commercially available ponds do not have a place in most people's budgets. But don't be put off! Ponds can be constructed at a very low cost, look attractive, and also serve the needs of the bird community.

There are three options available to you if you decide to install your own pond or water feature. You can purchase a ready-made pond shell, use a pond liner, or – if you are energetic – construct your own cement feature. Whichever option you choose, you will have to begin by digging a hole.

WATER IN THE GARDEN

A fibreglass pond shell was used to create this small garden feature. This type of pond is easy to install and takes on a natural look once border vegetation becomes established.

READY-MADE POND SHELLS

Pond shells can be bought at most nurseries or garden centres. Although the most costly of the three options, these ponds are easy to install, durable, and are not prone to leaking. When digging the hole for this pond, make it about 10 cm deeper and wider than the mould itself. Line the bottom of the hole with a layer of river sand and position the pond on top of this, adding or removing sand to achieve the right height. The edges of the pond should be slightly higher than the surrounding ground so that soil will not be washed into it. Use a spirit-level on a straight plank to ensure that the pond is level. If you intend creating a wetland area adjacent to the pond, you may want to tilt the pond slightly so that any overflow will run in the direction of the wetland. Alternatively, drill a hole into the side of the pond nearest the wetland to create a flow of water in that direction. The hole should be at least 2 cm in diameter or it may get blocked.

Once you have established your levels, fill in the spaces around the pond with river sand. This will ensure that the water pressure on the pond wall is even, and will guarantee a longer life for the pond, particularly in the case of a fibreglass structure.

POND LINERS

The use of pond liners, such as PVC (polyvinyl chloride), butyl rubber or bentonite clay, allows for more creativity on your part. You can incorporate islands, streams, deep pot holes and shallow shelves to create a feature that will be utilized by several bird species. In designing your pond, try to include a section that is about 50-75 cm deep:

this will ensure temperature stability of the water, which is important for fish and other pond life. Once you have sculptured your masterpiece, line the cavity with a 1-cm-layer of plaster sand (available from most hardware stores) before laying the membrane. Remove any sharp stones from the hole as these may puncture a plastic liner.

PVC liners are available through some nurseries, and can be specially made up to suit your design. They come in different strengths but, for long life, use one that is at least 550 microns thick. It is best to purchase a liner that is made for the job rather than glue separate sheets together. PVC material can be repaired if it is torn, and extensions can be joined on with a special compound that ensures a water-tight seal.

Polyethylene sheeting can also be used but will have a much shorter life than PVC, which should last up to 20 years. If you choose polyethylene, be sure to select one that is made from virgin material and at least 250 microns thick. Once it is in position, cover any exposed pieces of plastic around the edges of the pond with sand. This will protect the plastic from ultraviolet light and will also help to achieve a more natural look.

Instead of plastic sheeting, you can use bentonite clay as a pond liner. This substance is derived from volcanic ash, and swells as it absorbs water. Once you have dug the hole, mix the clay into the top layer of the soil and compact it to form a dense, impermeable layer. Contact with water will cause the clay particles to swell, which in turn will close any pores through which the water might have drained. This process does not exclude plants, however, which are able to grow through the clay, helping to complete a natural picture. Bentonite clay is susceptible to

A pond liner is one of the least expensive methods of installing a pond. Here, black polyethylene sheeting, 500 microns thick, is used to create a garden pond.

erosion and is, therefore, best used in a pond of standing water rather than in one with a waterfall or running water. Follow the supplier's instructions carefully when using the clay, as incorrect application can result in leaks.

CEMENT POND CONSTRUCTION

The use of concrete to build your own pond is certainly the most difficult option, and should be carefully planned before you tackle it. This structure can be shaped as you please, will not be affected by the elements, and also has the advantage of permanence. Careful preparation of the soil and concrete is paramount, and if not carried out correctly will lead to leaks, which are often difficult to seal.

Plan your pond in the same way as you would if using a pond liner, letting your creativity guide you. After digging, compact the soil very well so as to prevent cracking later. Line the excavation with galvanized chicken wire; this will serve as reinforcement within the concrete. When casting the concrete, ensure that there is a gap of about 2,5 cm between the soil surface and the wire, so that the concrete sets on both sides of this reinforcing. You can achieve this by pulling up the wire as you cast the concrete, or by using stones as props beneath the wire. It is essential to lay all of the concrete in one day; if joins are made over several days, leaks are likely to develop. Speak to your local building expert about the correct mix of cement and sand for concrete, and about the thickness required for the size of pond you have planned. These factors will vary according to the clay content of the soil in your area.

When you fill this type of pond with water, the concrete will release toxic salts. Because of this, the pond should be left to stand for at least two to three weeks, and should be drained and filled with a fresh supply of water before any fish are introduced into it.

Breathing Life into the Pond

It is one thing to install a pond but, having done this, you now have to introduce life into it. If possible, use borehole water or rain-water, rather than treated water, to fill a new pond. Your garden loses a valuable asset when rain-water running off the roof of the house is fed into the city's storm-water drains. It is a simple enough task to channel this supply from the gutter downpipes into a pond by preparing a grass-lined gulley in the lawn, or by running a polythene pipe underground. The pipe should have a bore of at least 5 cm to prevent it from blocking. The regular flushing of a pond with rain-water will maintain the quality of the water and ensure healthy life within it.

The Ultimate Water Feature

This prize creation is available to gardeners who fall into the upper tax-bracket. To install it, you will have to call in experts, who will cast a fibre-crete pond complete with all the trappings. The use of fibre-crete in the manufacture of water features over the last few years has revolutionized design, particularly in larger landscapes. This substance is made to resemble real rocks which only on very close inspection can be identified as not the real thing. The rocks are first moulded with bird netting and then plastered with a special compound which is later painted to look like natural rock. Water pipes can be built into the rocks to allow for waterfall simulation, and ledges, caves and plant boxes can also be incorporated. In time, moss, lichens and other plant material will grow, enhancing this feature and making it look like one of nature's own creations.

A spectacular waterfall, created with artificial rocks.

WATER IN THE GARDEN

Achieving the Ecological Balance

A pond is not performing as it should if you have to clean it out every month, or if it is so green with algae that even the fish are struggling to survive. The idea is to establish life in the pond and to try to get it working as well as nature would. Here are some basic rules for a successful pond.

- At least half the surface area of the pond should be covered by plant material in order to protect it from full sun. Sunlight stimulates the growth of algae, which dominate at the expense of other pond life. Water lilies are attractive and suit this purpose.
- The pond should have an open approach on at least one side. This should be an uncluttered area occupied by a lawn or low-growing plants.
- A densely planted section should border the pond along one edge. Bulrushes and indigenous reeds are ideal for this area.
- A wetland or bog section should ideally border on the pond. Such areas support a great deal of life associated with water.
- The pond must accommodate fish. They are an important component as they feed on mosquito larvae, which are always present in standing water.
- At least one section of the pond should slope gently downwards from the edge and should incorporate a shallow shelf for smaller birds to bath on.
- Ideally, the pond should have a section with a depth of 50-75 cm to ensure an area of stable temperature.

A well-balanced pond incorporates surface plant material to screen out sunlight, and is bordered by dense plantings of reeds, Papyrus and other water-loving vegetation.

A great deal of pond life will arrive under its own steam, but if you 'inject' the feature with water from another pond you will speed up the colonization process. Fish, of course, will have to be introduced. A popular choice are the brightly coloured Japanese Koi Carp. These fish are an excellent bonus for kingfishers, the Hamerkop and other angling birds because they are slow-moving and, with their bright colours emphasized against the dark pond, make easy targets. Several of the indigenous fresh-water fish are also worthwhile for a garden pond (*see* box feature on Banded Tilapia). Indigenous fish can be netted in rivers and dams, or obtained from certain fish dealers. Contact the Department of Environment Affairs (Conservation Division) for direction and advice in this regard. (Also refer to the back of the book for relevant addresses.) Avoid introducing barbel into a pond as these will devour any other fish species in the water.

If you are fortunate enough to have a large pond, it may be possible to attract jacanas, bitterns and some of the smaller herons, all of which will appreciate the type of food that is found in a well-balanced water feature. Delicacies such as snails, crabs and water scorpions all need to be accommodated, so try to imitate nature as far as possible by placing logs and rocks in the water, a thick layer of sand on the pond floor, and by allowing leaves and other organic matter to float on the surface. A great deal of enjoyment will be had discovering the vast range of plant and animal species that will collect in your pond if the conditions are right.

Banded Tilapia

This indigenous fresh-water fish is an ideal choice for a garden pond. It is small and fast-moving and has a far greater chance of evading capture by birds than does the slow, easily spotted Koi.

Banded Tilapia (*Tilapia sparrmanii*) are carnivorous and as such an asset to a pond, where they will keep frog, toad and mosquito populations in check by consuming tadpoles and larvae. They will readily breed in a pond if there are areas of cover provided by water plants. A fair number of the offspring will be consumed by predators in the pond and even by fellow Tilapia which are feeling peckish.

WATER IN THE GARDEN

A Cape Weaver perches on the stalk of a Papyrus plant overhanging the water. These colourful birds are attracted to reedbeds (even in small clumps) for nesting.

CREATING A GARDEN WETLAND

In nature, wetlands are often associated with open water; many, in fact, act as filters through which the water passes before reaching the deeper expanses, and sieve out excess sediment and pollution. Establishing a wetland adjacent to a pond in the garden can function in a similar way, and has other practical advantages. The concentration of water in one sector of the garden will in turn lead to a concentration of birds and other life here.

Select a site for your wetland, and dig out the soil to a minimum depth of 75 cm over an area of at least two square metres. The extent of the excavation will depend on your physical ability, or financial ability to employ workers to do what is truly an arduous task. Once you have removed the soil, line the hole with plastic sheeting. The overlapped sections may be glued together to limit leakage, although it is not essential. Then fill the hole with the soil you removed. (This request might elicit some interesting responses if you have hired help.) The idea is to retain as much water as possible in the wetland area, the plastic lining obviously serving to prevent water from draining into the surrounding soil.

Once the soil has been returned to its rightful position, it is time to turn on the waterworks. A leaking pipe or dripping hose placed in the wetland

A Malachite Kingfisher will visit a well-established pond and wetland.

WETLANDS – THE BIRD HAVENS

Southern Africa has a great many wetland areas – rich ecosystems which are renowned for the diversity of birdlife they support. Sadly, however, there is a shortage of well-designed water features in city areas, and wetlands there are almost non-existent. A mini-wetland system, properly set up in a private garden, can in time function as successfully as a natural one, just on a smaller scale.

Wetlands provide protection and nesting sites for a large number of bird species, in the almost impenetrable mass of plant material growing in the water. The combination of water and dense vegetation also creates an ideal habitat for many other life forms which make up part of the avian diet.

Start by converting a small section of your garden into a wetland, but be warned: once you get a taste of what this area can offer, you may join the ranks of the more fanatical 'wetlanders', some of whom have converted the entire garden area into a series of ponds and swamps.

Masked Weavers are a common sight around water and wetlands, and utilize the vegetation surrounding these areas for nesting sites.

Red Bishops (breeding male featured here) will probably be the most frequent visitors to a garden wetland and pond.

The Thickbilled Weaver inhabits areas of dense vegetation but breeds in reeds close to water and uses the leaves of wetland plants for nest material.

WATER IN THE GARDEN

OBTAINING PLANTS FOR A WETLAND

Plants for a wetland will not be easy to lay your hands on as few nurseries carry large stocks of these. Most of your plants can be extracted from established farm dams or existing wetlands, with the farmers' permission, of course, and with minimal damage to the environment. You need only plant a few specimens of Bulrushes and Phragmites Reed. Both grow fast in wet soil, and will be utilized by birds like the Red Bishop and Cape Weaver for nesting. Some of the more attractive plant species, the Crinums and Wild Iris (*Dietes grandiflora*) for instance, could be planted near the pond side of the wetland. The Bloodroot (*Wachendorfia thyrsiflora*), despite its off-putting name, creates a pleasing display of yellow flowers in spring and will grow successfully at the water's edge or even within the wetland. Do not be tempted to plant Spanish Reed (*Arundo donax*). This invader has choked many of our river systems since its introduction into the region and will have a similar effect on your garden wetland.

The Wild Iris makes a colourful addition to a wetland area. It will spread rapidly and is fairly undemanding, requiring little maintenance.

Bulrushes are aquatic plants and will grow only in water or wet soil. The slender leaves and flowers (here releasing seed) provide valuable nesting material.

Crinums can be planted near the pond side of a wetland. A variety of species is available, all producing beautiful flowers that will enhance any wetland area.

The Blue Water Lily (Nymphaea capensis) *grows naturally throughout the region and produces blue or pink flowers from spring to late summer.*

will do the trick, but a supply of overflow water from the pond is a better option. This will ensure that the pond life receives a regular supply of fresh, oxygenated water. If you are installing a pond at the same time as a wetland, it is simple enough to tilt it slightly in the direction of the wetland so that when it is full, the water automatically flows towards the wetland. If the pond is already in position, however, it is possible to create an overflow by breaking through a section of the pond wall. Ensure that the break is at least 5 cm wide or it will block.

If you are creating a garden landscape from scratch, it would be wise to shape the lawn area in such a way that it acts as a channel, directing water into the pond or wetland. A 'dished' or concave lawn is a very effective way of retaining rain-water in the garden where it is needed.

People with larger gardens may be able to create a stream system between two ponds and establish a wetland at the entrance to the lower pond. If the ground slopes drastically and the distance between the ponds is marked, you can install a series of mini-wetlands with weirs separating each one. The weirs can be constructed from rock, packed carefully to form a wall and then covered with soil and plants. At the point of overflow, however, it is advisable to use large, solid rocks or to build a small concreted section which will withstand erosion from the flowing water. If the garden is really steep, a small waterfall can be created, which will help to oxygenate the water. Recycling can be achieved by placing a small pump in the lowest pond to direct water back up to the highest pond. Little nooks and crannies surrounding the waterfall can be filled with ferns and other plants that enjoy wet conditions.

WATER IN THE GARDEN

CLEANING THE POND

Many people recoil at the idea of a pond in the garden because, like a swimming pool, it begs the question: who is going to clean it? This fear can safely be dispensed with because a well-designed pond should seldom, if ever, be cleaned. Cleaning a pond is an intrusion on the delicate life systems that have developed over time in association with the water, and where possible should be avoided.

Among the factors which can influence the need to clean a pond are size and depth, the smaller and shallower pond (less than 40 cm deep) being the most likely to need cleaning. Deeper and larger bodies of water tend to have a more stable temperature, which in turn is conducive to a more balanced system, one that in effect is self-supporting. Other factors detrimental to the balance in a pond are goldfish and sunlight. Goldfish have a tendency to rapidly deposit large quantities of fish manure on the pond floor, and are not a good choice if you want to avoid having to clean it (another reason to try the indigenous Tilapia – *see* page 44). And sunlight, particularly in excess, results in the rapid growth of algae, which lower the oxygen content of the water and initiate the rotting process. This is especially true of shallow ponds (less than 40 cm deep), which tend to heat up quickly, making conditions optimal for algae growth. Whatever the size of your pond, try to ensure that at least half of its surface is covered with plant material.

Even when cleaning seems necessary, it need not be extreme. Simple flushing of the pond with rain-water or tap water can help to keep it healthy and clean. More active cleaning will be needed, however, should the pond start filling up with silt. If this happens, try to intrude as little as possible. A suction pipe, about 3 cm in diameter, will vacuum the silt out effectively. Sucking on the pipe to get the siphon started can be risky and may leave a bad taste in your mouth, so rather fill the pipe before placing it in the pond and then allow the water to drain. Have someone watch that the fish don't get sucked through and deposited on the flowerbed. Alternatively, a sump pump can be hired and is usually quite effective in removing silt with minimal disturbance to life in the pond. Elaborate biological filters can be manufactured or bought, but they are normally used in larger water features and are often criticized for overdoing the job.

Do not use agents, such as chlorine, when cleaning a pond as these may be toxic to the fish and other pond life. In fact, never scrub a pond at all.

DRAGONFLIES

Dragonflies are a common sight around water where they are usually seen skimming the surface or perching delicately on waterside vegetation. These graceful and often beautiful insects are an important part of the diet of fish and many bird species. Although the adults inhabit the areas outside of the pond, they always lay their eggs in water and will only select well-balanced waterbodies as habitats for the life-cycle of the immature forms.

Phragmites Reeds provide a valuable habitat for a variety of birds, including some of the migrant warbler species.

If you still feel that a garden pond or water feature is beyond your means or capability, go back to basics. A dripping tap, a bird drinking-fountain, or a shallow dish of water will provide a welcome change in a garden which previously offered no water, and will go some way towards satisfying the birds' watering needs.

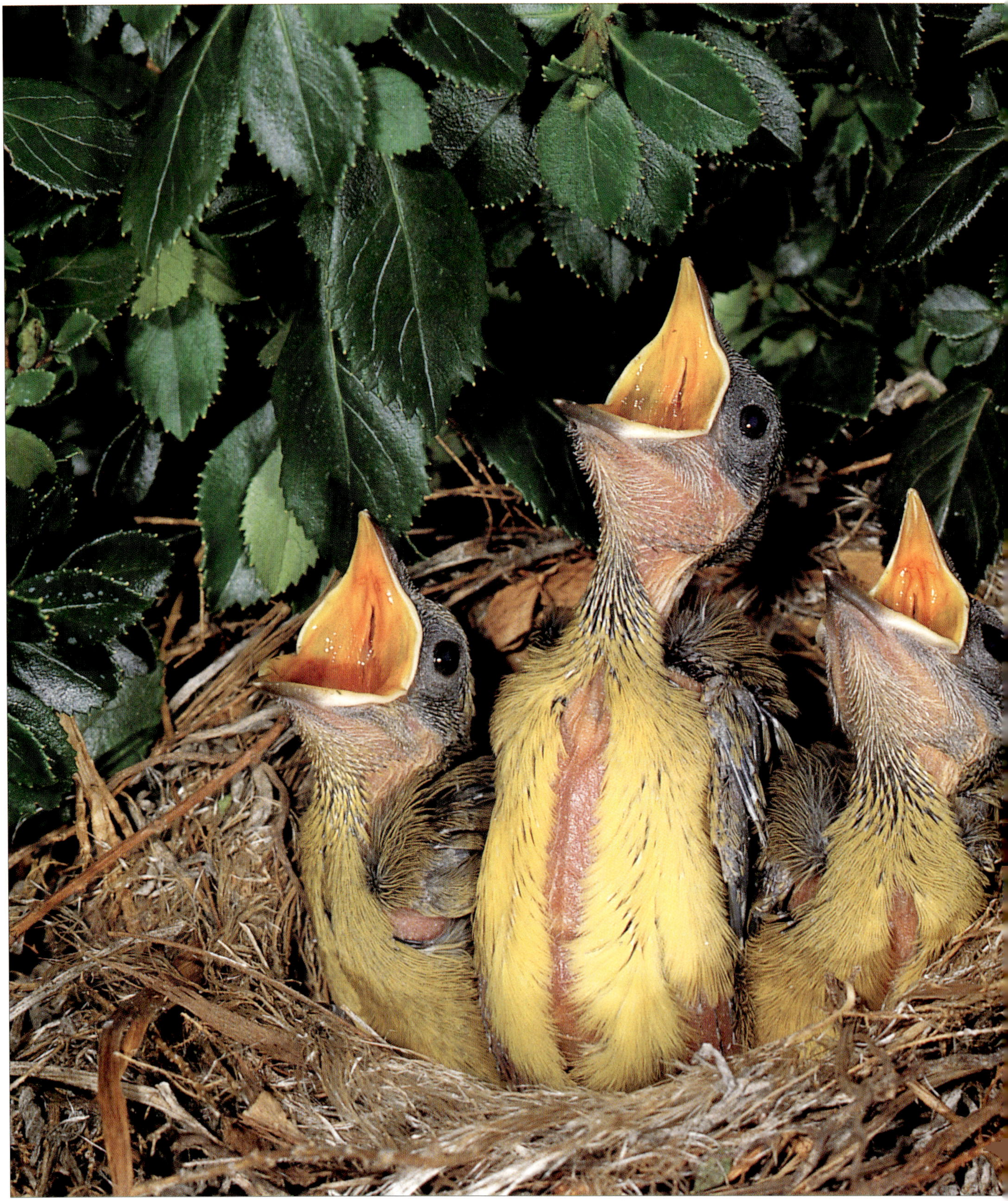

4
NESTING

*S*pring and summer bring a surge of life and activity to every garden when the inhabitants, both plant and animal, respond to the season with new energy and purpose. And the bird community is no exception. Birds are seen darting between trees and bushes, busily seeking out suitable nest sites and nest-building materials. A good stock of trees, shrubs and creepers will be a strong incentive for birds to nest in the garden, but a selection of artificial nests will bring even more birds and will be welcomed by many of the home builders.

Bokmakierie (Telophorus zeylonus) *chicks*

NESTING

NESTING

Getting birds to nest in your garden will provide the opportunity to study the complex breeding behaviour of different species, from courtship and nest-building to egg-laying and chick-rearing, and will give you greater insight into the varying life-cycles of different birds.

Encouraging birds to feed and drink in your garden will be a fairly easy task if you follow a few basic rules, but when you succeed in attracting them to nest within the boundaries of your property, you will have achieved the ultimate. Birds and animals will only breed when completely satisfied with the conditions, although many urban birds have had to let their standards slip in order to ensure the survival of the species. You may well have the House Sparrow and Laughing Dove as breeding residents, but the challenge lies in attracting less prominent species to the garden and convincing them that it is a suitable environment in which to raise their offspring.

Territorial behaviour is integral to the breeding cycle, and birds will strongly defend an area they have chosen for breeding against intruders. It can be quite entertaining to watch a barbet chasing competitors away from its nest site. This behaviour is not always directed at the same species only, and breeding individuals will often drive away other species while in an aggressive mood. There is also a strong pecking order between birds, and dominant species, such as drongos, Fiscal Shrikes and Indian Mynas, may inhibit other birds which would like to breed in the garden.

NATURAL NESTING SITES

In most gardens, and certainly in one planned for birds, there are several natural sites that will be used for nesting. If you have chosen your trees and shrubs with the needs of birds in mind, created an exclusion area, and established a wetland and area of open water, birds will find

Above: *The common Laughing Dove will build its flimsy stick nest in almost any bush or tree.*
Left: *One of the garden's busiest builders, the Masked Weaver.*

NESTING

A thorn tree is a must for the garden if you want to encourage nesting birds. Here, weavers have taken advantage of just such a site to build their nests.

you and will move in with a view to nesting and raising a family in this unexpected paradise. There are several areas in the garden which offer natural nesting sites.

THE CANOPY CORRIDOR

Most bird species nest above the ground and will naturally look to the tree tops for suitable sites. Thus, the canopy corridor is a very important area in this regard. Acacia trees, with their thorny reinforcements, offer prime nesting sites for birds but practically any tall tree with dense foliage will appeal to tree-nesting birds. Even a Bluegum tree (*Eucalyptus* species) will serve a purpose in terms of birds' need to nest. In fact, the rare Bat Hawk favours this tree as a nesting site, as does the Black Sparrowhawk, which can be found on the fringes of urban areas. The exotic Pin Oak is a favourite nesting site for some weavers, and the Blackheaded Oriole also selects tree canopies for nesting, as do the Grey and Purplecrested louries, the Blackeyed Bulbul and Olive Thrush. Tall trees, both exotic and indigenous, have an important role to play in providing nesting sites; and any specimens you intend replacing should be left standing until the preferred varieties have been planted and given a chance to establish some height.

The Paradise Flycatcher usually selects a drooping branch in which to build its delicate, lichen-covered nest.

Other sites within the canopy corridor that will attract nesting birds are dead branches. These are generally in short supply in urban areas because most gardeners remove them. Dead wood is favoured by hole-nesting species, like barbets and woodpeckers, and once these species have moved on, will attract secondary nesters, such as hoopoes and starlings. A dead tree should ideally be left standing unless it is a real eye-sore, and as long as it does not pose any danger. It is guaranteed to tempt at least one hole-nesting bird which is probably desperate for a home cooler than the steel fence-post that it may otherwise be forced to use.

THE EXCLUSION AREA

Because of the less tended character of this area, it will appeal to many nesting birds. For those that build their own nests, the Acacia species are among the most favoured trees. The thorns on these trees form an ideal foundation for a new nest, and double up as security against cats and egg-collectors. There are many different Acacia species available, but not all will be suited to local

*The sharp spines of the Natal Plum (*Carissa macrocarpa*) provide protection for nesting and roosting birds, and the large fruit it produces in summer is an added bonus.*

climatic conditions, so do some research before selecting any for your garden. Most Acacias are fairly fast-growing if conditions are right; you will be amazed to see how quickly birds take to them, often nesting there before the trees have reached two metres in height. By planting a group of Acacia species together you will find that the stronger plants grow tall while the weaker specimens fill in areas below them, so creating levels of vegetation, each of which will suit different birds.

NESTING

A Crowned Plover spreads its wings and stoops threateningly to defend its eggs. These birds are very aggressive when breeding and go to great lengths to protect their nests and chicks.

The Cape Robin is just one of several species that will make use of a well-established creeper for nesting.

Shrubs in the exclusion area, particularly those armed with thorns, will be popular nesting sites for the same reasons as are trees with thorns. Plants like the Natal Plum (*Carissa macrocarpa*) and the Kei Apple (*Dovyalis caffra*) also make good choices and have the added advantage of providing a food source in the form of succulent fruit.

GROUND-FLOOR FACILITIES

Although most birds will only look to great heights at which to build a nest, there are some species that make their homes on the ground. The first that probably come to mind are the gamebirds, like guineafowl and francolins, but there are others – dikkops and plovers, for instance – that also choose to nest here. Guineafowl may be found (after some determined searching) on their well-hidden nests between grass or herbaceous plants. Their nests are really hollows scratched in the ground, and often contain a large number of eggs. Dikkops and plovers lay their eggs on bare ground, often without creating any depression at all. These nests are also extremely difficult to locate and the parents are very careful to lead any snoopers away from them. A plover will even feign a broken wing to distract an intruder. The best way to locate a plover's nest is to sit down as if uninterested, while keeping track of the bird's progress. Patience will pay off and, once you have discovered the nest, you will be able to keep a check on the eggs and ultimately on the chicks too.

Ground-floor nesting facilities can be prepared by planting veld grass adjacent to a mown lawn, and allowing it to grow tall. Guinea Grass (*Panicum maximum*) and Weeping Love Grass (*Eragrostis teff*) make ideal grassland habitats, and the seeds of both are commercially available. The Spotted Eagle Owl may well nest between rocks and logs in this part of the garden. Bear in mind that all ground-nesting birds prefer an undisturbed area for breeding and will shy away from any areas of human activity.

OTHER AREAS

A well-trained creeper is worth nurturing, particularly in a quiet section of the garden, as this will provide a prime nesting site for a wagtail, robin, dove or sparrow. Birds selecting this location usually build their nests between a wall or fence and the branches of a creeper, so that they are well hidden by the leaves of the plant. If you are planning to plant a creeper, first nail a few wooden batons onto the wall or fence so that the plant is forced to grow slightly away from it. This will ensure that nesting birds have a wider area in which to construct their homes.

ARTIFICIAL NESTING SITES

One might argue that the whole garden is artificial, having been created or contrived according to human decisions and effort. However, there are more direct ways in which you can encourage birds to nest in the garden, which

The Blackcollared Barbet is a hole-nesting bird and will readily inhabit an artificial nest provided in the garden. It prefers to hollow out its own nest but will also use a nest-box if solid wood options are not available.

NESTING

involve more than just planting and then allowing nature to take its course. Artificial nests are built to the tastes of different birds, and should be strategically placed to tempt them. These nests are particularly useful in young gardens or small gardens which do not have any tall trees or dense habitats; but even in an established garden they will appeal to hole-nesting birds, which often struggle to find suitable accommodation in an urban context.

If you find dead wood unsightly and are reluctant to leave withering branches in your garden, artificial nests are an ideal option: they will satisfy the needs of hole-nesting birds, and keep you happy too. There will be great excitement when a nesting log or box has been provided and you are able to witness the birds flying back and forth to investigate the new facility.

NESTING LOGS

Nesting logs may be solid or hollow, depending on which bird species you wish to attract. Solid logs will appeal to primary nesting birds, like barbets and woodpeckers, which prefer to do their own hollowing and have the right 'tools' for the job. These birds generally have stout, pointed bills and adequate skull reinforcing to enable them to hollow out wood. Secondary nesting birds, the Redbilled Woodhoopoe and many of the starlings, for instance, are not able to hollow wood themselves and will readily occupy a hollow log provided for them, or will take over the nest of a primary nesting bird once it has abandoned the cavity. Hollow nesting logs are available from most nurseries and garden centres but you can very easily make your own (*see* box feature opposite).

Solid nesting logs made from the stem of the sisal plant are also available from most retail nurseries. These are sealed on the top and bottom sections with an epoxy coating to protect them against the weather, and usually contain the beginnings of a hole (about 40 mm diameter) to give the birds a head start in getting through the hard outer shell of the sisal. You can also make your own solid nesting log with minimal effort (*see* opposite).

A nesting log must be sited at least two metres above the ground and should be secured to the underside of a branch to prevent rain from entering the hole. Attach the

MAKING YOUR OWN NESTING LOGS

Use a sisal log or logs of softwood trees, such as Syringa (*Melia azedarach*) and Bluegum, to create your own nesting logs.

To make a hollow nest, select a branch with a diameter of at least 200 mm and cut off a 500 mm length. Saw off a section, about 30 mm wide, from one of the cut ends of the log. Hollowing can be done with a hammer and sharp wood chisel if you do not have the powerful equipment needed to drill out the pulp. When you have created a cavity, glue the section you removed back onto the log and seal any cracks to prevent light from entering. Seal the cut ends of the log with a non-toxic roof sealer, and cut a hole in the upper one-third of the log for an entrance. The size and shape of the hole you create is important as birds differ in their needs. A barbet, for example, generally will not breed in a log with a hole bigger than 50 mm in diameter. Hornbills, on the other hand, favour a much larger, oval-shaped hole which they plaster closed with mud, leaving open just a slit through which to feed the nest's occupants.

A hollow log will also be used by ducks for nesting. Follow the same procedure to hollow out a much larger log, and create an entrance hole that is big enough for a duck to enter and settle comfortably. Place the log among plants near the pond.

To make a solid nesting log, select a log with the same dimensions (200 mm diameter and 500 mm long). Again, seal the cut ends of the log with a non-toxic roof sealer. Start the entrance hole by drilling through the outer bark with a 50 mm wood drill bit but leave the actual hole-making to the birds.

Nesting logs in various shapes and sizes are made to suit different birds.

NESTING

SPOTTED EAGLE OWL NEST-BOX

Any scrap pieces of wood or split pole planks can be used to build a simple open nest-box with a roof. The base should be about 45 cm square and the roof supported by four pieces of wood about 45 cm in length. Attach sides, 10-15 cm high, around the base and to the roof supports; this will reduce wind chill and help to keep the eggs and owl chicks safely in the box. To help prevent the eggs from rolling around, place a layer of sawdust on the base of the box. Use a good quality exterior varnish to seal all external surfaces of the structure.

Place the box in a tree, against a building, or on top of a roof in a shaded position, remembering to select a secluded site as the birds are aggressive when breeding.

This open nest-box, placed on the ground in a quiet part of the garden, may also be used by an Egyptian Goose for breeding.

---

log firmly around the top and bottom with wire. Make sure that the entrance does not face north as this will cause overheating in the summer. Check the wire at the end of the breeding season and, if necessary, adjust it so that the branch is not damaged as it grows and expands.

NEST-BOXES

Although less natural-looking than a nesting log, a nest-box will appeal to several birds, like robins, sparrows and owls, and has the advantage of permitting you to follow the breeding cycle more closely than you could in any other type of nest. Nest-boxes vary in design according to the needs of different bird species. Some birds will only nest in a box that is completely enclosed, except for a small entrance hole; others are not fussy about the size of the opening but like to be covered on all other sides, while some species will nest in a structure that is much more open.

The conventional budgie or cockatiel nest-box – available from pet shops but also very easily built at home (*see* pages 56-57) – will be used by birds like the House and Cape sparrows and some of the starlings. It is a worthwhile addition to the garden (fixed beneath the eaves of the roof) because it will discourage these birds from entering the roof of the house where they can be a problem.

Open nest-boxes (*see* box feature above) are simple to build and can be placed in a tree or on the ground in a quiet part of the garden to encourage the Egyptian Goose to nest. The Spotted Eagle Owl will use the same type of nest, but for this species select a more secluded site – a tree or building in a remote part of the property – as these birds are very aggressive when breeding.

When building a nest-box, choose a material like plywood to ensure a longer life for the nest, and use brass screws rather than steel nails, which tend to rust and loosen in wet conditions. If you are going to use a wood preservative then do so on the outside of the box only; a yacht varnish is ideal but avoid any of the creosote- or arsenic-based wood preservatives.

Bees might be attracted to nest-boxes, particularly those with large cavities. If this happens plug the entrance with rags soaked in a strong-smelling liquid, like bleach. Once the bees have moved off, scrub the wood to remove any 'bee smells' or else they will be back to try again. Remember that bees can be dangerous, and you may feel happier contacting your nearest fire department who will recommend a bee-keeper to remove the swarm.

EXTRAORDINARY NESTS

Some birds nest in unusual places, often using the most surprising material. The challenge for you lies in dreaming up as many possible nesting receptacles as you can and encouraging birds to use them. Birds are known to use

NESTING

light fittings, umbrellas, plant pots and many other unusual items for nesting, and the rightful owners have to wait until after the breeding cycle to reclaim them. Old kettles hung in trees, saucepans and hanging plant bowls are among the objects which may be utilized by urban birds for nesting. Let your imagination run wild, and involve the whole family in manufacturing and putting all of your creations to the test.

Calabashes make ideal nesting sites once you have cut a hole in the side and secured them in a tree. Platforms and shallow wire baskets, lined with thin branches to create a natural look and placed high up in a tree, might attract open-nesters like egrets, herons and Hadedas. These species are unlikely to nest in the average urban garden but often make use of gardens bordering a green belt, sanctuary or natural area.

A truly extraordinary nest. This dove has made use of an old car headlight in which to make its home.

Birds do not let any nesting opportunity elude them. Odd corners, like this timeworn wall nook, are not overlooked.

FEATHERING THE NEST

You can greatly assist birds during the breeding season by making available a range of natural and artificial materials for nest-building. Leave piles of material at different points in the garden or offer a 'mixed bag' by filling a loosely woven bag with various items and suspending it from a tree.

Feathers are used by some birds for lining the nest. They are soft and provide essential warmth for incubating eggs.

Twigs and sticks provide stability and structure and form the foundation of many birds' nests.

Birds will use whatever is available and easy to carry, including scraps of fabric.

A bag of assorted items makes a bird's task of gathering suitable material so much easier.

NESTING

Barn Owls

Barn Owls have a tendency to nest in the roofs of houses. The nest's eventual occupants, usually in a clutch of three to six, often generate noise and smell, much to the ire of the house owners. It is not uncommon for the chicks to be dumped at a rehabilitation centre where a great deal of time and money is spent on rearing them, teaching them to hunt and releasing them. If your roof is selected as such a nesting site, try to bear with the problem until the young birds leave the nest, and be sure to evict the adults before sealing up the entrance hole. If, however, the situation becomes unbearable, simply place the chicks into a wooden box and attach it to the side of the house nearest the original opening to the roof, and allow the adults to rear their chicks in the open.

Barn Owls, as the name suggests, are often associated with buildings, and favour roof cavities in particular.

A clutch of Barn Owl chicks may number as many as ten and may well cause disturbance in a house roof.

How to Build a Standard Nest-box

The standard nest-box will be used by a variety of small birds, among them the House Sparrow, the Redbilled Woodhoopoe and some of the barbets and starlings.

Materials:
1 x 1720 mm x 220 mm x 20 mm length of pine
wood glue
14 brass screws (4,5 mm x 30 mm)
3 mm, 8 mm and 40 mm wood drill bits
yacht varnish

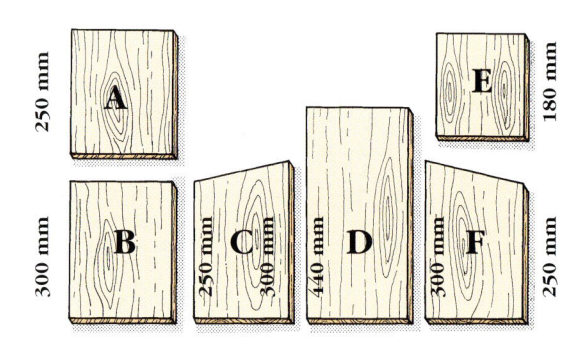

Cut the 1720 mm length of pine into six pieces (A–F) as illustrated.

Mark the positions for each side panel on the back panel (D) using a square (above). Glue side panels (C & F) to back (D) and once dry, screw in position (right). Attach base (E) to sides and back in the same way using wood glue and screws.

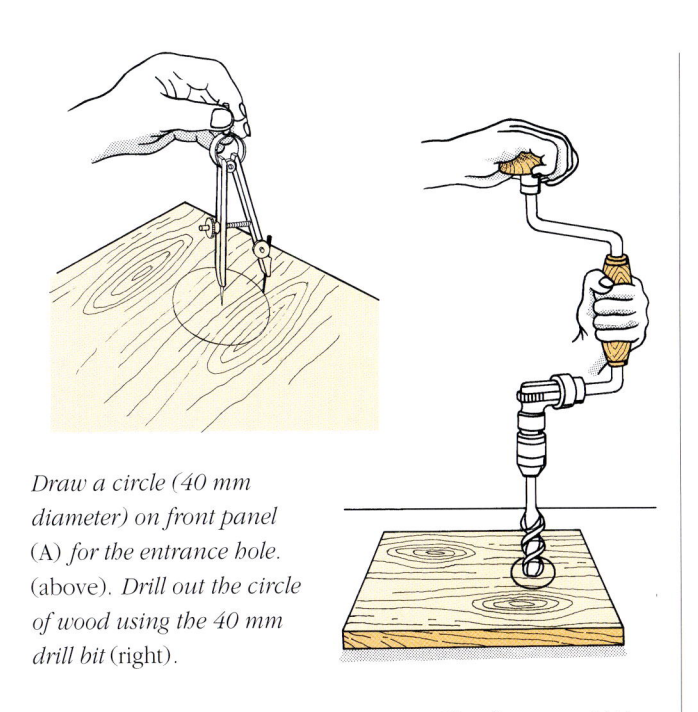

NESTING

Draw a circle (40 mm diameter) on front panel (A) for the entrance hole. (above). Drill out the circle of wood using the 40 mm drill bit (right).

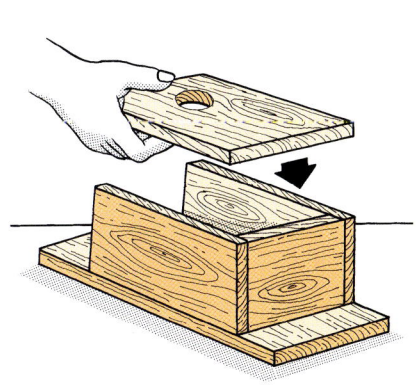

Glue front panel (A) to the structure, and screw down in position. Then attach roof (B) in the same way. Seal any cracks with a mixture of sawdust and wood glue. Varnish all exterior surfaces three times, sanding lightly between each coat.

If you want to keep an eye on the breeding cycle, you can hinge the top of the box with a piece of rubber. Lifting the lid may cause shyer species to abandon the nest, so only monitor the cycle in this way when bolder species move in.

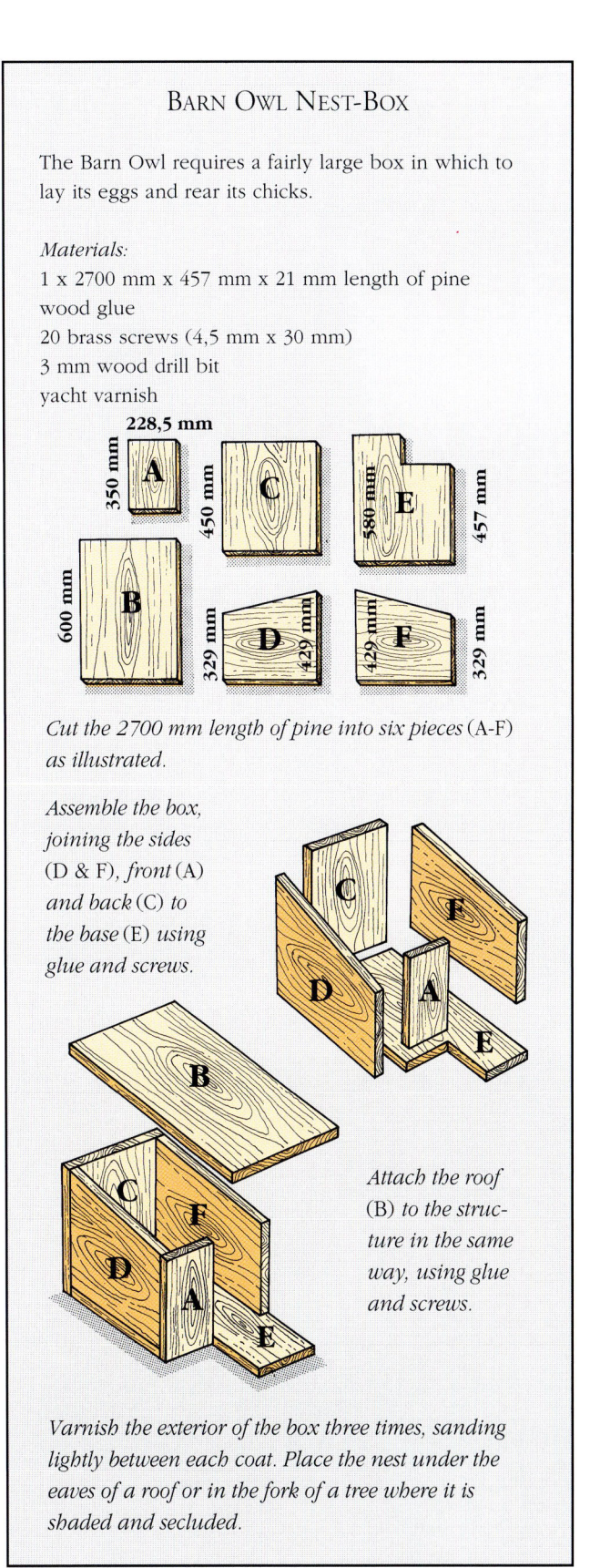

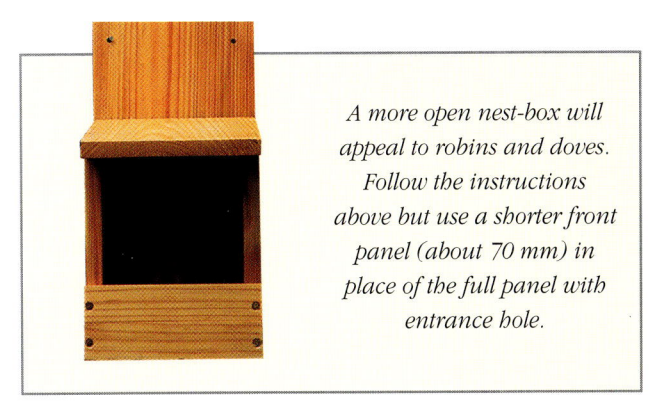

A more open nest-box will appeal to robins and doves. Follow the instructions above but use a shorter front panel (about 70 mm) in place of the full panel with entrance hole.

Barn Owl Nest-Box

The Barn Owl requires a fairly large box in which to lay its eggs and rear its chicks.

Materials:
1 x 2700 mm x 457 mm x 21 mm length of pine
wood glue
20 brass screws (4,5 mm x 30 mm)
3 mm wood drill bit
yacht varnish

Cut the 2700 mm length of pine into six pieces (A-F) as illustrated.

Assemble the box, joining the sides (D & F), front (A) and back (C) to the base (E) using glue and screws.

Attach the roof (B) to the structure in the same way, using glue and screws.

Varnish the exterior of the box three times, sanding lightly between each coat. Place the nest under the eaves of a roof or in the fork of a tree where it is shaded and secluded.

NESTING

Nesting Material

Even in an urban setting, birds are generally able to collect suitable nesting material and some, like crows and the House Sparrow, have adapted to an urban lifestyle and make use of artificial materials (wire, plastic, string, etc.) in building their nests. Obviously though, you can make life a lot easier for our feathered friends by ensuring a supply of nesting material, be it natural or artificial, on site.

A well-designed bird garden will provide a great deal of natural nesting material. Long grasses and palm leaves will be collected by the weavers, while the sunbirds will make for the exclusion area to gather spider webs to line their new homes. Mud from the wetland area will appeal to the swallows for the creation of their unique abodes, and any dead twigs will be collected by a host of different birds for nest-building. Try to resist removing all the dead branches and twigs from trees. You can even go so far as to actively collect dead wood for the exclusion area where it will be well out of your sight but readily available to birds.

Even if your garden offers sufficient nesting material, it's fun to watch birds building their nests and is worth hanging up a bag filled with feathers, grass and scraps of fabric or cloth to ensure that you can witness the activity more directly. Do not include cotton wool or material with a lot of threads as these can get caught up on the legs of young birds, which may result in their death. Use a woven plastic fruit bag to hold the material so that it can easily be extracted. Don't be tempted to stuff material into a nest-box or nesting log. Birds prefer to determine their own design, layout and 'colour scheme', and some, like the barbets, which use only the few wood shavings left in a log for nesting, will not appreciate the addition of anything else.

Baby Birds in the Garden

Having birds breed in the garden is very exciting for now, like first-time parents, you will experience the thrill of the young fledgling on its first flight. Many questions will go through your mind as you observe the new offspring: Where are the parents? Has the baby been abandoned? Is it not too small to be out of the nest? So many mistakes are made at this stage and many birds are lost because of human interference.

Birds like the Spotted Eagle Owl and Burchell's Coucal may cause alarm because the young leave the nest at an early stage, before they have a full set of feathers; some, in fact, looking as if they should still be in the egg. This is a completely natural occurrence and the parents will follow their young at close range, feeding and protecting them until they are old enough to fend for themselves. The young birds are very 'tame' at this stage and can easily be picked up, but don't be tempted. To remove a nestling and try to rear it can be disastrous and may result in it being killed by territorial birds once it is released again. So many of the young birds that have ended up in rehabilitation centres and zoos could have been successfully reared by their parents had they been left in the gardens where they were found.

If you suspect that a young bird's parents have been killed or gone missing and the youngster is in real danger, you can catch the bird. Before taking this step, however, observe the chick for a few hours and ensure that there is no hope of the parents returning. Once you are certain,

A garden planned for birds will offer many opportunities for natural nesting, and also a wealth of natural material to gather for nest-building.

NESTING

Bird Rehabilitation

The intricacies of bird rehabilitation are well illustrated by the case of abandoned owl chicks. These chicks are commonly handed over to rehabilitation centres, and it takes an enormous amount of time and money to rear them. Owl chicks need a balanced diet of mice and birds in order to develop properly, and any substitute foods offered by well-meaning 'rescuers' can cause severe damage.

Once the chicks are reared they have to be taught how to hunt. When they are proficient at catching mice in a large cage, the birds are ready to be placed in a 'hacking' cage which is built and located in the area where the birds are to be released. This area is selected according to the needs of the particular species in terms of habitat, natural distribution, etc. After a period of three weeks this cage is opened and the birds are free to go, or return for the meal which is put out for them each night. Gradually, the birds adapt to the new area and learn to fend for themselves.

Most birds in the care of reputable centres are rehabilitated using the hacking method. Incorrect rehabilitation, no matter how well intended, will result in the death of a bird.

Spotted Eagle Owl chicks leave the nest at a very early stage, and are often 'rescued' by well-meaning citizens.

place the bird in a cardboard box lined with a towel or piece of carpet. Do not use cotton wool or any material with loose threads attached as these can get caught up in the chick's feet. The dark cardboard box will keep the bird calm and stress-free, and a light shining on the outside of the box will help to keep it warm. Contact a rehabilitation centre or zoo (*see* Useful Addresses at the back of the book) as soon as possible and arrange to deliver the bird. If it is essential to feed the bird before you hand it over to professionals, use a mix of regular Pronutro and water. All birds can be fed with this mixture for a short time and it won't upset their delicate stomachs. Do not feed birds with milk or white bread as these can cause damage. Birds should not be fed if they are dehydrated. It is advisable, in fact, to give small, regular amounts of an electrolyte solution before attempting to feed any bird.

A young bird that has been thrown out of its nest in a storm can be placed back in the nest without a problem. The parents will not mind you touching the chick as long as your hands do not smell of perfume or any other strong-smelling substance. If the whole nest and its occupants have fallen out of a tree, place the offspring in a small basket or container and hang this up in the same tree. To make the birds more comfortable, line the container with nesting material similar to that of the natural nest. Keep a keen eye on the birds and wait: in most instances the parents will yield to the hungry calls of their young, and will return to feed them. The parent-chick bond is a great deal stronger than many people suppose.

Fiscal Shrike chicks gape widely in anticipation of a meal. Most young birds are fed on insects and other invertebrates, which provide essential proteins for healthy development.

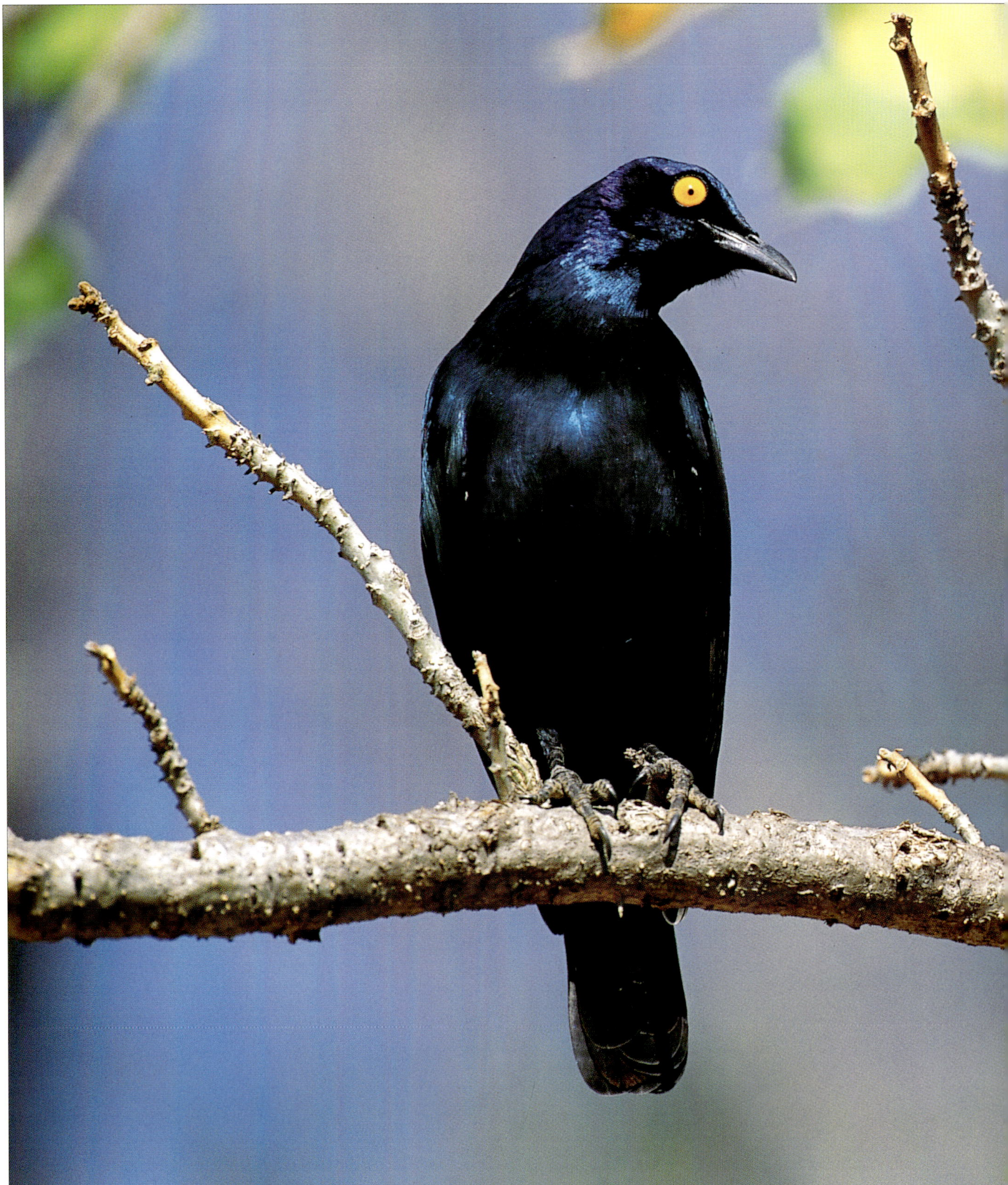

5
MAINTAINING THE INDIGENOUS GARDEN

Many myths prevail around indigenous plants, their requirements, growth patterns and their potential. In actual fact, these plants respond very well to nurturing and care, and in most cases can be grown to look as good as exotic plants. More importantly, indigenous plants are integral to any garden planned for birds.

Glossy Starling (Lamprotornis nitens)

Maintaining the Indigenous Garden

There is a common perception among people that indigenous plants should just be planted and left. This is fine so long as you like an 'untamed' look, but it is certainly not the only way to grow indigenous plants, and is no reason to avoid buying them for your garden.

The word 'indigenous' is used to describe plants and animals that occur naturally in a region. The term may be used broadly to describe plants that are native to southern African, or more specifically to refer to plants that occur naturally in a part of the region, say the Transvaal Highveld, Natal coast or Karoo.

Indigenous plants are often overlooked for gardening purposes because of their generally drab appearance in the nursery container. A Puzzle Bush (*Ehretia rigida*), for instance, would definitely not qualify as an impulse line because in its young stages it is dull and unappealing. At maturity, however, this plant bears sweetly scented, pale lavender or white flowers from August to February, and fleshy, bright orange-red fruit which is edible. Indigenous plants, with exceptions, do not compete well with most exotic plants, which are bred to look good at all stages, from their beginnings in a nursery container through to full size. It is best not to judge indigenous plants by their appearance at the nursery, but rather to look at their function in attracting birds and at their potential beauty at maturity.

Above: *The Cape White-eye lacks the long, probing tongue of the sunbirds and often splits the flowers of plants like this Aloe to reach the sweet nectar.*
Left: *A Lesser Doublecollared Sunbird on an Erica plant.*

Dispelling the Myths

In addition to the misinformed notion that indigenous plants make for an unkempt garden, there is a prevailing belief that all indigenous plants have the following requirements:
- a poor, sandy soil
- little or no fertilizer
- very little water.

Many people believe that indigenous plants will wither and die if exposed to irrigation systems, good quality soils or compost. There certainly are plants that will only grow in a sandy, unfertilized soil and with little water, but these are not generally available in nurseries and garden centres

MAINTAINING THE INDIGENOUS GARDEN

Fever trees, once established, require little management although regular removal of the side shoots will encourage straight and upright growth.

and, therefore, are unlikely to find their way into city gardens. Nurserymen do not have time to attend to the needs of individual species; most of the indigenous plants available to the public through nursery outlets are able to survive average garden conditions, and many of them will thrive on good feeding and watering.

The belief that all indigenous plants are slow-growing also prevails, and is without truth. Slow-growing plants are not economically viable to nurserymen and, like plants that require special nurturing, are left to the attentions of the avid plant collector.

Another myth has been generated around the life span of southern African Acacias or thorn-tree species, which is often reported to be in the order of ten to 15 years. This has definite origins in the average life of Australian Acacias, which generally fall down or are blown over by wind before they reach 15 years. Most local Acacias are long-lived and can safely be planted with a view to a long, shade-providing future.

Having dispelled some of the myths about indigenous plants, hopefully you will look more attentively at the selection of these plants next time you visit the nursery. Before making your choice, find out a bit about the different species and their requirements. Although you need not provide a separate set of conditions for each variety, it is advisable to have some idea of the preferred habitat of a plant before you earmark the spot in your garden for it. It would not be a good idea, for example, to plant a Sweet Thorn (*Acacia karroo*) in a wetland area as it prefers a drier location and would die within a few weeks. Its relative, the Fever Tree (*Acacia xanthophloea*), however, will thrive near water. All species have minimum growing requirements and will only succeed if these are met; local conditions, such as wind and climate, will also have to be taken into consideration before you make your selection. Generally, however, your local nursery will only stock plants that are suited to your area.

Managing Indigenous Plants

Indigenous plants can be managed in two ways, and depending on the type of management you adopt, your garden may be characterized by
- an untamed look, or
- a manicured look.

THE UNTAMED INDIGENOUS GARDEN

To many gardeners committed to growing indigenous plants, the untamed indigenous garden is the ultimate achievement. People dedicated to this gardening strategy are generally those with a deep interest in local fauna and flora, and many of them will choose to plant only those species that are indigenous to their specific area.

If this type of garden appeals to you, and if you can brush aside the type of comments it will bring from more conventional citizens, then this style of gardening is worth pursuing and will bring many rewards in terms of birds and other animal life that it attracts.

Pruning and manicuring does not have a place in the untamed garden. New plants brought in may be irrigated and fertilized until they become established, but hereafter are left to grow unattended. If you are happy with this

An untamed garden takes on a 'wild and woolly' look, and has special appeal for gardeners committed to growing indigenous plants but, more particularly, for the birds that visit it.

MAINTAINING THE INDIGENOUS GARDEN

Fynbos: The Cape's Floral Wealth

The winter-rainfall region of South Africa, a tiny belt stretching along the southern and south-western coasts, is distinguished from the rest of southern Africa by more than its climate. It is one the world's seven floral kingdoms and supports an astonishing variety of plants known collectively as fynbos; these include the beautiful ericas and numerous protea species. Many of the fynbos plants make ideal garden specimens and will attract a variety of birds but, because they are adapted to local conditions, are best suited to gardens of the region; it takes a great deal of effort and expertise to grow them elsewhere. The plants below are selected for their value in providing feeding or nesting opportunities for birds.

SOME PLANTS SUITED TO GARDENS IN THE WINTER-RAINFALL REGION

Botanical Name	Common Name	Height x Spread
Arctotis 'Silver Lining'	Silver Arctotis	0,1 m x 0,3 m
Agathosma ovata	Oval-leaf Buchu	1,75 m x 1 m
Athanasia crithmifolia	Klaas-louw Bush	1 m x 1 m
Cassine peragua	Bastard Saffron	5 m x 3 m
Chondropetalum tectorum	Thatching Reed	1,5 m x 1 m
Chironia baccifera	Christmas Berry	0,45 m x 0,45 m
Coleonema pulchellum	Confetti Bush	1,5 m x 1,5 m
Elegia capensis	Broom Reed	2,5 m x 1,5 m
Erica gracilis	Erica	0,5 m x 0,3 m
Geranium incanum var. *incanum*	Carpet Geranium	0,3 m x 0,3 m
Gladiolus carneus	Painted Lady	0,2 m x 0,8 m
Haemanthus coccineus	March Flower	0,25 m x 0,25 m
Haemanthus sanguineus	April Fool	0,30 m x 0,30 m
Helichrysum splendidum	Cape Gold	1 m x 0,5 m
Leucadendron argenteum	Silver Tree	7 m x 3 m
Leucospermum conocarpodendron	Tree Pincushion	4 m x 3 m
Mimetes cucullatus	Rooistompie	1,25 m x 1 m
Monopsis lutea	Yellow Lobelia	0,2 m x 0,3 m
Myrica serrata	Lance-leaved Waxberry	3 m x 1,5 m
Olea capensis subsp. *capensis*	Ironwood	10 m x 6 m
Orphium frutescens	Orphium	0,6 m x 0,45 m
Podalyria calyptrata	Sweetpea Bush	3 m x 3 m
Polygala myrtifolia	Bloukappie	3 m x 3 m
Protea compacta	Bot River Protea	3 m x 2 m
Protea neriifolia	Bearded Sugarbush	3 m x 3 m
Protea repens	Sugarbush	3 m x 3 m
Rapanea melanophloeos	Cape Beech	15 m x 3 m
Rhus laevigata	Dune Taaibos	2 m x 1,5 m
Rhus lucida	Blink Taaibos	1,5 m x 1,5 m
Ursinia sericea	Magriet	0,4 m x 0,2 m
Watsonia borbonica subsp. *ardernei*	Witkanol	1,5 m x 0,5 m
Watsonia fourcadei	Suurkanol	1,2 m x 0,3 m
Widdringtonia cedarbergensis	Clanwilliam Cedar	10 m x 4 m
Widdringtonia nodiflora	Mountain Cypress	5 m x 4 m

MAINTAINING THE INDIGENOUS GARDEN

Indigenous plants can be grown very successfully by applying conventional gardening practices. Here, a selection of native plants has been nurtured to create a pleasing, ordered effect.

type of garden, you will be comfortable with the fact that it demands no water other than rain and that the diverse life forms here, some in the form of recognized pests, all have a role to play and should not be interfered with. This is a 'hands off' garden with its own special appeal.

Take note of the preferred habitat of plants you select for the garden before planting them. A Fever Tree, as mentioned, enjoys water and ideally should be planted in a low-lying part where it can be assured of extra moisture from runoff water. The Highveld Cabbage Tree (*Cussonia paniculata*), on the other hand, prefers drier conditions and should be planted higher up in the garden and in soil that is well drained. Fortunately, however, there are many indigenous plants that are able to survive in a variety of habitats with varying climatic conditions.

If you find the concept of an untamed garden appealing but perhaps too fanatical, why not devote a small section of the garden to the wild look? You could even make it an experimental plot that you will evaluate after a period of two years. If your garden includes an exclusion area, you can take the concept one step further by planting only indigenous plants here, and resolve not to interfere with the natural processes at work. It will be fascinating to watch the birdlife in the garden and see which areas attract the most interest.

THE MANICURED INDIGENOUS GARDEN

Most gardeners will be more comfortable with this style of management, where traditional practices such as pruning, weeding and spraying have a place. With this approach, the aim is to get the most out of your indigenous plants, pampering them and giving them as much attention as you would exotic plants, so that they are able to compete more fairly in terms of beauty and general condition. Very often, intensive management of indigenous species increases productivity in terms of flower and fruit production, which, of course, is an added bonus for birds.

PRUNING

Many indigenous plants respond well to pruning and will flourish if cut back aggressively once a year. Generally, the more vigorous a plant's growth, the greater the chance that pruning will be successful. Slower-growing varieties can be killed with excessive pruning, however, and require more sensitivity in handling.

The Cape Leadwort (*Plumbago auriculata*) and Cape Honeysuckle (*Tecomaria capensis*) are two good examples of plants that can be cut back to within a half a metre of the ground each year – ideally just before spring. Severe frost will often do the job for you in colder parts of the Highveld and Orange Free State, after which the plants will begin to produce shoots from the underground stem and roots. Spectacular hedges of Leadwort can be fashioned by regular pruning and, along with this, you will notice an increase in the number of flowers produced.

Unlike the pruning of fruit trees which requires a level of expertise, indigenous shrubs can generally be cut back with little or no pruning knowledge. Use a sharp pair of pruning shears to cut back all branches, and leave a strong, well-branched base. If you have a large shrub that has grown unchecked for several years, take a less severe approach as heavy pruning could kill it. In this case, prune just a section of the shrub and wait for new growth to sprout. Once this is established, you can safely prune the remaining branches. Cut thicker branches with a sharp saw and seal the cut surface with a tree sealing compound to prevent fungal infections from entering.

Never prune shrubs while there is still a danger of frost, because leaves and branches help to protect the base of a plant from the cold. Staunch horticulturists do not support the idea of pruning plants while they are actively growing, but in the case of most indigenous plants, no harm is done. Ideally, plants should be

The Cape Honeysuckle will produce more flowers, and so a richer supply of nectar, if pruned.

MAINTAINING THE INDIGENOUS GARDEN

pruned just prior to the growing season, but the job can be done as late as mid-summer if you have not been able to do it sooner. If you are worried about the effects of a late prune, experiment on a section of the plant and wait for the new growth to sprout before finishing the task.

For best results, be sure to shape plants from an early stage. When pruning trees, decide the height at which you would like a tree to start branching and then keep the main trunk clean of side shoots up to this point. Canopy shape can also be determined from early on by selecting a few main branches to form the basic structure and removing all the others. Young branches can be trained to grow in certain directions; you can even tie love-knots in them if you wish. Creative plant management, which includes the shaping of plants into topiaries and hedges, need not be limited to exotic species and can just as easily be applied to indigenous plants, with the same pleasing results. The Cape Leadwort, for example, can be very successfully shaped into a hedge or topiary.

Creative gardening in the form of a tree topiary. This type of plant management need not be restricted to exotic species; several indigenous plants can also be shaped as they grow.

WATERING AND FEEDING

Indigenous plants are often able to survive the harshest of conditions and will still be standing after many exotic species have perished. This is because over the centuries they have adapted to the climatic conditions of the region. Thus, the use of indigenous plants rather than the water-sapping exotics makes a lot of sense. This option becomes even more sound when one considers the unpredictability – and so often scarcity – of rain from season to season. One of the greatest criticisms that conservationists aim at private gardening relates to the vast quantities of water

The Broom Reed, an indigenous bog plant, likes its 'feet' in water and will require regular watering throughout the year if planted in any location other than a wetland or pond border.

that are required to keep city gardens aesthetically pleasing. Water requirements are drastically reduced by growing indigenous plants, and well-planned water collection from runoff areas will make a garden even less dependent on tap water (*see* page 43).

In nature, indigenous plants are exposed to adverse and changeable conditions and may take many years to mature. When exposed to slightly better and often ideal conditions in the garden, these same plants will surprise you with their rate of growth and general condition. Reference books on indigenous plants tend to present the growth rate of a plant in nature rather then its potential growth rate, which may be off-putting when you consider the years that it will take for a White Stinkwood (*Celtis africana*), for instance, to reach maturity. Unfortunately, information on growing indigenous plants is still lacking, except in the case of a few well-known species. But don't be discouraged, and take comfort in the fact that a little nurturing will bring many rewards from these plants.

Most indigenous plants will respond well to a fertilizing or feeding programme: the rate of growth will increase, the foliage will flourish, and fruiting (if applicable) will be more prolific. For example, the Puzzle Bush produces small berries in its natural environment, but with additional water and fertilizer will produce large, fleshy fruit which even the gardener can enjoy. Composting and fertilizing at the planting stage will ensure that a plant becomes established quickly and enjoys rapid growth in its initial stages.

A superphosphate fertilizer will stimulate root growth and should be mixed into the soil at the recommended rate during planting. A general fertilizer (3:2:1 or 2:3:2) for trees and shrubs will encourage top growth, and can also be incorporated into the soil at planting, or used as a top dressing. These fertilizers contain nitrogen, phosphate and potassium – all essential elements for plant growth and present in varying quantities in different fertilizers. The

MAINTAINING THE INDIGENOUS GARDEN

numbers in 3:2:1, for instance, refer to the ratio (in the sequence listed) of each element in the fertilizer.

Fertilizers do not last forever and, depending on the type used and climatic conditions of the area, may have to be re-applied every two to three months during summer.

As winter approaches, refrain from fertilizing plants so as to limit growth and ensure that no soft, new shoots are exposed to freezing. (As the warm weather returns, you can begin fertilizing again, which will help the plant with early growth.) In the summer-rainfall region, watering should also be kept to a minimum in winter and only undertaken once the sun has warmed the soil. Never water plants after midday in winter as this will mean that they 'go to sleep' with 'wet feet' and will increase the risk of freezing. Evergreen species will obviously need more water in winter than deciduous plants, which are dormant until air temperatures rise.

In the winter-rainfall region, new plants will need to be watered once a week through their first summer season and should also be mulched. However, plants that are well mulched will cope adequately through subsequent summers with minimal watering. Since summer is the growing season, the best time to fertilize plants in this region is at the end of winter, that is, around September.

When to Plant

In the summer-rainfall region, the best time to plant new additions to the garden is at the start of spring. This will allow the plants to enjoy a long growing period before the harsh, dry, winter conditions set in. The importance of a long growing season becomes clearer in light of the fact that some large nurseries specializing in growing plants tend to force specimens to grow faster than they would naturally. This means that the plants develop a lot of soft growth points which are particularly susceptible to cold conditions. Even hardy varieties may be frosted in a severe winter if they have not had the benefit of a reasonable period of growth. A long growing season allows a plant to 'harden' and gives the root system a chance to develop.

If you do happen to plant a young specimen late in the season, make sure that the plant is well protected during winter. Hessian sacking or long veld grass can be placed around the stem of the plant to prevent it from freezing. Even frost-tender species can be grown in cold areas if they are well protected through their first few winters. A thick mulch layer at the base of the plant will also help the situation, preventing soil temperatures from dropping too low and so sparing the roots from excessive cold. Cold-sensitive species planted in front of a north-facing wall will enjoy warmer conditions and, generally, less frost due to radiation from the walls. Well-established and hardy plants can also be planted around more sensitive species to protect them.

In the winter-rainfall region, different forces are at work because of the very wet conditions which plants experience during winter and the particularly dry conditions to which they are subjected in summer. Thus, in terms of planting, the reverse is true and species indigenous to these areas should ideally be planted in autumn or at the start of winter so that they can benefit from the many months of steady rain. Although plants may not show a great deal of growth in this season (summer being the

Fynbos plants make for a rich garden paradise. Cape gardeners need to be encouraged to use the natural beauty of their area.

A Leucospermum *species, one of the plants indigenous to the winter-rainfall region, will need watering through summer in its young stages, but thereafter will survive the dry season.*

MAINTAINING THE INDIGENOUS GARDEN

The Cape Leadwort responds well to severe pruning and with this treatment will rival many exotic shrubs for beauty.

growing season here too), their root systems become well established during the winter months because of the soaking rains, and when spring arrives they flourish from this solid foundation. There is no fear of young plants freezing during winter because there is no threat of frost.

Where to Find Plants

Very often indigenous plants are kept towards the back of the nursery and, because of this inconspicuous position and the generally low demand for them, have usually been in stock for a long time. Times are changing, however, and along with the trend towards 'natural' options – free range eggs and organically grown vegetables, for instance – so the demand for indigenous plants has increased, and many nurserymen are becoming more aware of their importance. You may struggle to find staff with any knowledge of indigenous plants, even of the limited varieties available, but this will make the trip to the nursery all the more challenging. Don't be afraid to take along your books on the subject so that you can expand your knowledge as you look – and help the nursery staff expand theirs!

Try to find a nursery that is committed to helping you and don't give up at the first "we don't have any" that you hear. Nurseries are often able to source plants, and once you have established a working relationship with your local nurseryman, this is what you should expect. You may have to phone a selection of nurseries in your area to find out which of them stock a good range of indigenous plants, but already there are many that have started to make an effort in this regard.

Botanical gardens situated throughout southern Africa (*see* Useful Addresses at the back of the book) also have nursery outlets and often stock small quantities of unusual indigenous plants. By visiting the gardens you will have the opportunity of viewing the plants at maturity and will be able to get ideas for your own garden. Expertise is generally on hand at these nurseries, which makes buying a lot more rewarding.

Growing Your Own Indigenous Plants

If you have the time and the inclination, you may wish to grow your own indigenous plants. Don't be put off by talk about needing 'green fingers': with a little effort and perseverance anybody can grow plants.

Because of the general scarcity of indigenous plants, some people, out of sheer desperation, have turned to growing their own. A number of species are difficult to propagate, however, and this is often the reason why they are not seen in nurseries. Some of our more beautiful trees, like the Red Syringa (*Burkea africana*) and the Silver Terminalia (*Terminalia sericea*), are difficult to grow and have yet to be produced on a commercial scale.

GROWING FROM SEED

This is the easiest form of propagation and requires the least amount of equipment and after care. Seed can be harvested from indigenous trees in your area, but be sure to collect ripe seed only, that is, just prior to natural dispersal. Seed can also be purchased from the Department of Forestry. Another option is to become a member of the Botanical Society as this entitles you to a supply of seeds each year, and there is usually a wide range of different species from which to choose.

A two-litre plastic colddrink bottle can be modified to make an ideal germination chamber for seeds. Remove the plastic base from the bottom of the bottle and fill it with seedling soil. Scatter the seeds over the surface of the soil, cover them with a thin layer of river sand, and water well. Then take the plastic bottle and cut off the top section just above the label. Invert the bottle and insert it into the base. You now have a mini-greenhouse which will help to maintain high levels of humidity while the seeds are germinating. Store the germination chamber in a cool spot which receives plenty of natural light. Watering is seldom necessary, but keep a careful check on the soil to ensure that it never dries out.

As soon as the seedlings develop four leaves, remove the bottle and allow them to 'harden off'. Once they have strengthened, transplant each individually into a plastic nursery bag or tin can; punch holes around the edges of the base of the container to allow for drainage. A commercially available potting soil is ideal for planting at this stage, although top soil can also be used. If you choose top soil, growth will be very slow, however, and a great deal of patience will be needed while you wait for the plants to develop further.

GROWING FROM CUTTINGS

This procedure is often more difficult than growing from seed, and should only be undertaken when seed is not produced by a plant or when germination is poor. The same greenhouse can be set up in a modified colddrink bottle, but instead of a seedling soil, use a mixture of half river sand and half fine bark. Nurseries use automated fogging or misting systems which come on every few minutes to keep cuttings moist but the bottle-greenhouse system will work well in maintaining high levels of humidity.

When taking cuttings, select those with firm tips rather than the hardwood sections which are slow to root. Make the cut just below a node (area from which a leaf grows) and ensure that the cutting is no longer than 10 cm. Remove the bottom leaves where the cutting will lie in the sand, but leave at least two leaves at the top of it; don't have more than four leaves on a cutting. Large leaves can be cut in half to limit transpiration, an excess of which can kill a cutting. Avoid taking cuttings early in the growing season when the plant tissues are still very soft as this may lead to them rotting.

A two-litre, plastic colddrink bottle can easily be modified to make a suitable germination chamber for seeds or a mini-greenhouse for growing plant cuttings.

THE SEED BITE TEST

Some seeds with hard outer coats need to be treated before they will germinate. To test for hardness, use the 'bite test' to show which seeds require treatment: those which are unaffected by your best bite will need to be immersed in water that has just boiled, and left to soak for 24 hours. This will soften the seed coat and facilitate germination. Never place seeds into water that is still boiling as this will kill them.

After three weeks you will be able to see whether or not you have been successful in your venture. Some plant varieties can take several months to root; as long as the top part of a cutting is healthy, you will not have failed and rooting may still take place. Hormone powders can be used to enhance rooting, but many nurseries do not support this method of growth.

There are several books available on plant propagation if you feel that you would like to go into it further. Alternatively, speak to your local nurseryman or botanical garden expert, who should be able to give you advice on propagating plants that you are having trouble with.

HARVESTING SEEDLINGS

Mother Nature is most successful at germinating her own seeds, and it is often easier to harvest seedlings that have sprouted below an adult tree rather than undertake the task of germination yourself. Once they have developed four leaves, transplant the seedlings into a plastic nursery bag or tin can, keeping as much of the soil around the roots as possible so as to minimize shock.

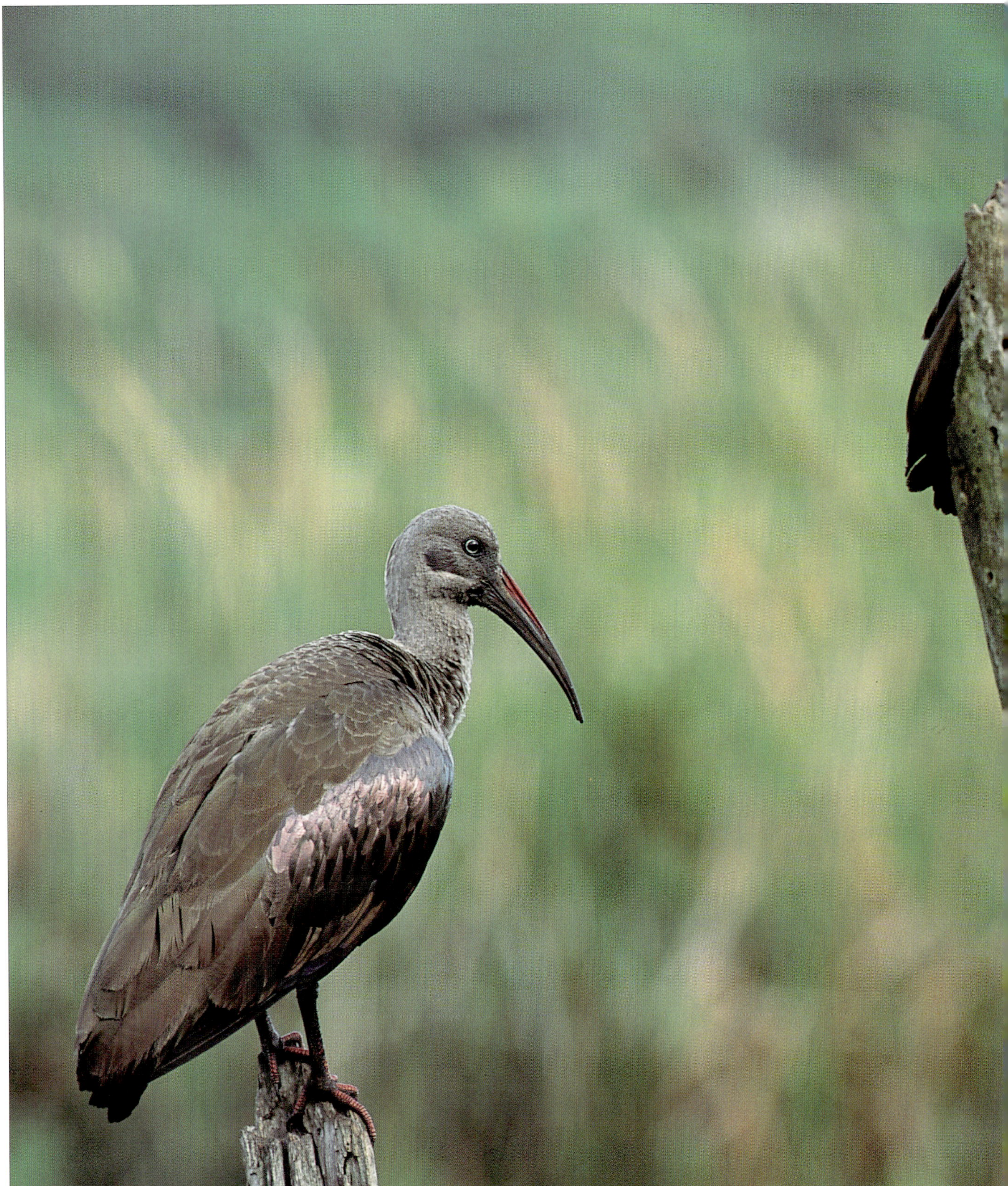

6
Pest Control

Plant pests, from scale insects, common aphids, mealybugs and ants to slugs, snails and moles, have plagued every garden at some time or another, and to varying degrees. There are different ways, both natural and artificial, of dealing with these problems, but the remedy adopted impacts to some degree and either positively or negatively on the birds that visit the garden.

Hadeda Ibis (Bostrychia hagedash)

Pest Control

The role of the gardener in controlling pest problems can range from non-intervention, to partial intervention through the use of 'soft' chemicals in conjunction with natural remedies, to full chemical control aimed at containing pest attacks through the application of a wide range of chemical products.

The use of chemicals to control pests has caused more deaths among birds than any other single human interference factor. Birds may adapt with relative ease to dogs, cats, fences, power lines and other such hazards, but it is impossible for them to escape an invisible killer such as a poison. Pesticides have had a detrimental impact on insectivorous birds, such as wagtails and coucals, while rodenticides have all but eliminated the Barn Owl from urban areas. Fungicides which are used to control plant diseases such as mildew, rust and damping off, however, seem to have little impact on birds and other 'wildlife'.

It is no use taking a fanatical approach, and banning the use of chemicals altogether. Because of human interference in nature – the planting of large areas under one crop, the importation of exotic plants, and with them exotic pests, and the clearance of massive tracts of indigenous plants for urban development, for example – chemicals have become an essential means of control. Without chemicals, we could not survive; but the manner in which we apply them is of paramount importance.

The Barn Owl (above) *has been adversely affected by the use of rodenticides in urban areas.*

Human interference in nature, including the planting of large areas with exotics, such as Eucalyptus *species* (above), *has resulted in the extensive use of chemicals to control pests.*

The Chemical Solution

The folly in choosing chemicals as the immediate and only solution to the problem of pests in your garden hardly needs reiteration. We read each day about the adverse effects of chemicals and spray-can products on the natural environment and its inhabitants, and the message that is put across is always one of warning and caution.

There is a vast range of chemical controls for plant pests on offer and it is difficult to know which ones to use. Many chemicals are indiscriminate in their action and can result in the death of many beneficial organisms in the garden along with the pest. Some have a long-term resid-

PEST CONTROL

Fruit beetles are common garden pests, but seldom attack in force, and therefore are easy to control.

ual effect on plants and soil, and have a sustained action over some weeks. In the worst scenario some indirectly target far more than the garden pest: birds eating the dead or dying insect can similarly be affected by the poison and die. This is known as secondary poisoning.

BIOLOGICAL CONTROL

In a truly natural context, that is, one that has not been interfered with or altered in any way by human influence, there are no pests. All elements of the environment are kept in check naturally, and nothing dominates at the expense of anything else. Biological control means allowing nature to maintain a balance and control any pests, and is acceptable in a natural context. However, in today's world natural forces have been distorted, and this distortion has necessitated an 'unnatural' response. The garden itself is a corruption of nature, with its mix of indigenous and exotic plants, and its artificial fertilizing and watering programmes. Since nature is no longer in control, it cannot be expected to deal with all the problems that arise. Although natural predators are often able to contain small outbreaks of pests, more serious afflictions are difficult to manage solely through biological control.

INTEGRATED PEST MANAGEMENT

This is a fancy term for a strategy which proposes the careful use of selected chemicals, in conjunction with the use of natural predators, for pest control in the garden. Where it is not possible to rely purely on biological control, integrated pest management offers a solution.

This approach encourages you to stand back and assess a situation of afflicted plants in your garden before embarking upon a campaign of pest destruction. What you need to do before instinctively reaching for a spray-can is to ask yourself a few questions:-

- Is the situation out of control, that is, are the pests taking over in the garden?
- Is the problem localized, or is the whole garden affected? Pests are most often localized in their activities and it is not normally necessary to spray anything other than the affected plant.
- Is there any non-chemical way that the pests can be dealt with (for example, leaving it to natural predators, removing affected branches or hand-picking off large bugs and destroying them)?
- How will spraying affect the other inhabitants in the garden, and how can the damage done be minimized? 'Spot' treatment involves spraying the infected plant only or even a single infected twig on a plant, and has minimal impact on the rest of the garden, while the 'shotgun' approach means spraying large areas randomly with non-specific chemicals and impacts enormously on other life in the garden.

Your aim in dealing with each of these questions is to avoid the chemical solution if possible, and where it is not, to take great care in choosing a product. Select a chemical that is suitable for the particular problem, and make sure that it is safe to use on the affected plant. Try using insecticides that have a short residual effect, such as the pyrethroid-based chemicals, as these tend to do the least damage to bird species. If you are spraying to control pests, you may wish to collect up the useful pest preda-

Caterpillars should be picked off affected plants by hand, rather than controlled using chemical pesticides.

PEST CONTROL

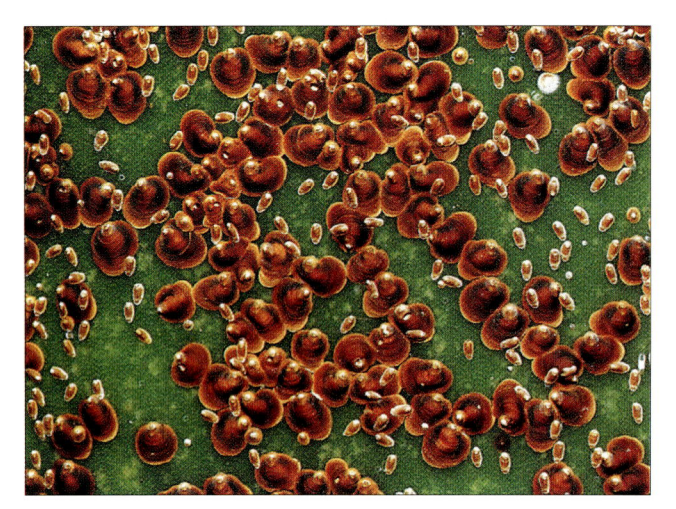

Before treating an ailing plant, such as this Aloe which has fallen victim to scale insects, establish the cause of the problem, which may have to do with unfavourable growing conditions.

tors, such as ladybirds and praying mantises, before spraying, and then release them later to clean up any stragglers.

Use a commercial sticker or spreading agent (if recommended) when spraying as this will ensure penetration of the waxy outer coating that protects many garden pest species. A cheap spreading agent can be concocted using the standard green dishwashing liquid. Add one teaspoon of the liquid to every five litres of the poison solution.

Never become involved in preventative spraying which aims to prevent pests from ever reaching the garden through the use of chemicals on a regular basis. Such measures often lead to a higher population of pests than would be the case with no spraying at all. Practise only symptomatic control using well-selected chemicals.

If you decide to adopt a new strategy, and reduce or stop spraying at certain times of the year, for example, be prepared for a full attack by pests for the first season or two while the natural predators in your garden build up their numbers to 'war readiness'. Then, once the predator-prey ratios have stabilized, you should be able to sit back and enjoy the results of a healthy garden which requires the occasional use of chemicals only.

Understanding Plants and Pests

Plants that are continually covered in aphids or scale, or suffering from mildew, rust or some other affliction, are usually plants that are not happy. The reasons for this may be various. They may be receiving too much sun, too little sun, too much water or too little water. So often, the gardener is at fault, having planted the species at the wrong time, in the wrong soil, in too windy a position or even in a climate that is altogether unsuitable.

Environmental conditions play an enormous part in a plant's well-being: take note of the origin of an ailing or afflicted plant and compare its natural growing conditions and habitat with those it experiences in your garden. You can always change the position of the plant if it is young enough to transplant. If the problem persists after you have tried a variety of remedies it may be better to remove the plant completely: the last thing you need is to be continually doctoring such plants.

Seasonal Scourges

Many of the indigenous Karee trees (*Rhus* species) are covered in aphids for a short period each summer but the trees appear to survive this attack without any ill-effects, and new leaves continue to 'grow through' the problem. A panic-stricken gardener may well waste money, time and the lives of other garden species by applying a chemical spray to solve the problem. In actual fact, the aphids disappear of their own accord, and no amount of spraying will prevent them from returning the following summer. The Wild Peach (*Kiggelaria africana*) experiences a similar seasonal problem, but with hairy caterpillars, and although young trees can be adversely affected, larger specimens survive the attack without a problem. Always monitor a pest infestation over a few days and then decide whether or not to intervene.

The Karee (Rhus lancea).

PEST CONTROL

Certain plants are more susceptible to disease or attack by pests than others. Indigenous plants are well adapted to our soils and climate and are therefore often capable of surviving attacks by indigenous pests. Many exotic species, however, are not as resistant and some are particularly vulnerable to attack. Roses, for instance, are one of the greatest attractants to pests. A bed of roses covered in aphids often sees a gardener treating the whole garden with the strongest chemical available. This does not always succeed in eradicating the problem, as aphids can reproduce very quickly and in a short space of time; but it may result in the obliteration of any ladybirds which were feeding on the aphids. Any surviving ladybirds will take longer to reproduce and, when they do, will only produce a few offspring by comparison. The result is an imbalance of predators (ladybirds) and prey (aphids) – and the spraying never stops. To maintain a population of predators in the garden, it is obvious that there needs to be a source of food – the pests. Most plants can cope with a small number of pests, and generally plants are affected adversely only when conditions are right for the pest to breed rapidly. A healthy garden will have a sustained balance between predators and prey.

FOOD PRODUCTION VERSUS BIRDS

It is a well-known fact that fruit and vegetables are especially prone to attack by pests and diseases, and if you want to succeed in producing edible produce, chemicals are necessary for keeping destructive forces at bay. Birds, too, will relish any fresh produce that a garden has to offer, but the 'treated' fruit and vegetables will obviously have detrimental effects on the birds. This situation of potential conflict can be overcome, and you need not sacrifice either one for the other.

Vegetables can be grown under a light shade cloth or bird netting. This will enable you to practise chemical control without any fear of harming birds. Fruit can be protected from birds by placing plastic mesh bags over young, selected produce. This means that you can secure the choicest fruit for yourself and leave the rest – untreated with chemicals – for the birds, which will need no invitation to the feast. If you wish to protect the entire crop, it

Rose bushes and trees are particularly susceptible to attack by pests and diseases, and generally require some degree of chemical protection in order to thrive.

BEHIND THE BLEMISH

Many people will happily accept a few moth-eaten leaves or discoloured and blemished fruit on trees in the garden but do not welcome the same condition in fresh produce they are going to eat. Perfect, blemish-free produce is generally the result of intensive spraying programmes, however, which is undesirable in food production. Although some form of chemical control may be necessary to protect fruit and vegetables, excessive use of insecticides and fungicides may contribute to serious health problems (including cancer). A few blemishes do not change the taste of a fruit or vegetable, and probably indicate that the food has been grown more naturally. Behind the blemish is often a tastier, more wholesome and healthy product.

Unblemished fruit, although most appealing, is often an indication of extensive chemical use in cultivation.

PEST CONTROL

is possible to cover a tree completely with bird netting for the fruiting period. Netting is relatively inexpensive and will spare a great deal of frustration and cursing while flocks of mousebirds systematically devour a fruit crop.

To alleviate the situation, ensure that feeding tables are kept well stocked with inviting, second-grade fruit during the fruiting season. This may help to divert the birds away from the trees, but there are no guarantees!

RODENTICIDES AND OWLS

Most homes have been plagued by rats or mice at some time. Of these, the Norwegian Rat and Brown Rat normally pose the greatest problem as they prefer to be indoors and generally move into the house or outbuildings. Indigenous rodents, on the other hand, usually remain in the garden and are less of a problem. Rodents are not the most pleasant of companions in a house and obviously present a health hazard, so it is necessary to take some action to control them. Apart from borrowing a few snakes from the local zoo, little can be done other than to place traps or put down some form of poison. Rodents often become 'trap-shy', and are adept at evading them, which leaves poisoning as the only viable method of control.

THE MANTIS MIXTURE

A young group of conservationists, the 'Mantis Team', has come up with a 'natural' remedy to control aphids, woolly plant lice and similar garden pests.

What you need:
500 g fresh kakiebos leaves, seeds, flowers and twigs
2,5 litres boiling water
10 ml sunflower oil
30 ml liquid soap

Cut up the pieces of kakiebos into a bowl, then pour the boiling water over them and leave to stand. Once cool, filter the mixture through a cloth and add the oil and soap. Use this mixture to spray the affected parts of a plant, and repeat weekly if necessary.

Barn Owls are the main victims of rodenticides. The use of poisons to control rodents has had a detrimental effect on owls which are killed through secondary poisoning.

Although targeted at rodents, the effects of rat poisons do not end with these pests. Barn Owls, once plentiful in most towns and cities in southern Africa, have almost been eradicated from these areas. The reason for this is simply poison. New rodenticides, known as the second-generation rodenticides, are even more deadly than previous forms, most of them causing death after the victim has fed on the bait only once. The poisoned rate carcass may be picked up by a hungry Barn Owl, only to seal its fate too.

If you need to use a rodenticide, use a multi-feed poison that is metabolized by the rodent. In other words, even if the carcass is fed on by an owl, secondary poisoning is unlikely to occur. This type of poison requires that the rodent feed for a minimum of three days on the bait before its death is guaranteed. These types of poisons are also safer to use if there are children or pets about, as large amounts would have to be eaten over a few days before there is any real danger. All poisons should be applied with great care, and should be used in areas beyond the reach of children or pets or, better still, in enclosed areas, such as the roof of the house.

Owls, and in particular the Barn Owl, offer the best form of biological control of rodents, and if the irresponsible use of rodenticides is brought to an end, these owls may slowly begin to recolonize urban areas. Many farmers have begun to realize that the indiscriminate use of poorly selected rodenticides can cost them dearly in the long term, and efforts are being made to entice these owls back to the barns where they belong.

PEST CONTROL

Common Pests and How to Control Them

By using integrated pest management as a basis for controlling the following common garden pests, you can protect your plants *and* the birds that visit your garden.

SNAILS

These garden pests are particularly unpopular with gardeners who enjoy Agapanthus species. Snails are particularly fond of these plants but do, of course, attack a wide range of garden plants. A pair of ducks is a sure way of solving this problem. There are several spectacular, exotic, small duck species available, which could be quite an attraction in the garden. Small ducks will not damage the plants while feeding, but will need to be fenced off from a swimming pool. Do not purchase Mallard Ducks as they pose a serious threat to the indigenous Yellowbilled Duck through interbreeding. Other birds, such as Burchell's Coucal and the Hadeda, will also feed on snails, so if your garden is bird-friendly, you may be able to attract these predators to come and work for you.

Another way of controlling snails is to lay a wet sack down at night on the flowerbed where the problem is greatest. Beer poured over the sack will act as an additional attraction to snails, which will congregate beneath it. Simply lift the sack in the morning and squash the offenders. Broken egg shell will also act as a deterrent to snails and can be placed on garden beds to discourage them.

If you use snail bait, do so with caution. It is highly toxic and should be placed in a 'snail jail' or alternative holder which prevents birds and pets from accessing the bait. It is probable that many Burchell's Coucals have been killed unwittingly through the use of snail bait.

TERMITES AND ANTS

The Harvester Termite is notorious for the destruction it causes in lawns, many of which have died through its invasion. Trees are also susceptible to attack by a related species of termite which causes the death of the tree. Because of their very deep burrow systems, these pests are not easy to get rid of.

Guineafowl provide the best means of biological control of these pests, and if your property is not too small you may consider purchasing a pair of the domesticated strain. The domestic guineafowl tends to 'home' more readily

Gardeners' Friends

The following visitors to the urban garden are useful because they feed on the harmful pests that are found there.

Ladybirds are often brightly coloured and will not be eaten by birds. They help to control a variety of garden pests, including aphids and wood lice.

Chameleons have been decimated in many urban areas by poisons. They are excellent hunters, eating many garden pests by catching them with their long, sticky tongues.

Certain wasp species lay their eggs on the bodies of worms that they first paralyze with a shot of venom from their sting. The newly hatched larvae then feed on the dead worm.

The praying mantis is an active hunter in the garden and should be actively encouraged as it helps to control problem pests such as worms and moths.

PEST CONTROL

Harvester Termites attack in large numbers and can kill a lawn. Guineafowl act as an effective control.

than the wild variety, and you do not need a permit to keep them. Farming magazines often advertise these birds and they are relatively inexpensive. Study your municipal bylaws before spending any money, however, and check with your neighbours as well; they may not find the calls of roosting guineafowl as attractive as you do. Fears that interbreeding may occur between the domesticated and wild guineafowl have been put forward by some conservationists, but this is unlikely as the two appear to be disinterested in each other, even when crossing paths.

Fortunately, chemicals used on ants and termites usually result in the insects dying underground which means that birdlife is not affected. Try to apply chemicals directly into the burrows and avoid spraying ants or termites on the soil surface where the contaminated bodies may be taken by birds. Another way of controlling ants (which is safe for birds) is to sprinkle agricultural lime around their holes and walk-ways.

RED SPIDER MITE

These pests are normally seen on the underside of plant leaves and appear as red specks accompanied by a fine web-like material. They can be controlled by making a mixture of 250 ml sugar to 1,5 litres water and spraying it

The Red Spider Mite, a sucking insect pest, is particularly troublesome in hot, dry weather, and typically congregates on the underside of leaves.

on the underside of the leaves. This should kill the pests, but if the infection is bad, it is best to cut the plant back and wait for new, clean growth. Burn the branches that you remove to ensure that the garden is rid of the pests.

APHIDS

Well known to most gardeners, aphids probably provide the greatest stimulus to buying poisons. They are in fact not too difficult to control without the use of conventional chemicals. A jet of soapy water will remove these pests from a stem, but more intricate concoctions can be made up and sprayed (*see* page 76).

Interplanting beds with Marigolds and Wild Garlic (*Tulbaghia* species) will also help to keep aphids at bay.

MOLES

These small mammals are not favoured by many gardeners, their burrows serving to dislodge plants and disfigure garden beds and grassed areas. Certain parts of the region are plagued to a greater degree than others. The bad news

PEST CONTROL

Some plant species serve as effective pest deterrents and can be cultivated for this specific reason. Euphorbia *species (above) may help to control moles and Marigolds (opposite, bottom) will discourage aphids.*

is that very little can be done to keep these pests at bay. Perimeter planting of *Euphorbia* species may have some effect on moles because of the poisonous nature of the sap, but reported results vary. The use of plastic two-litre colddrink bottles, buried near a mole hole and with the screw cap removed, is also reported to discourage moles due to the noise generated by wind blowing over the open neck of the bottle. A toxic fumigation tablet can also be used and, because it is applied underground, ensures that the animal dies there and that it is not picked up by any predatory birds.

FRUIT BEETLES

These common plant pests seem to plague most gardens and are particularly fond of roses. Their distinctive black and yellow colouring serves as a warning that the insects are inedible, poisonous or both, and birds, taking heed of this, do not eat them. If your plants are heavily plagued by fruit beetles, use a chemical control to protect the plants.

Compost heaps often harbour the juicy, white larvae of these pests, so if you have a compost heap in your garden, harvest the worms and offer them on the feeding table for insectivorous birds.

WORMS

The lawn caterpillar can be a problem in the hot summer months, its presence indicated by the appearance of brown patches at different points in the lawn.

Birds like plovers, dikkops and the Hadeda Ibis will feed on these pests and, in conjunction with other predators found in the garden, may be able to bring the situation under control, but if the problem gets out of hand, there is a 4:1:1 lawn fertilizer available which contains a

The Crowned Plover is a useful garden visitor as it patrols lawns, seeking out its insect prey which includes several varieties of garden pest.

chemical suitable for killing these worms, and which appears not to affect birds. Any other worms found on plants in the garden are usually present in insignificant numbers, and can be removed by hand.

Although many other pests are seen from time to time in the garden, few have a major impact on the plants. All too often our aim is to obliterate all unwanted pests, but in so doing we move towards a sterile garden, which is not only unnatural, but which limits the number and variety of birds that might otherwise visit.

Fruit Beetles have a predilection for roses.

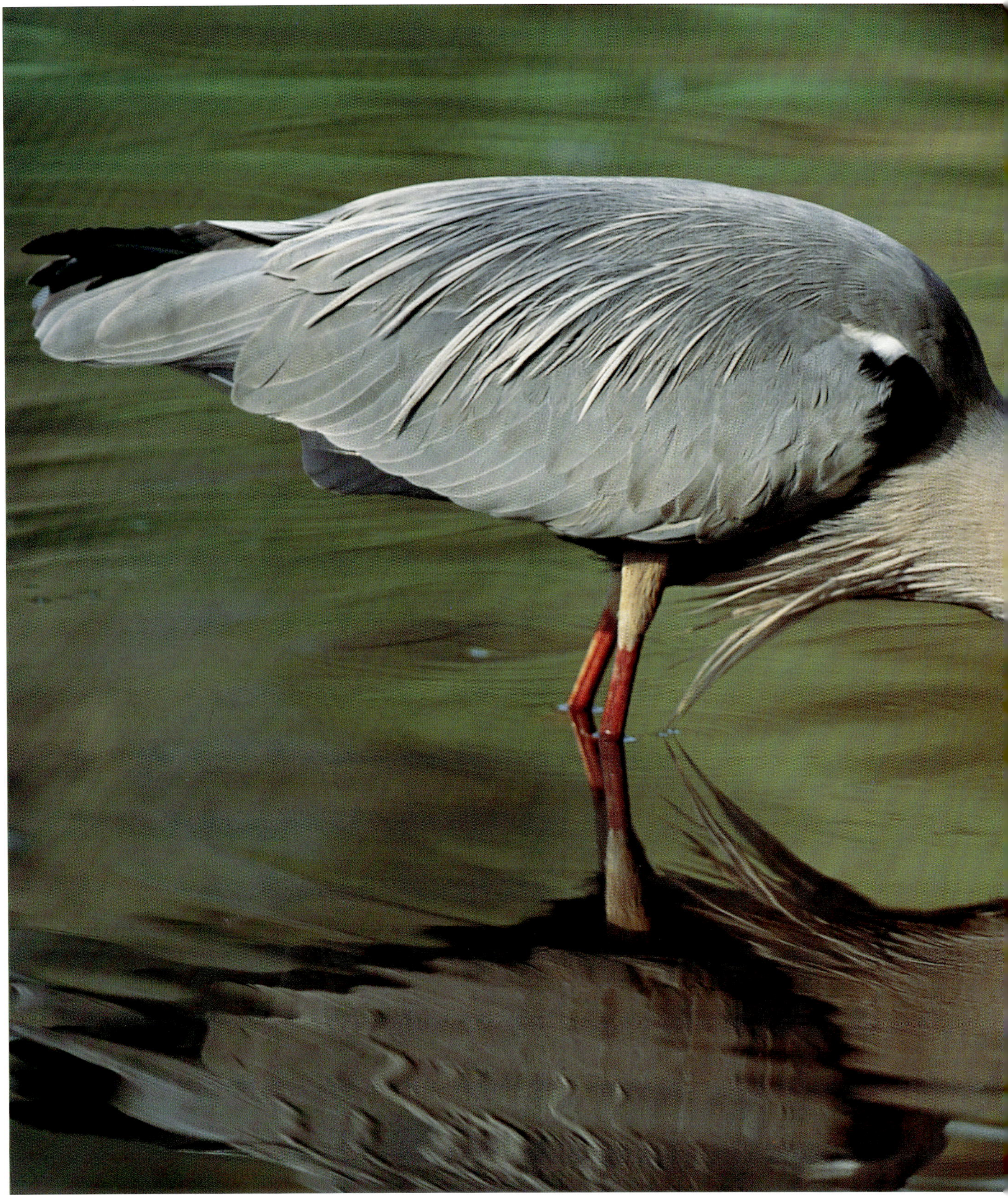

7
BIRDS ON SMALLHOLDINGS

Unlike the urban environment, farms and smallholdings still attract an enormous variety of bird species. Many occur here because conditions are such that they are easily able to survive, even thrive; others because they have been pushed out of the town and city areas by the increasing concentrations of people and buildings there.

Left: *Grey Heron* (Ardea cinerea)
Above: *Ovambo Sparrowhawk* (Accipiter ovampensis)

BIRDS ON SMALLHOLDINGS

Birds on Smallholdings

Properties on the fringes of urban areas are in a unique position to sustain a diversity of birdlife and, through the efforts of the residents here, further encourage birds so as to ensure their wellbeing and continued survival at this important interface between city and farm land.

As an owner of farmland on the fringes of a city or town, you are in a privileged position. Not only is the extent of your land an asset, but its location and size are favourable in terms of attracting and supporting a variety of bird and animal life. You may wish to play the role of custodian of the birds on your land, and ensure their survival merely by protecting them from hunting, egg-collecting and other threats they may face. However, you also have enormous scope to make your garden an 'oasis' for birds, and a place where you can watch and enjoy a concentration of species nearby.

The same basic principles already covered in the book apply, but can be practised on a far grander scale. Ponds can become dams, exclusion areas mini-woodlands, and feeding tables even 'vulture restaurants'.

Planning a Bird-friendly Environment

When planning the garden in a rural area, try not to look at it in isolation, but rather as continuous with the surrounding bush. The principle of a golf course illustrates the concept perfectly, the finest lawn being around the holes, with a gradual decrease in the amount of manicuring from the surrounding fairways to the rough. So too, with your house as the 'hole', your cultivated garden can gradually give way to less tended areas and ultimately to the outlying natural area.

OPEN AREA

A well-manicured lawn, in conjunction with areas of veld grass, will satisfy the requirements of an open area. You may wish to mow pathways through the veld grass to provide access through the wilder areas. Avoid creating too many pathways and ensure that the areas between them are large enough to attract guineafowl and francolins to

Right: *There are many attractive veld grasses that can be planted in an open area. Thatching Grass is a good option, and also grows well next to water. Grasses with full seed heads are worthwhile too, providing a valuable source of food for birds.*
Top left: *Black-shouldered Kite.*

82

BIRDS ON SMALLHOLDINGS

Although exotic, Bluegum trees provide roosting and nesting sites for many birds of prey, including falcons and eagles.

breed here. There is a wide range of veld grasses available which you can use to your advantage, selecting some which provide full seed heads for seed-eating birds and others that provide birds with ample cover from predators.

EXCLUSION AREA

In the urban garden the exclusion area is largely determined by the size of the property; in a rural setting, the extent of this area need only be limited by your budget. Here you have an opportunity to create a true woodland that will make your farm a sought-after home for birds.

If you want to establish an area that approximates nature, start by identifying the tree species which occur naturally in and around your property, and then attempt to source them from garden centres and botanical-garden nurseries. If some of the species are not available commercially you might want to harvest seed from the existing trees on the property. This method of propagation is, of course, a lengthy process and is often more difficult than it first appears. Don't be tempted to transplant trees from natural bush areas to your garden; this is a specialized procedure and unless carried out properly can result in the tree dying. If you are not fussy about using plants indigenous to your area, then consult the list of plants suggested for exclusion areas on page 16.

Plant trees close together so that the canopies will ultimately interlink, and try to include a number of different species so as to provide a variety of feeding and nesting opportunities. If you live in an area prone to very cold weather, it would be wise to plant hardy tree species for the first few years and only once these are established to add frost-tender varieties beneath the hardy specimens.

Sagewood (*Buddleja salviifolia*) is an excellent 'nurse' plant and will provide some protection for less hardy specimens against the cold.

Plant a selection of shrubs under the tree canopies to create a dense stand of plant material. Be sure to select drought-resistant varieties as it will not be practical to water this area artificially: rain-water will have to suffice.

When planting out trees and shrubs, avoid making the 'traditional' wells around the bases of the plants as this will prevent runoff water from reaching them. Rather build contours that direct runoff to different plants and help distribute it evenly over the area. In the dry Negev region of Israel, this arrangement has ensured that tree seedlings planted in areas receiving less than 250 mm of rain per annum, survive without ever being hand watered.

The exclusion area should be well stocked with rocks and logs to provide habitat options for bird species and their food items. Any trees that have been cleared from your property for road building or any other reason can be placed here, as well as all organic material deriving from the more manicured section of the garden.

Above left: *The African Goshawk, a woodland bird, will actively hunt in the exclusion area.*
Above right: *The Fever Tree can be planted in exclusion areas.*

Don't be tempted to remove any of the large Bluegum trees (*Eucalyptus* species) that are so often found on smallholdings. These provide roosting and nesting sites for birds like the African Hawk Eagle, Wahlberg's Eagle, and various kestrel species, which are still to be found on the edges of urban areas. If it is necessary to kill off any trees, then do so by ring-barking, and leave the tree standing so that it can still be of some use to birds.

BIRDS ON SMALLHOLDINGS

CANOPY HABITAT

The canopy habitat will come into its own through the planting of tree species in your mini-woodland. Aim to link the tree canopies in your garden with those of the surrounding bush. In natural habitats dense stands of trees are often found along drainage or seep lines because of the high concentration of water there. Should you have such a stand near your property, try to link the trees you have planted with those along the seep line; this will help to create an extensive corridor, right through your property and into the bush, along which birds can move.

WATER AND WETLAND AREAS

These areas are probably the most exciting to create in the rural garden as space is not usually a limiting factor and you can use your creative talents to the full. Surface water is a scarce commodity in many outlying areas, so by providing a well-planned facility, you can be sure of attracting large numbers of birds to feed, drink and breed.

Generally, all that is on offer waterwise in farmland areas are the circular, concrete dams which, because of their design, hold water that is inaccessible to birds. Ponds, dams and wetlands all have an enormous role to play in serving birds (*see* pages 40-46), and are a worthwhile investment if you have the interest and inclination to create or adapt one to suit birdlife.

CREATING A BIRD-FRIENDLY DAM

Earth dams are normally constructed by bulldozing or grading a dam wall at the lowest end of the structure to hold back the water. Although most birds favour something that has been excavated and the soil removed (high, compacted walls obscure the view and make some birds nervous when drinking or bathing), there are several birds that will benefit from just such a wall. Kingfishers and bee-eaters will use the wall for nesting and, if it includes a very steep section, will be safe from most predators here. You can ensure that a dam wall includes a steep section by erecting sheets of corrugated-iron and filling in behind

---

RURAL WETLANDS

The ideal spot for a wetland is at the entrance to a dam, where water naturally flows in. To prepare the site, start by shaping a level shelf at this point, as well as a small, earth overflow bank to ensure that water collects on the shelf before flowing into the dam. Depending on the gradient of the land, a series of shelves (and ultimately wetlands) could be formed at different levels on a slope, each serving to collect the water before it overflows down to the one below.

The shelves you create will soon fill up naturally with wetland plants, which will act as filters, cleansing the water before it enters the dam. The plants will also slow the water down, which means that silt will settle here rather than in the dam. Another benefit of the plants is that they will absorb nutrients and pollutants from the water, particularly those that wash off the farmlands. Too great a nutrient content in the water can result in excessive algae growth which in turn lowers oxygen levels. Not only would the water turn pea-green but the fish would die off, and the combination of excessive algae and rotting fish is not a desirable one.

If you have a regular or continual flow of water into the dam, you can take advantage of this by locating your wetland at the point of overflow, using a similar shelf-type design here too.

Top: *Wetland plants provide refuge for nesting birds.*
Bottom: *The Hamerkop is a frequent visitor to a wetland.*

84

BIRDS ON SMALLHOLDINGS

A newly built, bird-friendly farm dam with shallow edges and a deeper central area. The ground surrounding the dam will rapidly be colonized by natural vegetation.

them with soil. Leave the soil to settle for several weeks, watering well throughout this period, and then remove the sheets of iron. Your task complete, the birds will happily excavate their nest holes in the steep soil bank.

Although a uniformly deep dam is not a practical option where birds are concerned, a uniformly shallow one is not either. A shallow section is an essential part of a dam if birds are going to benefit, but it is equally important to include a deep section. Dams that are shallow throughout tend to become choked with plant material until no open water remains, which will upset grebes and ducks, among other species. Be sure to incorporate areas with a depth of more than 1,5 metres; these parts will stay clear of plants and will help to maintain a healthy balance in the dam.

If the size of your dam will allow for it, include an island as part of this feature. This will provide a breeding haven – out of reach of predators and human interference – for ducks, geese and other waterbirds. Transplant veld grass onto the island to help speed up the plant cover and you may be lucky enough to have birds breeding here by the second season. Guinea grass (*Panicum maximum*) can also be sown here and will spread rapidly. Place plenty of logs on the island – including hollowed-out ones – to provide nesting sites for ducks.

GREENING THE DAM

Many people are concerned about planting up a new dam, but seasoned farmers will tell you that a dam wall and island will rapidly be colonized by grasses, reeds and bulrushes without any intervention from you. The first season in the life of a dam is normally greeted by herbaceous

RESCUE PLATFORMS

Circular farm dams are the cause of thousands of birds and animals drowning each year. Having fallen in accidentally, the creatures are often unable to get out, most of them swimming round and round against the wall even when a float is available in the middle of the dam.

To make a dam 'animal safe' install a rescue platform. A rough wooden ramp constructed with cross batons will suffice, and should be anchored to the side of the dam by means of a rubber hinge to allow for changes in the water level. Large branches and logs placed in the water near the edges of the dam will function similarly, enabling any animals or birds that have fallen in to alight to safety.

A shelf built on the inside wall of a dam ensures that any birds falling into the water can get out. A wooden ramp or floating log will serve the same purpose.

weeds, like Blackjack and Kakiebos, which you may wish to cut back to prevent them seeding. Do not turn the soil with ploughs or other implements as this will only result in a new crop of weeds. The second season will herald the arrival of grasses, and it won't be long before the new structure is surrounded by plant material.

You may want to plant a few trees on the island and around the sides of the dam to provide roosting and breeding sites for birds. Be sure to select species that enjoy having their 'feet' in water, such as the River Bushwillow (*Combretum erythrophyllum*), White Stinkwood (*Celtis africana*) and the Fever Tree (*Acacia xanthophloea*).

BIRDS ON SMALLHOLDINGS

THE BLUE CRANE'S DEMISE

A plea must be made for the endangered Blue Crane of southern Africa. This species has been killed off at an alarming rate, largely by the irresponsible use of chemicals in farmland areas. The cranes are guilty of feeding on grain that has just been sown and because of this do not endear themselves to farmers. To overcome this problem, some farmers actively target these birds by soaking grain that is to be sown in a mixture of chemicals. The unsuspecting birds then eat the grain. The unfortunate outcome of this situation is that South Africa's national bird is now a highly endangered species.

With a little effort, farmers could, in fact, be the key protectors of this beautiful bird. For example, hired help could be employed to scare the birds off the lands shortly after planting; and feeding sites could be established in an effort to divert the birds from the agricultural crops.

Cranes are still known to breed on smallholdings and need to be protected to ensure their survival. If you have any of these birds on your property, regard it as a privilege rather than a curse, and cater for them directly by providing food. This will ensure that they do not have to travel in search of other food supplies (which may well be poisoned), and will go some way towards protecting the species.

INTRODUCING FISH

When selecting fish for the dam, avoid Barbel as they generally limit (by devouring) the population of other useful species like Tilapia. The Mozambique Tilapia (*Oreochromis mossambicus*) and the smaller Banded Tilapia (*Tilapia sparrmanii*) are both good choices for a dam and make for excellent eating once they mature. Barbel will often, almost inexplicably, find their way into a dam – even over great distances from other sources of water. These fish are able to move overland in search of new water, particularly during a drought spell, and have an uncanny ability to locate dams the owners of which are intent on keeping them out!

Fish in the dam will come under strain until water plants become established and are able to afford some protection from predators. Darters, cormorants and herons will move in the moment a free meal is on offer, and an exposed fish is a delicacy that will not be overlooked. Place thorn branches in a section of the dam to help provide some cover for the fish until the water plants take over.

A Darter is a certain visitor to a farm dam that is well stocked with fish.

WORKING WITH NATURE

Many small farms and outlying plots are bought with the idea of 'weekend' or 'part-time' farming in the hope of generating wealth. So often these dreams are destroyed by the realities of managing a farm. Having dispensed with the farming idea, the owners abandon the lands. The natural cycle can take many years to re-establish itself, and a phase of bush-encroachment is typical. This is nature's way of protecting the soil from further damage by climatic influences, erosion and use by wildlife, and a dense mass of plant material spreads through the once-open pastures.

If you fall into the category of a once 'weekend farmer', or if you have any areas of 'old land' with scars from earlier farming, you can actively contribute to the situation by speeding up nature's recovery process. The aim is to create a savanna-type vegetation of trees interspersed with grasslands. To do this, you will need to clear a fair amount of the rapidly spreading plant material. Start by selectively removing trees so as to open up bush areas, and prune remaining trees to form erect, well-structured specimens. Avoid ploughing over any soil, if possible, as this will encourage weeds and prolong recovery.

This type of veld management will help to restore the land to its original splendour and will mean that the vegetation can be better utilized by birds. Study areas of undisturbed vegetation near your smallholding to use as a model for your own management. While the trees are growing it would be a good idea to erect a T-bar (*see* box feature opposite) to meet the needs of birds of prey.

BIRDS ON SMALLHOLDINGS

Pest Management

Although the same principles of pest control pertaining to urban gardens (*see* pages 72-74) will apply to smallholdings and farms, these need to be taken a step further in this context. This is because the nature of activities carried out in farmlands often leads to more aggressive use of chemicals, many of which (to compound the problem even further) are more lethal to wildlife than those sold to the average city gardener.

Integrated pest management is as viable, if not more so, in farming as in gardening. In fact, this approach is already widely used in citrus and soft fruit production; and other farming sectors are also beginning to practise more responsible pest management. Many farmers are now making an effort to retain bands of natural vegetation adjacent to farmlands so as to afford protection to natural predators. These areas house and support insectivorous birds (shrikes, coucals and egrets) and rodent-eating birds (owls, kites and hawks), as well as predatory insects, such as spiders, ladybirds and wasps, and other useful small predators like snakes, hedgehogs and genets.

A great deal of damage is done through the use of granular insecticides in farming, which are spread onto the ground between crop plants. The granules are often picked up by birds, some of the products causing more or less instant death. Seed-eating birds are especially prone to this type of poisoning, although secondary poisoning is also common and occurs when kites and other bird scavengers feed on the smaller bird carcasses. The use of water-soluble chemicals, which are applied in liquid form, is a more viable option for controlling pests on farms and lowers the risk of non-target poisoning.

Chemicals used in crop production should be carefully selected, and farmers should be encouraged to contact the manufacturers directly for further advice and information on the effects of their chemicals on wildlife. Many of these companies, and particularly those with international connections, are becoming more environmentally aware and will happily assist with any queries you might have.

Predator Perches

All too often farmers remove most if not all of the vegetation surrounding their farmlands, without realizing the ill-effects of such an exercise on other life forms. Many birds of prey depend on this vegetation for habitat, and these birds are extremely valuable in controlling pest populations, especially rodents, on farms. By obliterating this habitat, the farmers in fact lose out on a natural form of pest control. To overcome this situation and to encourage birds to hunt in and around farmlands, 'predator perches' can be erected.

Consisting of a pole of about 6 metres long and a crossbar of about 2 metres long, a T-bar can be secured in the ground on the edge of active farmlands or even in abandoned farms where trees have been removed. Birds of prey, including kites, buzzards and owls, will use the bar as a perch from which to search for prey items before stooping down on them.

A Barn Owl will use a T-bar from which to hunt prey.

One of the farmer's best friends: the Blackshouldered Kite consumes a large number of rodents each day.

Directory of Garden Birds

One of the joys of watching birds in your own garden is that you can pull up your favourite chair and settle in familiar surrounds to learn more about birds and their daily and seasonal habits. An important first step, however, is the identification of new visitors or residents.

This directory presents 100 of the most common garden birds occurring in southern Africa. Some of these birds will visit the garden for cover, others for food and water, and still others for roosting or nesting sites; some will visit to satisfy several of these needs, all depending on what your garden has to offer.

In order to get the most out of this opportunity, it is important to have the right equipment at hand. A good pair of binoculars is essential: a recommended size for bird-watching is the 10 x 40 combination (10 power with a 40 mm object lens). This will enable you to observe the finer details of individual birds, which will make identification that much easier.

You may wish to use tape-recordings of certain bird calls to attract those birds into the garden, but do so judiciously as these can be disconcerting and confusing to resident birds, and you may unwittingly end up being guilty of harassment.

A hide – if your garden can accommodate one – is an ideal way of viewing birds without intruding on their space. This can be built from various materials (such as canvas, cardboard, reeds or other plant material), but the more natural it looks, the better. If a hide is to become a permanent feature in your garden, place it near the main feeding area as this will be the centre of bird activity. Try to do most of the construction work away from the garden so that disturbance is kept to a minimum. Viewing slots in the hide should obviously be able to accommodate a camera lens and binoculars. If you wish to make the opening larger, a 300 mm x 300 mm slot is acceptable. Birds seem happy enough to see a human face but are alarmed by the entire human form. In short, either be invisible in a hide with a small opening for a lens, or let only your face be visible through a larger, more obvious viewing window.

The position of the hide should allow birds to fly down to food or water and to land without feeling threatened. In spite of the initial intrusion of a hide, birds will soon accept it as part of the garden. Noise and movement within the hide should obviously be kept to a minimum.

Contact your local bird club or wildlife society for checklists of birds in your area (*see* addresses at the back of this Directory – page 191). It would be a good idea to become a member of a club in order to increase your knowledge and share your own experiences of birds. The jargon associated with birding can be obtained only by word of mouth from fellow 'twitchers'. Soon you will be talking about BSKs (Blackshouldered Kites), pearlies (Pearlspotted Owls) and you will be able to PI (positively identify) all the species you record in your garden.

The Malachite Kingfisher is an inconspicuous bird and may well be a visitor without the gardener's knowledge.

IDENTIFYING BIRDS

forehead
crown
nape
throat
mantle
breast
wing
belly
leg
flank
vent
back
tail
rump

Use the labelled bird parts (above) *when recording details of birds you see in the garden. Take note of a bird's size, general colour, bill shape and colour, leg colour, and any distinctive markings on the face or body. Note the habitat or area of the garden which the bird is using, and any peculiar habits or behaviour it displays. The more detailed your written observations, the more chance you have of making a positive identification.*

HOW TO USE THIS DIRECTORY

This bird directory provides guidelines to identifying each species by means of photographs and, where necessary, a brief description. The birds are ordered taxonomically and follow the sequence used by *Roberts'* (Maclean 1993). Diet and breeding information are provided for the bird in nature, and there is a discussion on the role of the garden in satisfying the need of each species for habitat, food and nesting. This provides valuable information on where in the garden to look for a particular bird and, more importantly, on what to plant or to offer artificially to attract it to feed, rest or breed in the garden.

Birds are identified by their common name. The scientific name is printed in italics below this and is followed by the Roberts number in parentheses and by the length of each species (the measurement given being from the bill tip to the tail tip of an outstretched bird). For each species there is a map provided, depicting the bird's distribution within southern Africa, which will indicate at a glance whether or not the bird occurs in your area.

TERMS EXPLAINED

Incubation period refers to the time between the laying of the eggs and the hatching of the chicks.

Fledging period, as used in this book, refers to the time between the chicks' hatching and their leaving the nest. In the case of francolins, plovers and dikkops, whose young leave the nest soon after hatching, 'fledging period' refers to the time between the chicks' hatching and their first being able to fly.

DIRECTORY OF GARDEN BIRDS

CATTLE EGRET
Bubulcus ibis (71) Length: 54 cm

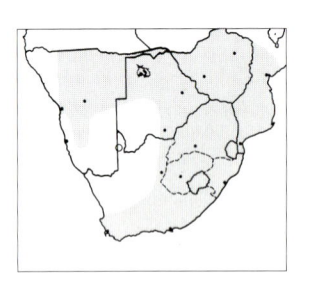

The Cattle Egret is a common visitor to urban gardens, particularly those with large open areas. It occurs in groups and is usually seen probing the lawn for insects. The common name derives from the bird's habit of accompanying cattle and feeding on insects, especially grasshoppers, disturbed by the moving animals. This bird is commonly seen on sports fields, golf courses and other grassy areas.

The Cattle Egret has buff plumes on the head, breast and back, and its legs turn red in colour during the breeding season.

DIET
Mainly insects; also fish, amphibians, rodents and reptiles if the opportunity arises.

BREEDING
Site: Trees or reeds close to water. Nests in colonies, sometimes very large ones, often in the company of other egrets, herons and cormorants. Nestling mortality results in a strong smell which is characteristic of the breeding sites of these birds.
Season: September to February in the Transvaal; slightly earlier in the Cape. **Clutch Size:** 2-4, rarely up to 7, laid at daily intervals. **Incubation Period:** 22-26 days. **Fledging Period:** About 30 days, but chicks leave the nest before this, at about 20 days old.

The saucer-shaped nest is often built between reeds in wetlands, but sometimes in trees, and two to four, bluish-white eggs are laid.

IN THE GARDEN
Habitat: The Cattle Egret is attracted to open areas which allow for a clear, all-round view. It tends to avoid gardens where there is a lot of activity and will often visit once children are at school and the area quietens down.
Food Requirements: The bird visits gardens most often during summer, when insects are abundant. It is attracted by outbreaks of lawn caterpillars, and is often able to control the problem, thus reducing the need for chemical control. It can be attracted to the garden with pieces of meat placed on the lawn, and if you establish a feeding routine will soon become a regular visitor.
Nesting: This bird will not breed in small urban gardens, but may roost or breed in nearby sanctuaries or green belts. Exotic Bluegums (*Eucalyptus* species) and the Weeping Willow (*Salix babylonica*) are often favoured as nest sites.

The open area of the garden is the hunting ground of this bird, where insects are taken.

DIRECTORY OF GARDEN BIRDS

Hamerkop

Scopus umbretta (81) Length: 56 cm

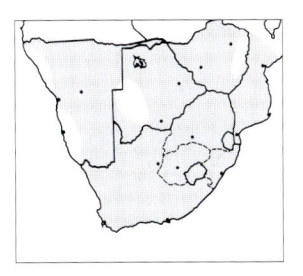

This large, brown bird favours aquatic habitats and is typically seen standing in shallow water watching for movement. It is often an unwelcome visitor in gardens because of its taste for goldfish. The Hamerkop is an interesting character, however, with a fascinating habit of shuffling its feet in shallow water so as to disturb prey that may be concealed.

The nest is a huge structure, a metre or more wide, and is often built in a fork of a tree.

The Hamerkop is often seen in shallow water, stirring up the mud with its feet in search of aquatic prey.

DIET
Fish, frogs, crustaceans and aquatic insects.

BREEDING
SITE: The huge, domed nest is unmistakable and is built in the fork of a tree or on a cliff face, normally near water. The nest incorporates sticks, mud and artificial materials – plastic bags, cardboard, even tin cans – and typically has an entrance on the least accessible side. It may be nearly two metres high and strong enough to bear the weight of a man.
SEASON: Mainly July to January in South Africa, but throughout the year in Zimbabwe. CLUTCH SIZE: Up to 5. INCUBATION PERIOD: About 30 days. FLEDGING PERIOD: About 45 days.

IN THE GARDEN
HABITAT: A productive wetland area incorporating a pond will encourage the Hamerkop to visit the garden on a regular basis.
FOOD REQUIREMENTS: The Hamerkop often depletes garden ponds of goldfish because the fish provide such an easy meal. The use of Tilapia instead will make the bird less of a nuisance because these fast-moving fish are better able to evade capture than the slow, brightly coloured goldfish. Frogs and aquatic insects will also be eaten. The birds may be attracted by bits of meat left on rocks around the pond.
NESTING: The Hamerkop is unlikely to breed in any urban gardens, except very large ones when the nest will be sited in a large tree.

91

DIRECTORY OF GARDEN BIRDS

Hadeda Ibis
Bostrychia hagedash (94) Length: 76 cm

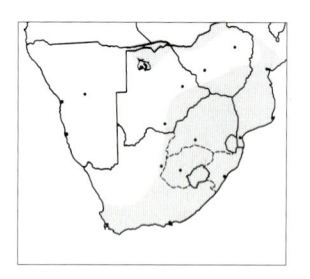

The Hadeda Ibis has extended its range in recent years and has adapted to even the smaller gardens in urban areas where it is a frequent visitor. Its call, from which it gets its name, is often heard as the birds fly to and from their roost sites at dusk and dawn.

The Hadeda Ibis may nest in larger gardens, selecting a tall tree as a site for its shallow stick nest.

SEASON: July to January. CLUTCH SIZE: Up to 4, usually 3. INCUBATION PERIOD: About 25 days. FLEDGING PERIOD: About 40 days.

IN THE GARDEN

HABITAT: The Hadeda Ibis is a common visitor to gardens with well-watered lawns which are easy to probe for food items. It is often chased by dogs and for this reason favours quiet gardens with plenty of 'runway space' for escape.

FOOD REQUIREMENTS: The bird's long beak is ideal for probing into the lawn to extract its insect prey. It is thus an excellent agent of biological pest control. A thick mulch layer with its rich insect population will be well utilized by the bird. You can also offer small pieces of meat or bone-meal on the lawn.

NESTING: The Hadeda Ibis will breed only in large, mature gardens, where the shallow nest of sticks and grass is likely to be placed high in the fork of a tall, densely foliated tree.

The drab, uniform, greyish colouring of the Hadeda Ibis is broken by a metallic sheen on the back and shoulders, which is seen only at close range.

DIET
Insects, snails, spiders and earthworms; also small rodents and reptiles when available.

BREEDING
SITE: Usually tree branches overhanging water. The nest consists of a stick platform lined with grass.

Slugs and snails are favourite food items and the Hadeda Ibis will make short work of these garden pests.

DIRECTORY OF GARDEN BIRDS

Egyptian Goose
Alopochen aegyptiacus (102) Length: 70 cm

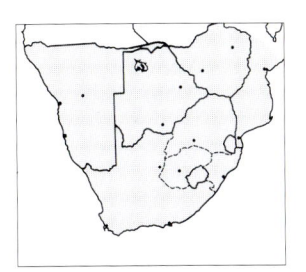

The Egyptian Goose is a common resident in southern Africa. It is often found in pairs but also forms large flocks, particularly in areas where food is plentiful. It would seem that a pair of birds selects a garden after an aerial survey, and may then spend some time there deciding whether or not to visit it regularly. The Egyptian Goose is, however, an occasional visitor rather than a permanent garden resident.

Egyptian Goose ducklings imprint on their mother, and at only a day old will leave the nest to follow her.

The common and widespread Egyptian Goose is a brownish bird with a characteristic dark brown eye patch.

DIET
A variety of plant material, including grain crops.

BREEDING
Site: Nests in various locations: at ground level near water, in hollow trees, in deserted raptor nests, on top of old Hamerkop nests; and even on top of buildings where suitable ledges are available.
Season: Year round. **Clutch Size:** 7-9. **Incubation Period:** About 30 days. **Fledging Period:** About 60 days.

IN THE GARDEN
Habitat: A wetland area and pond will encourage these birds to visit the garden.
Food Requirements: The Egyptian Goose is fond of lawn grass and will graze even when this is very short. Poultry pellets, sprinkled on the lawn where it feeds, will be relished by this bird.
Nesting: Egyptian Geese will utilize an open nest-box in the garden (*see* page 54), even displacing owls from it. Resident pairs, which bond for life, will defend their territories during the breeding season and chase away intruders, with much noisy display. The ducklings, which show well-developed imprinting behaviour, leave the nest simply by jumping, no matter what the height. At the Delta Park Environmental Centre in Johannesburg, ducklings slide down a drain pipe to reach ground level, having hatched on the roof of the building.

An open nest-box such as this, placed in larger gardens, will encourage this bird to nest.

DIRECTORY OF GARDEN BIRDS

Ovambo Sparrowhawk

Accipiter ovampensis (156) Length: 33-40 cm

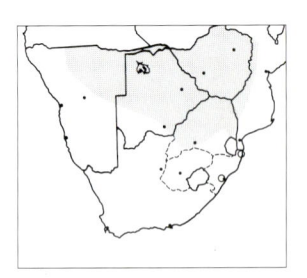

This agile bird is not a common visitor to urban gardens but its numbers appear to be increasing in this context, probably due to the wooded character of many gardens and the abundance of prey on offer here. A shy, unobtrusive bird, it is seldom seen except when making dashing flights between trees or when being mobbed by other birds.

The Ovambo Sparrowhawk feeds on a variety of small birds, plucking them before eating them.

DIET
Almost entirely small birds, including weavers, doves, cuckoos and flycatchers; but nothing larger than a Redeyed Dove.

BREEDING
SITE: A sparsely lined nest platform made of sticks is constructed high up in tall trees.
SEASON: September to November. CLUTCH SIZE: 1-5, usually 3. INCUBATION PERIOD: About 35 days, by female alone. FLEDGING PERIOD: About 33 days.

IN THE GARDEN
HABITAT: In some areas in the north of the region the Ovambo Sparrowhawk is commonly seen in large gardens and may become quite tame. It normally perches in the middle of a tree canopy and makes short, quick flights between perches. Tall trees, both in the garden and in surrounding areas, will provide an incentive for the bird to visit.
FOOD REQUIREMENTS: The Ovambo Sparrowhawk will feed on a variety of small garden birds, but is unlikely to attack large poultry. It hunts from a perch or in flight, often stooping from great heights on prey below. Bird prey is plucked before being eaten. There is no specific way of attracting this raptor to the garden, but it will visit regularly if enough prey items are available there and if there are suitable nesting trees in the vicinity.
NESTING: This bird is unlikely to breed in a garden, but may do so on a smallholding or farm. Tall trees, including the exotic Bluegums (*Eucalyptus* species) and the Grey Poplar (*Populus canescens*) make ideal nesting sites. The Ovambo Sparrowhawk normally builds a different nest each year.

The Ovambo Sparrowhawk selects tall trees as sites for its nest. A stand of Bluegums such as this may attract the bird in the breeding season. The nest may be as high as 26 metres off the ground. These birds also hunt from perches, either by hot pursuit or by stooping on prey.

DIRECTORY OF GARDEN BIRDS

Little Sparrowhawk

Accipiter minullus (157) Length: 23-25 cm

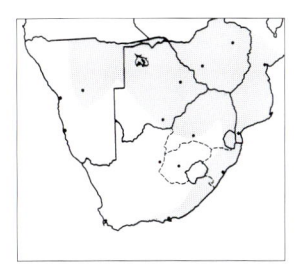

This tiny raptor is often present in urban gardens, particularly in areas which border on natural habitat. It is an elusive bird and is easily overlooked as it moves rapidly through the tree canopies and the exclusion area.

A favourite hunting technique employed by the Little Sparrowhawk is to ambush its small-bird prey. It selects a concealed vantage point in a tree near water and dashes out after a victim when the birds settle on the ground.

The Little Sparrowhawk is not often seen. It is a fairly small raptor with slate-grey upperparts, heavily barred underparts and a distinctive white rump.

DIET
Almost entirely small birds such as finches, warblers and weavers; occasionally insects and small reptiles.

BREEDING
SITE: A nest of twigs is constructed in a tall tree. The nest is lined with green leaves and is larger than one would expect for such a small bird.
SEASON: September to December. CLUTCH SIZE: 1-2.
INCUBATION PERIOD: About 32 days. FLEDGING PERIOD: About 25 days.

IN THE GARDEN
HABITAT: The Little Sparrowhawk may be encouraged to visit a garden with tall, large, leafy trees in which it is able to keep a low profile and remain inconspicuous. However, it is unlikely to be attracted as a permanent resident to the urban garden as it requires dense thickets in which to wait in ambush for its prey. This little, unobtrusive species occasionally becomes a visitor to bird-baths.
FOOD REQUIREMENTS: Gardens with a healthy population of small birds such as sunbirds, prinias, warblers and weavers, and an abundance of insects, will help make this bird a regular visitor.
NESTING: Although the Little Sparrowhawk is unlikely to breed in a garden environment, it may nest on larger properties bordering natural habitat. Exotic Bluegums (*Eucalyptus* species) and Grey Poplars (*Populus canescens*) are often selected as nest sites as these tall trees allow the birds to build their nests high up off the ground. The habit of laying a clutch of only two eggs is unusual for sparrowhawks and their eggs are distinctive in that they are white and unmarked. The parents defend the nest aggressively during the breeding cycle. This species often re-uses nests in subsequent breeding seasons, but may build a new nest near to that used in a previous year.

DIRECTORY OF GARDEN BIRDS

African Goshawk
Accipiter tachiro (160) Length: 36-39 cm

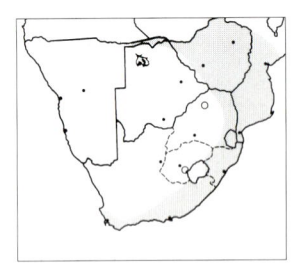

This bird is often overlooked as it prefers to hunt in dense vegetation. It is most conspicuous when flying high over the tree tops in the early morning, calling repeatedly as it goes.

This unobtrusive bird of prey hunts by watching from a concealed position, periodically changing perches, or by ambushing prey. It takes mainly birds and small mammals, particularly small rodents.

BREEDING
SITE: A platform of sticks, lined with green leaves, is built high up in tall trees.
SEASON: September to November. CLUTCH SIZE: 2-3. INCUBATION PERIOD: 35 days. FLEDGING PERIOD: 35 days.

IN THE GARDEN
HABITAT: This bird will frequent gardens which have large, leafy trees and dense vegetation, from which concealed positions it attempts to approach and catch its prey unawares.
FOOD REQUIREMENTS: A healthy population of small birds and reptiles, especially lizards, will make this species a regular visitor and possibly even a breeding resident in the urban garden. The African Goshawk has been known to visit a feeding table to take bone-meal.
NESTING: This bird favours indigenous trees, including *Ficus*, *Breonadia* and *Syzygium* species for nesting, but may also choose exotics such as Bluegums (*Eucalyptus* species). Although nests are occasionally built as low as four metres above the ground, the average height of nests is closer to eight metres.

The immature bird resembles the immature Little Sparrowhawk but is much larger and lacks white tail spots.

DIET
Mainly birds (including doves and bulbuls); occasionally also small mammals and reptiles.

DIRECTORY OF GARDEN BIRDS

Cape Francolin
Francolinus capensis (195) Length: 42 cm

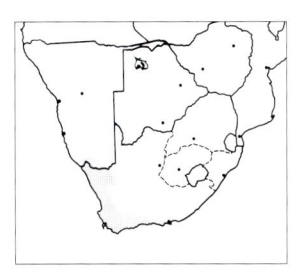

This shy bird visits urban gardens which offer ample plant cover and where there is not too much disturbance. Once resident in the garden it becomes quite tame. It is a fairly large francolin, and lacks the red throat area characteristic of several other large francolins. It will frequent the exclusion area and, once it feels secure, will venture into the open areas of the garden to feed on seeds and insects there.

Despite their shyness, Cape Francolins tame easily, and once they become accustomed to the garden will venture into the open area to feed on seeds, insects and any kitchen scraps that are offered there.

The lack of red on the throat distinguishes the Cape Francolin from other large francolins. The pale cheeks contrasting with a darker cap are seen only at close range.

DIET
Corms, bulbs, roots, seeds, berries, soft plant material and insects.

BREEDING
Site: A hollow, scraped out beneath a bush and well camouflaged between plant material.
Season: September to December. **Clutch Size:** 6-8.
Incubation Period: Not known in the wild; 22-25 days in an incubator. **Fledging Period:** First able to make short flights at 12 days old, but probably fledges at 25-28 days old.

IN THE GARDEN
Habitat: A well-developed exclusion area which offers ample protection will be well utilized by this bird. It will also make use of a wetland area and open areas in the garden. A sand patch (*see* page 13) will be used daily to keep its feathers in peak condition.
Food Requirements: A rich mulch layer in the garden beds will be a big attraction and the bird will spend a great deal of time scratching here to extract the juiciest insects (it is an excellent agent of biological pest control). It responds well to feeding, and poultry grain can be sprinkled in the exclusion area to supplement its diet. Once the bird becomes tamer, it will be possible to entice it into the open area with food.
Nesting: If this bird's needs for food (mulch layer) and cover (exclusion area) are met it will readily become a garden resident and may breed. The Cape Francolin is an attentive parent and the chicks are often only seen once they are a week old, or more. The young are able to fly when they are still very small, but remain with their parents until they are fully grown.

DIRECTORY OF GARDEN BIRDS

NATAL FRANCOLIN
Francolinus natalensis (196) Length: 30-38 cm

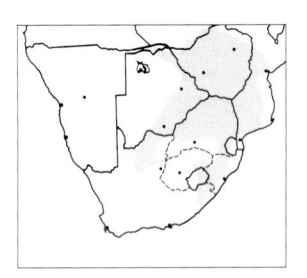

The Natal Francolin is widely distributed in the eastern parts of southern Africa and is a common resident in certain areas but a fairly shy visitor to urban gardens. It is often seen in groups with chicks and seldom strays very far from water. Like the Cape Francolin, this species does not have a red throat.

A rich mulch layer in the garden beds will provide a good source of food in the way of insects for the Natal Francolin, which will scratch busily in search of prey.

The Natal Francolin, unlike the Cape Francolin, has an orange bill and reddish-orange legs and feet. It readily forms small coveys, probably family groups.

DIET
Corms, bulbs, roots, fruit, seeds and insects.

BREEDING
SITE: A grass-lined scrape on the ground.
SEASON: Mostly mid-summer in South Africa; throughout the year in Zimbabwe with a peak in late summer and early autumn. CLUTCH SIZE: 5-8, usually 5. INCUBATION PERIOD: About 22 days (in captivity). FLEDGING PERIOD: Not known.

IN THE GARDEN
HABITAT: The exclusion area and open areas in the garden will be frequented by this bird, especially if the garden borders onto a natural area and if the boundaries include dense hedges and shrubbery. The Natal Francolin is very shy and will generally enter the garden only in the early morning and late evening. A suitable sand patch (*see* page 13) will be an added attraction to this bird.
FOOD REQUIREMENTS: Feeding at ground level, this bird will readily eat grain, bread crumbs, mealie meal, bone-meal, fruit and similar food items offered in the exclusion area. It becomes tame over time and can be persuaded to come into open areas if food is offered there on a regular basis. The bird is also fond of insects, particularly grasshoppers and termites, and will make a quick meal of any found in the garden.
NESTING: A well-developed exclusion area which offers ample cover will provide an incentive for this bird to breed. The chicks, which have greenish legs, are closely guarded by the mother and may only be seen when they are more than a week old.

DIRECTORY OF GARDEN BIRDS

Helmeted Guineafowl
Numida meleagris (203) Length: 56 cm

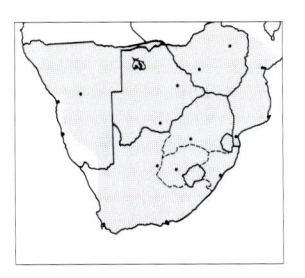

This guineafowl is common throughout southern Africa but only an occasional visitor to urban gardens. It is seen regularly on smallholdings, sports fields, golf courses and road verges. Gardens with large areas of lawn also attract the Helmeted Guineafowl. Outside of the breeding season it gathers in large flocks and prefers to visit farmlands or smallholdings where seed and insects are plentiful. Properties that border onto such areas also play host to this bird.

This guineafowl nest, well hidden between clumps of grass, is abounding with eggs. Several female birds often use one nest in which to lay their eggs.

DIET
Corms, bulbs, roots, seeds, berries and soft plant material, and insects such as ants and termites.

BREEDING
SITE: A shallow depression or nest hollow is scratched in the sand, often under a shrub or clump of long grass.
SEASON: October to March, coinciding with the onset of rains in the summer-rainfall region and the end of the rainy season in the winter-rainfall region. CLUTCH SIZE: 6-19; large clutches probably laid by more than one female. INCUBATION PERIOD: 24-25 days. FLEDGING PERIOD: First flies at about two weeks old; fully fledged at about four weeks old.

The Helmeted Guineafowl is unmistakable with its horny crown, blue and red facial skin, and blackish body heavily speckled with white.

IN THE GARDEN
HABITAT: Open areas and the exclusion area will be utilized by this bird.
FOOD REQUIREMENTS: The mulch layer will be valued as a food source, and insects will be exposed by scratching, much as a chicken would. This bird is valued by farmers for its role in combating pests – particularly harvester termites, which it relishes. Grasshoppers are also a favourite item, although most insects will be eaten. This guineafowl can also be attracted to the garden by sprinkling poultry grain on the lawn; once the food source has been discovered the bird will become a regular visitor.
NESTING: This bird, which has a high breeding success rate, will breed readily on smallholdings, and may well breed in large gardens with extensive exclusion areas. The breeding bird will not abandon the nest and will vigorously attack any intruders who might pose a threat. The chicks have characteristic striping down the length of the body.

DIRECTORY OF GARDEN BIRDS

CROWNED PLOVER
Vanellus coronatus (255) Length: 30 cm

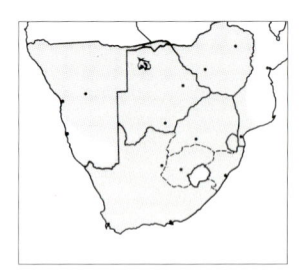

This common resident of the southern African region regularly visits urban gardens. It is usually seen in pairs or small groups in open areas of the garden, and is often heard calling loudly as it swoops down on the local cat or dog.

The eggs of the Crowned Plover are well camouflaged among these flowering annuals. Plovers do not build a nest but lay their eggs on bare ground.

The Crowned Plover, with its distinctive black cap encircled by white, is attracted to sandy, open areas.

DIET
Mainly insects and their larvae, including grasshoppers.

BREEDING
SITE: The nest is a scrape in the ground and is usually in an open area where eggs are well camouflaged against a sandy background.
SEASON: June to March; timing varies regionally in southern Africa. **CLUTCH SIZE:** 2-4. **INCUBATION PERIOD:** About 30 days. **FLEDGING PERIOD:** From about 30 days.

IN THE GARDEN
HABITAT: This frequent visitor to quiet gardens will spend most of its time on the lawn, hunting for food.
FOOD REQUIREMENTS: The Crowned Plover feeds on a variety of insects and insect larvae and is particularly successful at keeping the lawn free of caterpillars. It embarks on a short run with its head held down and then stops suddenly to stab at its prey with a rapid, forward movement of the head. It responds well to feeding and will relish any offerings of mealworms, bone-meal and small pieces of meat.
NESTING: This bird may breed in large gardens with open areas comprising veld grass and sand. The parents aggressively defend the nest and will dive down on any intruders, sometimes mobbing them in force. They may also feign a broken wing, dragging it along the ground to distract the intruder from the nest. The chicks lie flat against the sand to avoid detection, and it takes a sharp eye to discover them. They leave the nest very soon after hatching and forage for themselves from their first day out, although food items are pointed out to them by their parents.

The chicks lie flat against the sand to avoid detection.

Spotted Dikkop

Burhinus capensis (297) Length: 44 cm

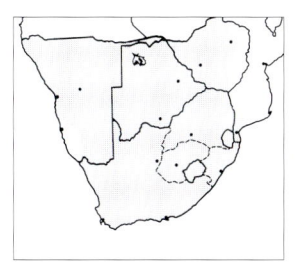

The Spotted Dikkop will visit some urban gardens, but is not often seen because it is active almost exclusively at night, when it is sometimes heard calling. It may occur singly or in pairs. The characteristic whistling call is often given while the bird is on the wing, and it displays a peculiar habit of flying almost vertically when disturbed from its ground position where it is usually well camouflaged.

Breeding birds will confront intruders with outstretched wings in a threatening display and may charge forward.

The large, yellow eyes of the Spotted Dikkop are adapted to nocturnal vision, enabling the bird to hunt for its insect prey after dark. The heavily speckled body makes it a difficult bird to spot, particularly when it sits motionless at rest during the hours of daylight.

DIET
Insects, small crustaceans, molluscs and grass seeds.

BREEDING
SITE: A scrape in the ground, usually in an open area.
SEASON: August to December, extending to April in winter-rainfall areas. CLUTCH SIZE: 2. INCUBATION PERIOD: About 25 days. FLEDGING PERIOD: 50-56 days.

IN THE GARDEN
HABITAT: The Spotted Dikkop may be attracted to an exclusion area adjacent to open veld, and will make use of this to rest during the day. At night (when it is active) it will forage in open areas of the garden but it is extremely wary of dogs.

FOOD REQUIREMENTS: Although shy, this bird will be attracted to a light hung in the open area at night, to take advantage of a free insect meal. Bone-meal, mealworms and small pieces of meat can also be offered once the bird becomes a regular visitor.

NESTING: The Spotted Dikkop is unlikely to breed in a small garden, but may be attracted to a larger garden which offers a large open area with sections of veld grass and sand. Chicks leave the nest shortly after hatching and, unlike Crowned Plover chicks, are fed by the parents for some time after this.

The Spotted Dikkop lays its well-camouflaged eggs in a scrape on the ground beneath a bush.

DIRECTORY OF GARDEN BIRDS

Feral Pigeon

Columba livia (348) Length: 33 cm

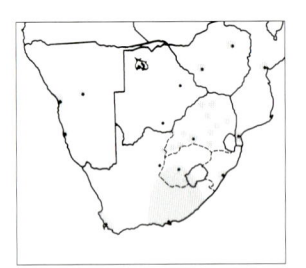

The Feral Pigeon is a common resident of urban areas. It was first introduced to the region from the Netherlands and, later, from other parts of Europe. It is often found in large flocks in city parks and other open areas, and is particularly well adapted to living alongside man. The Feral Pigeon has become a nuisance in many cities and is disliked for its habit of fouling building ledges and roofs with its droppings. It is one of the very few bird species in southern Africa whose distribution is tied almost exclusively to human habitation.

This pigeon commonly roosts on house roofs which become covered in the bird's droppings.

The Feral Pigeon displays a great deal of variation in colouring but is generally a shade of blue, grey or purple with some white markings.

DIET
Seeds, grains, fruits and food scraps.

BREEDING
SITE: Building ledges or crevices. The nest consists of a platform of sticks, plastic and other such items.
SEASON: Any month of the year. CLUTCH SIZE: Usually 2. INCUBATION PERIOD: About 18 days. FLEDGING PERIOD: About 30 days.

IN THE GARDEN
HABITAT: This bird will enter the garden to feed in open areas. Most people are happy not to have it visit the garden, however, as it is capable of consuming vast quantities of food from the feeding table and tends to bully other species. The Feral Pigeon also has a habit of roosting on house roofs which it rapidly litters with its droppings.
FOOD REQUIREMENTS: This bird's diet is almost entirely adapted to the human diet. It will feed on crumbs, seeds, fruit and any other items offered it. Its rapid rate of population growth and range expansion would not have been possible without the generous offerings left by 'friendly' humans.
NESTING: This species is most likely to breed on the house or outbuildings if there are suitable building ledges or crevices present, but most people would rather discourage it. Watching it go through its breeding cycle on a flat-block or office window-sill, however, can be both entertaining and educational.

DIRECTORY OF GARDEN BIRDS

ROCK PIGEON
Columba guinea (349) Length: 33 cm

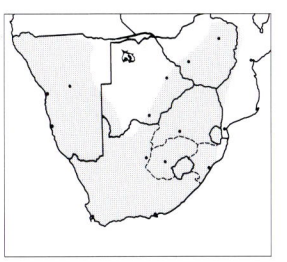

The Rock Pigeon is a common resident of urban areas and is regularly seen with the Feral Pigeon, with which it sometimes hybridizes and produces fertile offspring.

DIET
Seeds, grain, fruit, young shoots and kitchen scraps.

BREEDING
SITE: Building ledges, large palm trees and cliff faces. The nest consists of a thin stick platform lined with some green plant material.
SEASON: Any month of the year. CLUTCH SIZE: 2, occasionally 1. INCUBATION PERIOD: About 15 days. FLEDGING PERIOD: 25-30 days.

IN THE GARDEN
HABITAT: This species prefers to forage during the day in wide-open areas, especially cultivated fields. It is

The Rock Pigeon has a red skin patch around each eye. The wings speckled with white also serve as a distinguishing feature. Immatures lack the red face.

Above: *Rock Pigeons have successfully adapted to life in urban settings and are common garden residents. Seeds and grains such as sunflower seeds* (left) *form the bulk of this bird's diet and it is common throughout the grain-growing areas of the region. It will also enjoy pecking at a piece of bread offered on the ground.*

more likely to use the garden for a breeding site than as a feeding site.
FOOD REQUIREMENTS: The Rock Pigeon will feed at ground level in the open areas. It is not a common visitor to the feeding table, but if you are fortunate enough to have a breeding pair in the garden be sure to provide plenty of grain and seeds on the lawn or on a feeding platform.
NESTING: The Rock Pigeon, common in urban areas, uses any sheltered site to breed, so suitable ledges sited or large palm trees planted in the garden may encourage it to breed here. Alternatively, it may nest under the eaves of the roof of the main house or outbuildings.

DIRECTORY OF GARDEN BIRDS

Rameron Pigeon

Columba arquatrix (350) Length: 42 cm

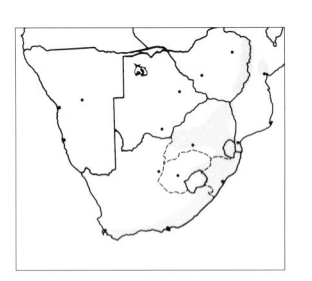

This is the largest of the southern African pigeons. It is nomadic and moves to wherever there are plants in fruit. This bird occurs in well-wooded gardens, especially those situated near tracts of indigenous forest.

DIET
Fruit; occasionally insect larvae, especially caterpillars.

BREEDING
SITE: A platform of sticks is built in the fork of a tree.
SEASON: Usually during summer but has been recorded in most months of the year. CLUTCH SIZE: 1. INCUBATION PERIOD: 16 days. FLEDGING PERIOD: About 20 days.

IN THE GARDEN
HABITAT: This is a shy bird, preferring to keep to the tree tops, but is sometimes seen flying powerfully from one tree canopy to another. It is most conspicuous early in the morning, when it forages close to the ground in relatively open trees such as figs.
FOOD REQUIREMENTS: The Rameron Pigeon is a fruit-eater, and is particularly attracted to the alien Bugweed (*Solanum mauritianum*) and other fruit-bearing plants, such as the Wild Olive (*Olea europaea africana*), White Stinkwood (*Celtis africana*), Yellowwoods (*Podocarpus* species), Pigeonwood (*Trema orientalis*), and the low-growing Inkberry (*Cestrum laevigatum*). It is unlikely to visit the feeding table but may be attracted to fruit that has been placed high up in trees in the exclusion area.
NESTING: The Rameron Pigeon is shy when breeding, and nests are rarely built in gardens. The nest is sited between one and 14 metres above the ground, usually in a well-leafed tree or bush.

The fruit of the Outeniqua Yellowwood (Podocarpus falcatus) *is one of the bird's favourite foods.*

Rameron Pigeons favour a forest habitat. They feed on the fruits produced by trees such as olives and wild figs.

The large Rameron Pigeon has yellow eye patches, a yellow bill and yellow feet.

DIRECTORY OF GARDEN BIRDS

Redeyed Dove

Streptopelia semitorquata (352) Length: 35 cm

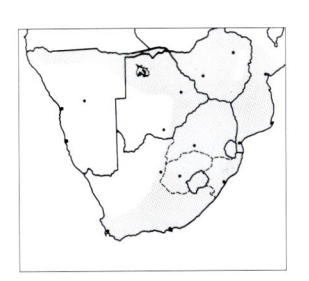

A common resident of urban areas, this bird is the largest of the ring-necked doves and can be recognized by its characteristic red eye, encircled by a dark pink eye-ring.

DIET

Seeds, fruit and insects.

BREEDING

Site: A platform of twigs is built in a tree or shrub.
Season: Any month of the year, with a preference for summer. **Clutch Size:** 2. **Incubation Period:** About 15 days.
Fledging Period: About 20 days.

The Redeyed Dove is a larger and darker bird than the similar Cape Turtle Dove, and is distinguished further from that species by its characteristic red eye-ring.

IN THE GARDEN

Habitat: The Redeyed Dove often rests in tall, open trees, including willows and Bluegums (*Eucalyptus* species), flying down to feed or display. It forages on the ground, often on lawns, and is a regular visitor to a bird-bath or garden pond.
Food Requirements: Although not as common at the feeding table as the Cape Turtle Dove, this bird is similar in its habits and will feed on various grains, bread crumbs, mealie meal, fruit and also insects. Most doves prefer to feed on the ground, so by sprinkling grain at ground level in the open area you can divert them from the feeding table and minimize competition there. Trees bearing small fruit will also be an attraction to these birds.

The Redeyed Dove eats a wide variety of food, taking seeds, tubers and insects as well as unshelled peanuts (which it swallows whole), maize and sorghum. It will also feed in trees and bushes where small fruits are available.

The Common Forest Grape (Rhoicissus tomentosa).

Nesting: The Redeyed Dove builds its nest anywhere from one metre above the ground right up to the tree canopy. Nests close to the ground are usually sited over water, but otherwise a nest may be built almost anywhere. This bird does not, however, nest on buildings.

The nest of the Redeyed Dove is more substantial than those of most other doves, and is usually built with twigs and lined with finer material.

DIRECTORY OF GARDEN BIRDS

CAPE TURTLE DOVE

Streptopelia capicola (354) Length: 28 cm

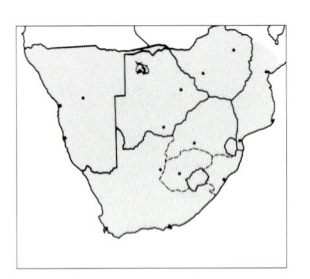

This is one of the most common residents in urban gardens throughout the region. It is often found in large numbers at feeding tables or on the ground in open areas. Feeding and drinking groups are highly wary of predators and often take to the air simultaneously in a flurry of wings if disturbed.

The Cape Turtle Dove is very fond of water and will utilize a bird-bath (above) or a larger body of water (below) in order to keep its feathers in peak condition.

The Cape Turtle Dove is distinguished from the Redeyed Dove by its dark eye which lacks a red eye-ring. In flight the white-tipped tail is conspicuous.

DIET
Seeds, grains such as millet and maize, and insects.

BREEDING
Site: A simple twig platform is built in a tree or shrub.
Season: Any month of the year, but mostly spring or late summer. **Clutch Size:** 2. **Incubation Period:** 12-16 days. **Fledging Period:** 20 days.

IN THE GARDEN
Habitat: Typically rests in open trees, bushes and vines, but forages on the ground. It is a frequent visitor to bird-baths and garden ponds.
Food Requirements: The Cape Turtle Dove will feed on grain, bread crumbs, mealie meal and various other items. Most garden-bird enthusiasts complain about the vast numbers of these doves in the garden, as they tend to drive more timid species away from the feeding table. Such pressure can be alleviated by sprinkling seed and grain on the grass. This ploy will also keep these bold birds busy for a while as they search for the food.
Nesting: This species will nest in a wide variety of trees and bushes, sometimes no more than a metre above the ground. Exotic Bluegums (*Eucalyptus* species) and *Acacia* species are favoured in the Cape, but further north in the region most nests are built in indigenous trees and bushes only.

DIRECTORY OF GARDEN BIRDS

Laughing Dove

Streptopelia senegalensis (355) Length: 25 cm

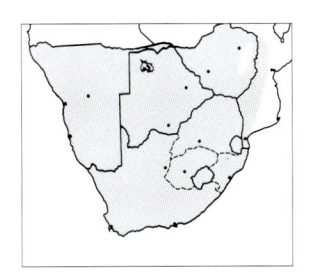

The Laughing Dove is another very common resident of urban gardens throughout the region and is commonly seen congregated in hundreds in city parks and open areas. Like the Turtle Dove, it displays by flying up, almost vertically, and then gliding down in a spiral with its wings and tail outstretched.

Both the male and female Laughing Dove incubate the eggs. Incubation lasts about two weeks.

IN THE GARDEN

Habitat: Commonly forages in open areas, often in the company of the Cape Turtle Dove and Redeyed Dove. These birds are often the victims of domestic cats and so reduce the risk of other birds falling prey to them.

Food Requirements: This bird feeds mainly on grain, and will eat bread crumbs, mealie meal and other similar food items offered on the ground. As with the other doves, feeding at ground level will limit competition with other birds at the feeding table where Laughing Doves may dominate by sheer numbers.

Nesting: Like the Cape Turtle Dove, this species nests in a wide variety of bushes and trees, favouring exotics in the Cape and indigenous trees further north. Nests are between two and five metres above ground level.

Although usually solitary, Laughing Doves will gather in force at a feeding table if seed is offered there, and may discourage other birds from visiting the table.

The Laughing Dove is characterized by a speckled cinnamon chest and blue-grey wing coverts.

DIET

Mostly seeds and grains but also insects and snails.

BREEDING

Site: A flimsy stick nest is built in a tree or shrub, although a convenient ledge, such as a horizontal drain pipe, may be used in urban areas.

Season: Any month of the year but mainly the dry season. **Clutch Size:** 2. **Incubation Period:** 12-16 days. **Fledging Period:** About 15 days.

DIRECTORY OF GARDEN BIRDS

Green Pigeon

Treron calva (361) Length: 30 cm

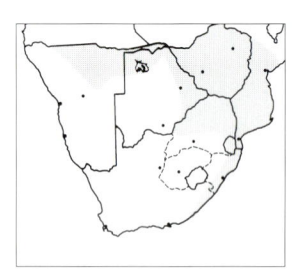

The Afrikaans common name of Papegaaiduif *(parrot pigeon) aptly describes this bird, which will often hang upside down on branches to obtain food. It is particularly fond of figs.*

Green Pigeons are attracted to wild fig trees where they will clamber among branches in search of the fruit.

BREEDING

Site: A flimsy nest of sticks is constructed on a branch which provides a good view of the surrounding area.
Season: Any month of the year, but mostly in summer.
Clutch Size: 1-2. **Incubation Period:** About 14 days.
Fledging Period: About 12 days.

IN THE GARDEN

Habitat: Green Pigeons rest in tall trees so the canopy habitat in the garden will be favoured by this bird, particularly if it includes fruit trees.
Food Requirements: The Green Pigeon is a fruit-eater and is particularly fond of wild figs, such as *Ficus sycomorus* and *Ficus sur*. It also feeds on the fruits of other trees, including the Transvaal Saffronwood (*Cassine transvaalensis*), Jacket Plum (*Pappea capesis*), Buffalo-thorn (*Ziziphus mucronata*), Water Berry (*Syzygium cordatum*) and Ebony Diospyros (*Diospyros mespiliformis*). The Green Pigeon also eats cultivated fruits such as mulberries and loquats. It will visit the feeding table regularly in some areas, where it will select all the fruit on offer. A variety of fruit placed on thorns in a tree or squashed between the scales of a pine cone will be welcomed.
Nesting: The Green Pigeon will nest in gardens, and sometimes several pairs nest in close proximity. It favours evergreen trees, starting to breed before the deciduous woodlands come into leaf.

The Green Pigeon is a predominantly green and yellow, parrot-like bird. The cere is scarlet, and the legs and feet are orange. The yellow tips on the outer tail feathers are most conspicuous when the bird is flying.

DIET
Fruit, especially wild figs, but also cultivated fruits.

DIRECTORY OF GARDEN BIRDS

PURPLECRESTED LOURIE
Tauraco porphyreolophus (371) Length: 46 cm

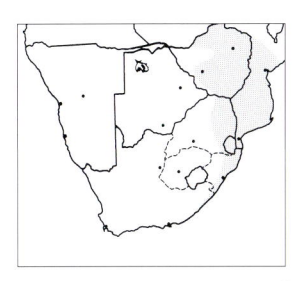

This striking bird is a fairly common resident, and in the eastern Transvaal Lowveld will regularly visit well-wooded gardens. It is usually seen in pairs or small groups but can be difficult to observe as it tends to keep to the denser tree canopies, jumping from branch to branch rather than making long flights.

DIET
Mainly fruit; the young are fed on invertebrates.

BREEDING
SITE: The nest consists of a stick platform which is built in a tree, thicket or creeper.
SEASON: October to January. CLUTCH SIZE: 1-4, usually 2 or 3. INCUBATION PERIOD: About 23 days. FLEDGING PERIOD: About 25-30 days, but are proficient fliers within about 10 days.

IN THE GARDEN
HABITAT: A well-developed canopy habitat in the garden will attract this shy bird. It is also fond of bathing and will readily make use of a water feature which is situated in the exclusion area or another quiet spot where it feels protected.
FOOD REQUIREMENTS: Fruit is taken from the canopies of a wide diversity of tree species. Favourite trees include the alien Bugweed (*Solanum mauritianum*), Cape Ash (*Ekebergia capensis*), Water Berry (*Syzygium cordatum*), Ebony Diospyros (*Diospyros mespiliformis*) and various figs (*Ficus* species). It also eats cultivated fruits, including guavas and mulberries. Fruit can be offered in the exclusion area or on feeders well covered by leafy growth.
NESTING: Trees supporting creepers are favoured nest sites, and thorny trees are preferred. The nest is normally less than five metres off the ground.

Above: *Although a generally shy bird, it will become tame with regular visits to the garden.*
Below: *Wild figs such as* Ficus sur *will attract this bird.*

The Purplecrested Lourie, a spectacular bird of the region, has a dark purple crest and conspicuous red wings which are seen in flight.

DIRECTORY OF GARDEN BIRDS

Grey Lourie

Corythaixoides concolor (373) Length: 48 cm

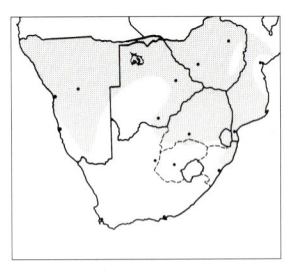

This bird is a common sight in some urban areas, most notably Pretoria and Johannesburg. It can often be heard making its characteristic 'kweh-h-h' call which has given rise to the vernacular name of the 'go-away bird'. Small groups of birds will call loudly when a cat or dog is sighted.

Thorn trees, especially Acacias, are favoured nesting sites of the Grey Lourie.

DIET
Fruit, seeds, soft plant material and insects.

BREEDING
SITE: A simple, slightly bowl-shaped, stick nest is made in a dense tree or shrub canopy.
SEASON: All months of the year, with a peak in late winter and spring. CLUTCH SIZE: 2-3. INCUBATION PERIOD: About 25 days. FLEDGING PERIOD: About 40 days, although the young generally leave the nest at about 20 days old.

IN THE GARDEN
HABITAT: The Grey Lourie will frequent the canopy habitat. Once it has entered the garden, it quickly overcomes its shyness and can be seen in pairs or small groups, 'shrieking' at the cat, dog or any other animal that may threaten it.
FOOD REQUIREMENTS: Fruit is a favourite item of this species, particularly over-ripe paw-paw. Groups of birds may spend hours feeding in fig trees (*Ficus* species), the Natal Plum (*Carissa macrocarpa*) and a variety of other fruit-producing plants. It is also partial to the buds of certain plants, in particular *Bauhinia*. The Grey Lourie will readily feed from a table on which fruit is offered. Secure the fruit by impaling pieces onto nails so that the bird is forced to eat at the table rather than carry fruit pieces away with it. This bird can cause havoc in vegetable gardens, eating the leaves of cabbages and lettuces. 
NESTING: The Grey Lourie will readily breed in the exclusion area of the garden, favouring thorny trees, especially Acacias. The young leave the nest before they are fully feathered, and no attempt should be made to 'rescue' them as they explore the garden.

When alarmed, the Grey Lourie raises and lowers its crest. It is usually conspicuous and noisy.

DIRECTORY OF GARDEN BIRDS

REDCHESTED CUCKOO
Cuculus solitarius (377) Length: 30 cm

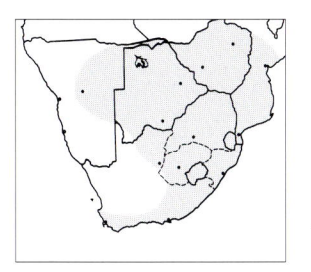

Although this bird is not often seen, most people will recognize the characteristic, three-noted call of the male bird, which is best described by the Afrikaans common name, Piet-my-vrou. *It sometimes calls at night, which has earned it the less friendly Afrikaans name of* Skiet-my-nou! *The Redchested Cuckoo is a breeding migrant from tropical Africa. It arrives in the northern parts of southern Africa during October and departs in about April. In the south, the main arrival and departure months are September and February respectively.*

The immature bird lacks the adult's red breast.

DIET
Insects, favouring caterpillars in particular.

A Cape Robin feeds a Redchested Cuckoo chick which has evicted the robin's own offspring from the nest.

BREEDING
SITE: As with most cuckoos, this bird is a brood parasite and lays its eggs in the nests of other species, including robins, thrushes, chats, and the Cape Wagtail. The young cuckoo ejects any other eggs and chicks from the nest within a few days of hatching, and keeps the adopted parents busy trying to satisfy its voracious appetite.
SEASON: October to January. CLUTCH SIZE: 1 egg per nest. INCUBATION PERIOD: About 15 days. FLEDGING PERIOD: About 20 days.

IN THE GARDEN
HABITAT: The Redchested Cuckoo is a difficult bird to attract to the garden and, even if you succeed, it will remain extremely shy and will seldom venture from the exclusion area. Here, perched high up in the canopy of a tree, it will make its presence known by calling at any time of the day or night.
FOOD REQUIREMENTS: This bird will feed within the tree canopies and may also take insects from the mulch layer in the garden. Mealworms and other insects offered on a feeding table may be taken in the early morning or late evening.
NESTING: The most frequent host of the Redchested Cuckoo is the Cape Robin. Owners of large and well-treed gardens may be lucky enough to see a fledgling cuckoo being fed by its host parents.

KLAAS'S CUCKOO

Chrysococcyx klaas (385) Length: 18 cm

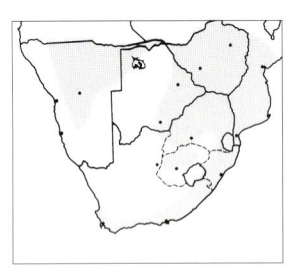

Predominantly an intra-African migrant, this bird arrives in southern Africa in August and September and departs in April; some birds remain throughout the year. It is a solitary bird and is not easily seen, but can be located by its familiar 'may-chee' call. Males often call for extended periods from a high, exposed perch and then are fairly easy to locate.

DIET
Insects, mainly caterpillars beetles and grasshoppers.

BREEDING
Site: Klaas's Cuckoo is a brood parasite, known to parasitize the nests of more than 20 other bird species. Hosts include many sunbird species and are typically birds much smaller than the cuckoo. The cuckoo chick evicts the chicks or eggs of the host species from the nest within the first few days of hatching, and is raised by the host species.
Season: Between October and March.
Clutch Size: 1 egg per nest. **Incubation Period:** 12 days.
Fledging Period: About 20 days.

The male of this species resembles the Diederik Cuckoo but lacks the white markings on the wings.

This Klaas's Cuckoo chick will probably be raised by one of the sunbird species, the cuckoo's favourite host.

IN THE GARDEN
Habitat: A well-developed canopy environment will attract Klaas's Cuckoo to the garden, and it will spend most of its time foraging there. It is one of the few species to eat the caterpillars of the distasteful butterfly, *Acraea horta*, which itself eats the leaves of the Wild Peach (*Kiggelaria africana*).
Food Requirements: This cuckoo feeds mostly in tree canopies or in flight, taking insects. Although unlikely to visit the feeding table, a healthy population of insects, and in particular caterpillars, will attract these birds to the garden.
Nesting: Any nests of host species, especially sunbirds, will attract this cuckoo to breed in the garden.

The Wild Peach (Kiggelaria africana).

DIRECTORY OF GARDEN BIRDS

Diederik Cuckoo

Chrysococcyx caprius (386) Length: 18 cm

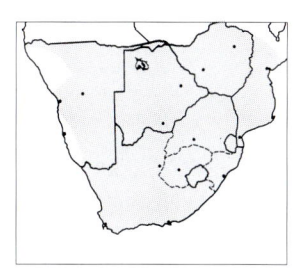

The Diederik Cuckoo is a breeding intra-African migrant, arriving in September and October and leaving the region between February and April. A few birds remain throughout the year. It is not as shy as the other cuckoos and is more easily seen than Klaas's Cuckoo due to its habit of calling from a conspicuous perch or while in flight. It is often seen and heard in the vicinity of weaver nests.

Above: *Acraea horta* larvae are a favourite food item.
Below: *The Diederik Cuckoo parasitizes a wide range of hosts, particularly various weaver species.*

The Diederik Cuckoo is difficult to distinguish from Klaas's Cuckoo but has white markings on the forewings

DIET
Insects, including caterpillars, beetles and termites.

BREEDING
Site: The Diederik Cuckoo is a brood parasite and lays eggs in the nests of at least 20 other bird species. The most common of these is the Cape Sparrow but other common hosts include weavers, bishops and the Cape Wagtail. The cuckoo chick will evict any other eggs or chicks from the nest within four days of its hatching.
Season: October to March. **Clutch Size:** 1 egg per nest. **Incubation Period:** About 12 days. **Fledging Period:** About 20 days.

IN THE GARDEN
Habitat: This bird prefers gardens with well-leafed trees and bushes, but regularly perches out in the open, especially when singing. Male birds make use of song posts.
Food Requirements: The Diederik Cuckoo will feed in tree canopies, in flight or on the ground. It is one of the very few species that eats caterpillars and pupae of the distasteful butterfly, *Acraea horta*. These caterpillars feed on the leaves of the Wild Peach tree (*Kiggelaria africana*). A healthy insect population in the garden will increase the chances of its visiting, but it is unlikely to visit the feeding table.
Nesting: The presence of nesting host birds will encourage this cuckoo to breed in the garden.

DIRECTORY OF GARDEN BIRDS

Burchell's Coucal
Centropus burchelli (391a) Length: 44 cm

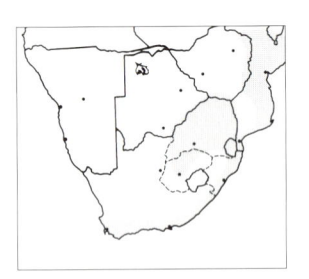

Burchell's Coucal has only recently been recognized as taxonomically distinct from the Whitebrowed Coucal (391b). Burchell's Coucal has become increasingly common in urban areas, probably due to the increased amount of plant cover and food offered in mature gardens. This bird eats snails and caution should be used if poison is put down for these pests, particularly the various toxic baits which should be used only in a covered 'snail jail'.

Burchell's Coucal has a long dark tail, brown and black upperparts and white underparts.

DIET
Insects, snails, small birds, lizards and frogs.

BREEDING
SITE: A large, untidy nest of twigs, grass and leaves is constructed in dense vegetation. It is often quite close to the ground.
SEASON: August to February. CLUTCH SIZE: 2-3. INCUBATION PERIOD: 15 days. FLEDGING PERIOD: About 20 days.

Burchell's Coucal keeps to the more protected parts of the garden and is most active at dawn and dusk. Here, a bird raises its feathers and opens its bill in a threatening pose.

IN THE GARDEN
HABITAT: This bird will be attracted to a well-developed exclusion area and canopy habitat. It is more often heard than seen, tending to skulk. It may occasionally be seen in flight, gliding between tree canopies. The bird is most active early in the morning and in the evening, when it searches for food in well-bushed borders or along lawn edges close to cover; it may perch conspicuously in the early morning.
FOOD REQUIREMENTS: Burchell's Coucal is among the gardener's best friends as it feeds on snails and insects. It becomes tame over time and will eventually venture down to the feeding table to feed on meat scraps, bone-meal, suet and insects offered there.
NESTING: The presence of dense thickets may encourage this bird to breed in the garden. The chicks leave the nest before they are fully feathered, and should not be 'rescued' out of concern. The chicks excrete a foul-smelling liquid when handled or threatened.

DIRECTORY OF GARDEN BIRDS

Barn Owl

Tyto alba (392) Length: 34 cm

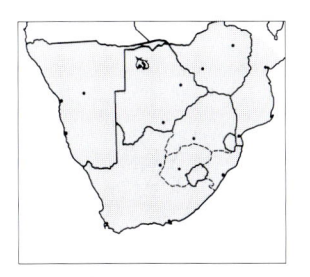

A once common resident of urban areas, the Barn Owl has been greatly affected by the use of modern rodenticides, and its numbers have been drastically reduced here. The provision of artificial nest-sites, typically the lofts or rafters of barns and other outbuildings has helped to increase the incidence of these owls in rural areas.

Right: *The Barn Owl has a distinctive white, heart-shaped face. The sharp talons are designed for killing its small-mammal prey.* Below: *Barn Owl pellets, consisting of undigested hair and bones of the prey, are degorged.*

DIET
Mainly rodents; occasionally small birds and insects.

BREEDING
SITE: In urban environments, most often a building or hollow tree.
SEASON: Mainly the late summer and autumn months in summer-rainfall areas but spring and early summer in the winter-rainfall region; throughout the year if food is plentiful. CLUTCH SIZE: 2-12, depending on food supply. INCUBATION PERIOD: About 30 days. FLEDGING PERIOD: 45-55 days, depending on food supply.

IN THE GARDEN

HABITAT: The Barn Owl is likely to be found only in large gardens or on smallholdings. The nest site is often used as a daytime roost.

FOOD REQUIREMENTS: You can encourage these birds of prey to visit the garden by offering food on a regular basis. A Barn Owl can be 'taught' to feed on dead mice but will need to be trained with live mice first (if you have the stomach for it). As it becomes used to the feeding schedule, dead mice can gradually be introduced. Never use mice that have been poisoned or that have died from an unknown cause. In the urban context, Barn Owls generally hunt from a perch, and having sighted a food item, the bird will

A close-up of a Barn Owl's wing feather. These feathers are especially adapted for silent flight.

swoop silently down onto the unsuspecting prey.
NESTING: The Barn Owl will readily nest in urban areas and is often found in the roofs of houses, where it can become a problem (*see* page 56). A Barn Owl nest-box (right), placed in a tree or against a wall which does not receive too much sun, will discourage this.

115

Spotted Eagle Owl

Bubo africanus (401) Length: 45 cm

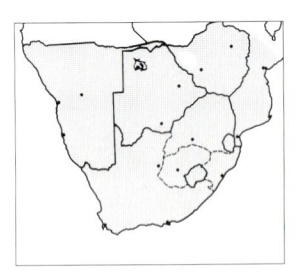

This is a common resident of urban areas but one whose survival is threatened by modern rodenticides and pesticides. The typical 'hooting' call is characteristic of the Spotted Eagle Owl, particularly when it is breeding.

The Spotted Eagle Owl can still be found in many urban areas. Small tufts of feathers on the head are erected into 'ears' when the bird is alert.

DIET
Insects, birds, rodents, toads and small mammals.

BREEDING
SITE: On the ground between rocks or logs; also on building ledges and even on top of old Hamerkop or Hadeda Ibis nests.
SEASON: July to November but later in the winter-rainfall region. CLUTCH SIZE: 2-4. INCUBATION PERIOD: 30 days. FLEDGING PERIOD: 35-50 days.

IN THE GARDEN
HABITAT: This owl will be attracted to large gardens or smallholdings where there are large trees or rocky outcrops. Its tendency to hunt from roadside perches at night places it at high risk from cars.
FOOD REQUIREMENTS: A high population of insects in the garden will attract this bird to feed, and a light suspended from a branch in the garden at night may encourage it to take the insects which gather there. A pond with resident toads will also prove an attraction. Hunting is often done from a perch, such as a convenient TV aerial, or on the lawn where insects may be chased on foot, often making a comical picture.
NESTING: This bird will breed in an exclusion area if it is sufficiently secluded. A nest-box, built to suitable proportions (*see* page 54), may also be used. The chicks are fed by the parents and remain near the nest for several months after fledging. Spotted Eagle Owl parents are very aggressive when breeding and will attack people if they feel threatened.

Spotted Eagle Owl chicks, even after fledging, depend on their parents for another six to seven weeks.

DIRECTORY OF GARDEN BIRDS

LITTLE SWIFT

Apus affinis (417) Length: 14 cm

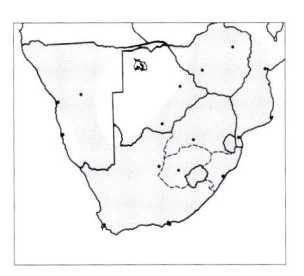

This bird is a common resident and partial migrant in southern Africa, with some birds moving out of the colder regions during the winter. The Little Swift is often overlooked because it spends much of the day in flight.

DIET
Exclusively aerial insects, and spiders.

BREEDING
SITE: Breeds in densely packed colonies under bridges over highways and under the eaves of tall buildings. The nest is bowl-shaped and made from feathers and grass glued together with the bird's saliva.
SEASON: Breeds from September to April or May with a peak between November and January.
CLUTCH SIZE: 1-3.
INCUBATION PERIOD: 22-24 days.
FLEDGING PERIOD: About 40 days.

IN THE GARDEN
HABITAT: Little Swifts will readily visit urban gardens to scoop liquid, in flight, from water features such as swimming pools and large ponds.
FOOD REQUIREMENTS: All feeding is done in the air and usually at great heights. Swifts are most likely to be seen low over the garden when rain is imminent.
NESTING: This species may breed under the eaves or overhang of a building, usually only a tall one. Both the adults and the offspring roost in their nests at night. Adult birds guide newly fledged offspring back into the nest by flying under them right up to the nest entrance and then veering away.

The Little Swift has a wide gape which enables it to catch insects and spiders in flight.

The Little Swift was once a rather uncommon bird but it has adapted well to human habitation. It frequently visits ponds and swimming pools, dipping its beak into the water while flying past.

The Little Swift is most likely to be seen in flight. It has a short, square tail and a white rump.

DIRECTORY OF GARDEN BIRDS

PALM SWIFT

Cypsiurus parvus (421) Length: 17 cm

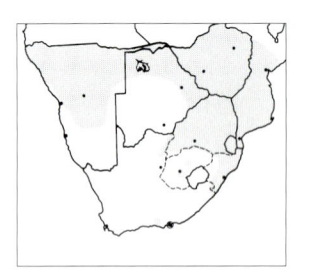

One of the smallest swifts in the region, the Palm Swift has a very slender build and a long, deeply forked tail. It is often seen near tall palm trees where it roosts and breeds. The planting of exotic palms in city gardens and parks has extended the distribution of this bird, and it sometimes breeds under bridges. It regularly feeds in flocks with other swifts and swallows.

The range of the Palm Swift has expanded westwards due to the planting of various exotic palms.

The little Palm Swift builds a curious nest consisting of a crescent of feathers which are glued with the bird's saliva to the underside of a pendant leaf of a palm tree. The incubating bird and its nestlings cling so tightly to the nest that it is almost impossible to pull them off.

IN THE GARDEN

HABITAT: The planting of indigenous and exotic palm trees will draw these birds into urban gardens in moist tropical and subtropical parts of the region.

FOOD REQUIREMENTS: Palm Swifts will not visit a feeding table in the garden (feeding as they do only on the wing), but a light hung from a palm tree where the birds are nesting will attract insects which may entice them to hunt at night.

NESTING: Indigenous and exotic palms in the garden may encourage the birds to breed here.

DIET

Exclusively aerial insects, and spiders.

BREEDING

SITE: A nest is built on the underside of a palm leaf and consists of a cluster of feathers glued together with the bird's saliva. Saliva is also used to glue the eggs to the lip of the nest. The parent clings in a vertical position to the nest while incubating.

SEASON: Throughout the year, except in very cold weather. CLUTCH SIZE: 2. INCUBATION PERIOD: About 18 days. FLEDGING PERIOD: About 30 days.

An exposed Palm Swift's nest shows the eggs which have been glued with the bird's saliva to the lip of the nest.

DIRECTORY OF GARDEN BIRDS

Speckled Mousebird
Colius striatus (424) Length: 35 cm

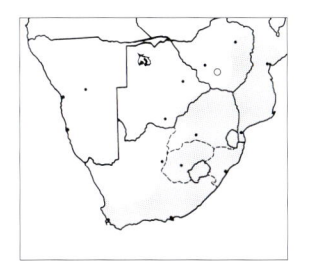

Mousebirds are generally cursed by gardeners trying to produce fruit and vegetables, as these birds are quick to locate a crop and feast on it, sometimes before it has even had a chance to ripen. The Speckled Mousebird is an ungainly flyer which has a habit of crashing into the tree it intends landing in. It is often seen in small flocks in urban gardens. The birds scramble up the branches, mouse-like, as they progressively devour the fruit that is 'on offer'.

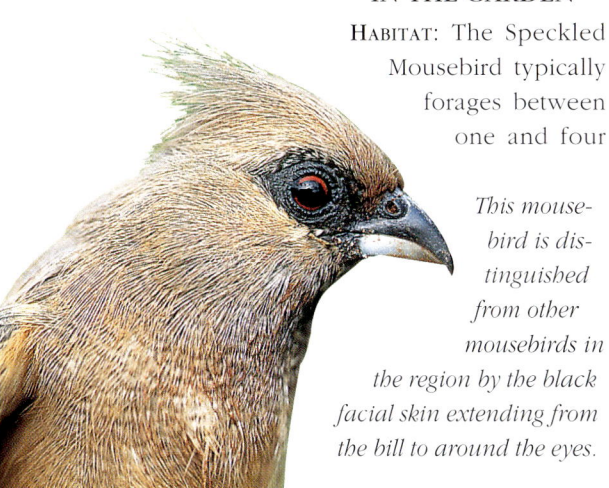

The gregarious mousebird is often an unwelcome visitor because of its voracious appetite and tendency to destroy fruit and vegetable crops, sometimes adopting curious postures in order to reach the offerings. The long tail and the habit of scrambling up branches account for the bird's common name.

DIET
Berries, fruit and vegetables, seed, leaves and nectar.

BREEDING
SITE: An untidy nest is made in dense shrubbery.
SEASON: August to March, with a peak between October and January. CLUTCH SIZE: 2-4. INCUBATION PERIOD: About 13 days. FLEDGING PERIOD: 17-18 days.

IN THE GARDEN
HABITAT: The Speckled Mousebird typically forages between one and four metres above the ground. Although most often found in the exclusion area, it occasionally forages in more isolated bushes and trees.

FOOD REQUIREMENTS: Mousebirds are not fussy eaters and will consume any fruit offered on the feeding table or pushed onto thorns or nails. They will also take bone-meal, bread crumbs and mealie meal. Fruit trees and vegetables should be protected with bird netting as these birds are capable of ruining entire crops. They will also feed on nectar and are unusual among arboreal birds in that they eat leaves.

NESTING: This bird may breed in areas of the garden with dense vegetation cover, such as tangled thickets of creepers. The nest is usually quite close to the ground, at heights of one to three metres.

This mousebird is distinguished from other mousebirds in the region by the black facial skin extending from the bill to around the eyes.

Fruit is a great attraction to mousebirds in the garden.

DIRECTORY OF GARDEN BIRDS

Redfaced Mousebird

Colius indicus (426) Length: 34 cm

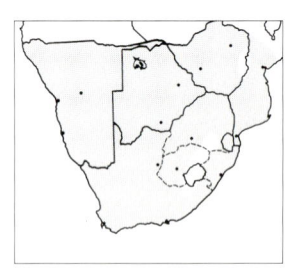

This is the most widely distributed of the mousebirds and is easily recognized by the bare red skin around the eye, and the greenish, rather than brown or grey, tinge to the plumage. This bird, like the other mousebirds, is social and flies in compact groups. It also has the habit of creeping, mouse-like, through the branches, often adopting strange postures to feed.

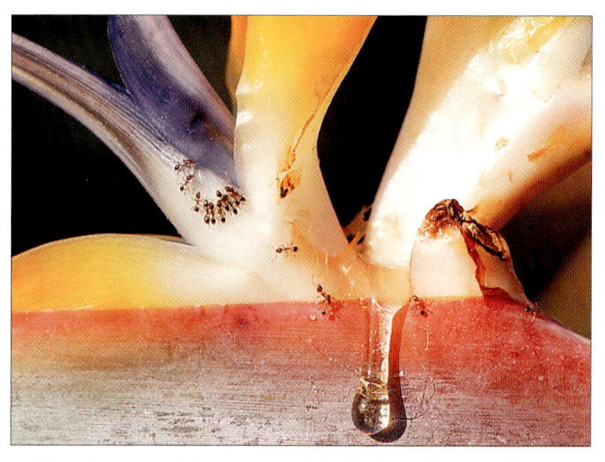

Although mousebirds eat mainly fruit and vegetables, they also take pollen and nectar of plants like Strelitzia.

DIET
Fruit, nectar, leaves, pollen and flowers.

BREEDING
SITE: An untidy, cup-shaped nest, constructed from plant material and lined with finer material, is built in dense shrubbery.
SEASON: Mainly August to January, but breeding has been recorded in all months of the year. CLUTCH SIZE: 2-4. INCUBATION PERIOD: About 15 days. FLEDGING PERIOD: About 17 days.

IN THE GARDEN
HABITAT: This bird will be attracted to the tree canopies in the garden.
FOOD REQUIREMENTS: Both exotic and indigenous fruit trees will be a major attraction to any mousebird. Protect selected fruit and vegetables for human consumption, and the mousebirds will devour the rest. It will also visit the feeding table for fruit, although not as boldly as will the Speckled Mousebird.
NESTING: The Redfaced Mousebird is shyer than the Speckled Mousebird and does not breed as readily as that species in urban habitats. Their nests are often sited in thorny vegetation and are placed slightly higher up than the nests of the Speckled Mousebird.

This species is easily distinguished from the Speckled Mousebird by the striking red facial skin. The colouring of this bird is lighter than that of the Speckled Mousebird.

DIRECTORY OF GARDEN BIRDS

Pied Kingfisher

Ceryle rudis (428) Length: 28 cm

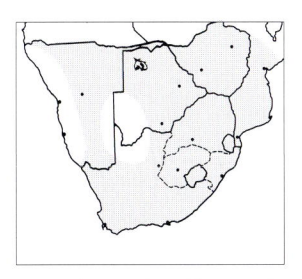

Although not often seen in urban gardens, the Pied Kingfisher will sometimes raid fish ponds and will pay the garden regular visits until the fish population has been depleted. It is often seen hovering over open expanses of water before diving in to capture fish.

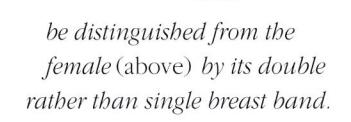

Although the Pied Kingfisher will not breed in the urban garden, a pond or larger water feature might attract it to feed there, especially if it is well stocked with fish. It may breed on farms if suitable sand banks are available.

BREEDING

Site: A hole is burrowed in a sand bank.
Season: Mainly early summer but will breed at any time throughout the year if food is available. Clutch Size: 2-3. Incubation Period: Not known. Fledging Period: Not known.

DIET

Mainly fish, but also crustaceans and insects.

The Pied Kingfisher is unmistakable with its black-and-white colouring and distinctive crest. The male bird (left) can easily be distinguished from the female (above) by its double rather than single breast band.

IN THE GARDEN

Habitat: Gardens with large water features or ponds may attract the Pied Kingfisher.
Food Requirements: The bird will visit to feed on fish, particularly the common goldfish or Koi, which are slow moving and easy to catch. Ponds with Tilapia do not provide the same attraction. The prey is generally carried back to a perch where it is beaten until it stops moving and can be swallowed.
Nesting: The Pied Kingfisher will not breed in an urban garden but may do so on a smallholding or farm with a pond or dam and suitable earth banks. This species is a co-operative breeder, whereby the young of previous years assist in feeding the new young. This behaviour accounts for the presence of several Pied Kingfishers at a single nest burrow.

DIRECTORY OF GARDEN BIRDS

BROWNHOODED KINGFISHER

Halcyon albiventris (435) Length: 24 cm

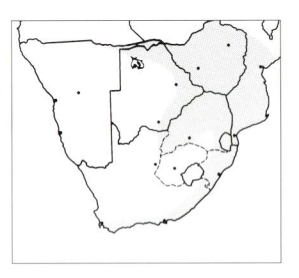

The Brownhooded Kingfisher is a fairly common garden bird in the eastern and north-eastern parts of the region. It may be seen singly or in pairs, and will often sit on a conspicuous perch, such as a fence or telephone wire, watching for movement of prey below.

DIET
Mainly insects; sometimes crabs, small rodents, reptiles and birds.

BREEDING
SITE: A one-metre tunnel ending in a chamber is burrowed into a sand bank.
SEASON: Spring and early summer. CLUTCH SIZE: 2-5. INCUBATION PERIOD: About 14 days. FLEDGING PERIOD: About 21 days.

IN THE GARDEN
HABITAT: The Brownhooded Kingfisher tends to favour wooded gardens with some suitable perches and open areas for hunting.

The Brownhooded Kingfisher has a characteristic brown head, a red beak and a blue rump, tail and flight feathers. It is often seen sitting on a prominent perch watching for insects, which it takes on the ground.

Above: *This kingfisher hunts from a perch.*
Below: *The Brownhooded Kingfisher often nests in a burrow in a sandbank, but occasionally occupies a hole in a bee-eater or sand martin colony.*

FOOD REQUIREMENTS: Gardens with a healthy insect population will prove an attraction to this bird. It will swoop into ponds and swimming pools to catch floating insects and to bathe. A bowl of mealworms, scorpions, 'Parktown Prawns' or insects offered on the feeding table may also encourage the Brownhooded Kingfisher, especially if provided on a regular basis.
NESTING: While urban gardens are popular foraging areas for this bird, the availability of nest sites, such as earth banks, in gardens is very low. Many move out of urban areas at the start of the breeding season to search for nests elsewhere.

DIRECTORY OF GARDEN BIRDS

HOOPOE

Upupa epops (451) Length: 28 cm

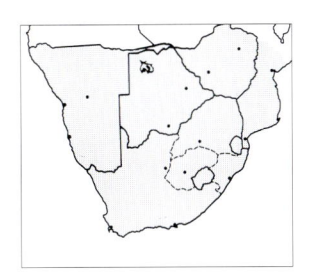

The Hoopoe is a common resident of urban gardens but has been threatened by the use of modern chemicals. Its favourite area is the lawn where it can be found singly or in pairs, probing the grass for insects and earthworms. The arrival of this bird in the garden is usually heralded by its characteristic 'hoop-poop' call, from which the bird gets its common name.

DIET
Insects and insect larvae; sometimes small reptiles.

BREEDING
SITE: A hollow termite mound, log, dry stone wall or other crevice.
SEASON: August to September. CLUTCH SIZE: 2-6. INCUBATION PERIOD: 18 days. FLEDGING PERIOD: About 30 days.

IN THE GARDEN
HABITAT: An open lawn is probably the greatest attraction to this bird. Another attraction will be fallen leaves under trees.
FOOD REQUIREMENTS: Invertebrates are caught on the ground or by probing with the long bill into the lawn. This bird is one of the agents of biological control for lawn caterpillars and is consequently affected by any chemicals that may be used to control these pests. It will seldom visit the feeding table, although it may take bone-meal provided on the table or in a feeding log.
NESTING: The Hoopoe is unable to hollow out its own nest and will therefore make use of an artificial hollow nest provided for it in the garden.

Above and below: The Hoopoe is a hole-nesting bird and often occupies the abandoned nests of barbets. The young are fed a variety of insects by the male bird.

The Hoopoe is unmistakable with its impressive crest and distinctive cinnamon, black and white plumage.

DIRECTORY OF GARDEN BIRDS

Redbilled Woodhoopoe

Phoeniculus purpureus (452) Length: 36 cm

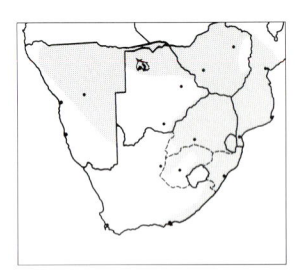

This noisy bird travels in small flocks of two to eight birds, occasionally more, and is normally heard before it is seen. The Zulu name for it, iNhlekabafazi, meaning 'laughing women', aptly describes the characteristic high-pitched cackling of these woodhoopoes, which is accompanied by head bobbing and tail fanning.

*While the Redbilled Woodhoopoe feeds mostly on insects, it is particularly partial to the nectar of the flowers of Coral trees (*Erythrina *species).*

With its long red bill and shiny black or purple colouring, this bird makes a striking addition to the urban garden.

DIET
Mostly insects; also lizards, and nectar from the flowers of Coral Trees (*Erythrina* species).

BREEDING
SITE: Natural cavities in trees and old nests of hole-making species such as woodpeckers are used.
SEASON: All months of the year but mostly spring and early summer. CLUTCH SIZE: 2-5. INCUBATION PERIOD: About 18 days. FLEDGING PERIOD: About 30 days.

IN THE GARDEN
HABITAT: The Redbilled Woodhoopoe favours medium-sized to large trees which have loose or convoluted bark where it can probe for insects and grubs. Acacia trees are favoured foraging sites, but generally lack suitable breeding cavities.
FOOD REQUIREMENTS: It feeds on insects in crevices and under the bark of trees, and will also take bone-meal offered at the feeding table or in a feeding log.
NESTING: This bird does not excavate its own nests, and will make use of a hollow log provided for it, particularly if it is placed in a tree in the exclusion area, or under the eaves of a roof. Favoured nest sites are vertical or near-vertical, with an entrance diameter of approximately 60 mm, an inner diameter of 120 mm and a depth of 650 mm. It is a co-operative breeder: only one pair within a flock breeds, and other flock members help to feed the offspring. The Redbilled Woodhoopoe not only breeds in cavities, but also roosts in them, in family units, every night.

DIRECTORY OF GARDEN BIRDS

BLACKCOLLARED BARBET

Lybius torquatus (464) Length: 20 cm

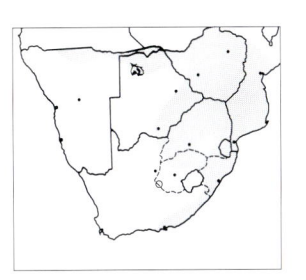

The Blackcollared Barbet readily enters urban gardens and will breed there. It is normally recognized by its characteristic duet, sung from the top of a tree. It competes strongly with the Crested Barbet for nest sites, and these two species may be found chasing each other around the garden as they 'bicker'.

The Blackcollared Barbet has a powerful bill which is strongly toothed. It eats fruits and berries, and also insects, sometimes hawking these in the air.

The bright red head and black collar are characteristic.

DIET
Fruit, berries and insects, including termite alates.

BREEDING
Site: Excavates a nest in dead branches or nests in a hollow log.
Season: Mostly September to December in South Africa, with a slightly more extended breeding season in Zimbabwe. **Clutch Size:** 2-5. **Incubation Period:** 18 days. **Fledging Period:** About 35 days.

IN THE GARDEN
Habitat: This bird keeps to the canopies of trees and will utilize the exclusion area and canopy habitat.
Food Requirements: This barbet may be wary of taking food from a feeding table but will readily consume fruit, such as paw-paw, apple, orange and banana, pushed onto branches or nails in trees.
Nesting: The Blackcollared Barbet will breed in urban gardens if nest sites are available. Nest-boxes can be provided, but as the birds prefer to excavate their own nests, a solid sisal log with a hole (40 mm diameter) drilled into the top third of the structure is probably a better option (*see* page 53). The birds will remove the fibre from the log and carefully carry it away to an area well hidden from the nesting site. Place several nests in the garden, if possible, to keep competition with other hole-nesting birds to a minimum.

Barbets are primary nesting birds and hollow out their own nests in branches and logs such as this (right).

DIRECTORY OF GARDEN BIRDS

Yellowfronted Tinker Barbet
Pogoniulus chrysoconus (470) Length: 11 cm

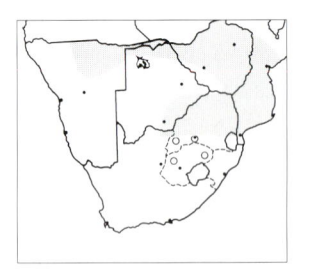

This is a common resident in the bushveld and escarpment regions of the Transvaal, and is widespread in Zimbabwe. The presence of the Yellowfronted Tinker Barbet is often given away by its repetitive 'tink-tink-tink' call, which carries on for long periods. It is inconspicuous, however, and seldom seen due to its habit of sitting high among the foliage of tall trees.

The yellow forehead (sometimes orange in the south of the bird's range), separated from the bill by a black line, is characteristic of this very small barbet.

DIET
Mainly insects; also fruit, particularly mistletoe berries.

BREEDING
SITE: A tiny hole is excavated in a dead branch.
SEASON: September to February in South Africa; September to December, occasionally throughout the year, in Zimbabwe. CLUTCH SIZE: 2-3. INCUBATION PERIOD: Not known, probably about 12 days. FLEDGING PERIOD: Not known, probably about 20 days.

Yellowfronted Tinker Barbets eat insects but also take both exotic and indigenous fruit.

IN THE GARDEN
HABITAT: This bird is likely to be found only in taller trees, especially fruiting trees. Do not cut down the large, dead branches which attract these birds as Yellowfronted Tinker Barbets excavate their own nest-holes in dead branches. These nest-holes are usually so tiny that they are easily overlooked.

FOOD REQUIREMENTS: This little bird is not a common visitor to the feeding table, but may be enticed to feed on fruit and bone-meal provided in the exclusion area. The Yellowfronted Tinker Barbet particularly favours the berries of parasites, such as mistletoe (*Loranthus* species). These are easy to cultivate but may kill host plants and spread throughout the garden, so care must be taken if they are introduced.

NESTING: The Yellowfronted Tinker Barbet prefers to excavate its own small nest-hole. If there is no dead wood in your garden, you could provide a solid sisal log, available from most nurseries or garden centres, as a nesting site (*see* page 53).

DIRECTORY OF GARDEN BIRDS

CRESTED BARBET
Trachyphonus vaillantii (473) Length: 23 cm

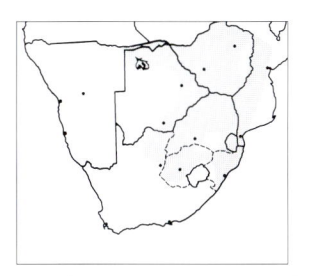

Well adapted to urban gardens and parks, this bird is one of the most colourful avian visitors and is a common garden resident. Its characteristic trilling 'alarm clock' call is uttered from the tops of trees and is a ubiquitous sound in many areas. The Crested Barbet is an obsessive excavator and spends a great deal of its time pecking at tree branches and logs. These birds have been known to peck holes right through split-pole fences and telephone poles.

DIET
Fruit including berries, insects, worms and snails.

BREEDING
SITE: A hollow is excavated in a dead branch of a tree. **SEASON:** Mainly between September and February in South Africa; all months (excluding early winter) in the north of the region. May rear up to four broods in a season. **CLUTCH SIZE:** 2-4. **INCUBATION PERIOD:** 15-17 days. **FLEDGING PERIOD:** About 30 days.

The Crested Barbet has a characteristic crest which it erects when it is alert.

Left: *The Crested Barbert is a compulsive excavator.*
Below: *Although omnivorous at feeding tables, in the wild it takes mainly insects and is not as dependent on fruit as other barbets. Nevertheless, it appreciates offerings of both indigenous and exotic fruits, including mulberries, peaches and apples.*

IN THE GARDEN
HABITAT: This species is not fussy about habitat and can be seen anywhere in the garden.
FOOD REQUIREMENTS: Fruit, such as paw-paw and apple, on the feeding table will be relished by these birds, and bonemeal will also be taken.
NESTING: Solid sisal logs (*see* page 53) secured in a tree will encourage these compulsive hole-makers to breed in the garden. Place several logs in different trees to reduce competition for nesting sites with other hole-nesting species.

DIRECTORY OF GARDEN BIRDS

Cardinal Woodpecker
Dendropicos fuscescens (486) Length: 15 cm

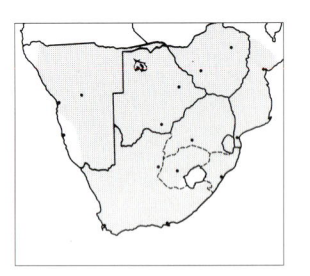

The Cardinal Woodpecker is the most common and widespread woodpecker in the region; however, it is a shy visitor to urban gardens. It may be seen pecking away at rough-barked trees in search of insects. The bird will often peck in rapid succession at a dead branch, presumably in an effort to locate cavities containing insect larvae but possibly also to advertise its presence in an area.

Cardinal Woodpecker chicks hatch after an incubation period of about two weeks, and fledge a month later. Both sexes incubate the eggs, and brood and feed the young.

The female Cardinal Woodpecker has a black nape while the nape of the male is red.

DIET
Insects, especially their larvae and pupae.

BREEDING
Site: A nest hole is excavated in a dead branch and may be used repeatedly each breeding season.
Season: Throughout the year with a peak from August to October. **Clutch Size:** 1-5. **Incubation Period:** 12-13 days. **Fledging Period:** 27 days.

IN THE GARDEN
Habitat: This bird will frequent the exclusion area and will forage in dead trees and those that have been attacked by borers and other insects.
Food Requirements: The presence of dead and rotting wood in the garden will attract many insects which, in turn, will attract this woodpecker. Mealworms and bone-meal may be taken but should be placed high up in a tree in the exclusion area.
Nesting: Although woodpeckers prefer to hollow out their own nests in natural tree branches, artificial nesting logs and even nest-boxes (*see* pages 53-57) provided for them may be used for nesting.

The Cardinal Woodpecker feeds mainly on the larvae and pupae of beetles, which it extracts from dead wood.

DIRECTORY OF GARDEN BIRDS

Redthroated Wryneck
Jynx ruficollis (489) Length: 19 cm

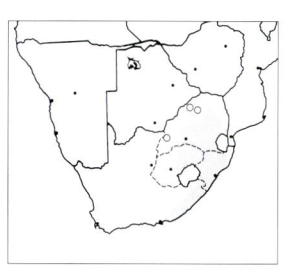

Although a fairly common resident in some parts, this bird is seldom seen due to its shy nature. It creeps along the tree branches with its body almost flattened and blends well with the bark of the tree. When calling, however, it often positions itself on a conspicuous perch.

The Redthroated Wryneck can be identified by its chestnut throat and upper breast.

DIET
Mainly ants (from eggs to adults); also other insects including termites and caterpillars.

BREEDING
Site: Abandoned barbet nests, cavities in roofs, and other hollow structures are used.
Season: August to February, with a peak between the months of September and November. **Clutch Size:** 1-4, usually 3. **Incubation Period:** About 13 days. **Fledging Period:** About 25 days.

IN THE GARDEN
Habitat: The Redthroated Wryneck is a shy bird and is most active in the early morning and late evening. Areas of dense cover in the garden will attract it.
Food Requirements: Bone-meal placed in a feeding log (*see* page 30) in a well-protected area may attract the bird, and, reportedly, avocado pear is also favoured.
Nesting: Provide hollow nesting logs (*see* page 53) in remote parts of the garden to encourage breeding.

Termites (above) *and ants are favourite food items; the bird uses its sticky tongue to mop up these insects.*

Areas of dense cover in the garden are necessary to attract the Redthroated Wryneck.

DIRECTORY OF GARDEN BIRDS

European Swallow

Hirundo rustica (518) Length: 18 cm

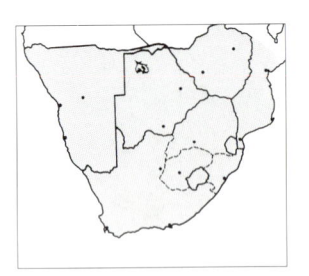

This species is one of the most common and conspicuous of the Palearctic migrants to the region, arriving in large numbers in September and leaving around May (a few birds will remain through winter). It may be seen congregated in large numbers on telephone lines before migrating northwards. The European Swallow is often found near water, open grasslands and agricultural lands. Flocks roost together in reedbeds and may number in the thousands.

These birds will scoop water in flight from a garden pond or even from a swimming pool.

IN THE GARDEN

HABITAT: The European Swallow will often fly into the garden to scoop water, in flight, from a swimming pool or pond.

FOOD REQUIREMENTS: The birds are often seen flying low over the ground in an almost grid pattern, feeding on insects that are disturbed from the vegetation. They may be attracted to a light hung in the garden in the late evening and will take insects in flight.

NESTING: Breeds outside of the southern African region.

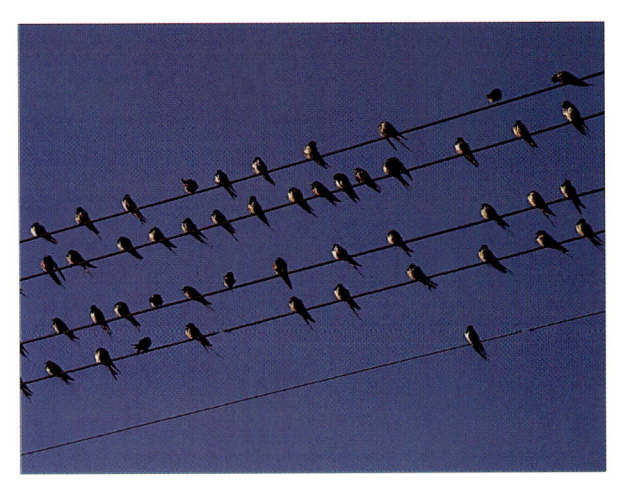

The European Swallow has metallic blue upperparts with a chestnut forehead and throat. The underparts are white, tinged with orange.

DIET
A variety of aerial insects including termite alates.

BREEDING
This species breeds in north Africa, Europe, northern Asia and North America.

European Swallows gather in flocks when resting but spend a great deal of time on the wing.

DIRECTORY OF GARDEN BIRDS

GREATER STRIPED SWALLOW

Hirundo cucullata (526) Length: 20 cm

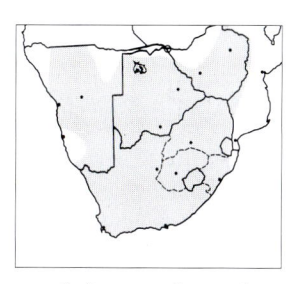

A common intra-African migrant, the Greater Striped Swallow arrives in August and departs from the region in April. It is easily confused with its smaller relative, the Lesser Striped Swallow, but is more common, ranging as far south as the southern Cape. This bird is seen in pairs when breeding, but in small groups towards the end of the breeding season. The Greater Striped Swallow often flies together with other swallows and swifts, and identification may then be difficult.

A nest is built out of mud, often under the eaves of a roof. The parents approach the nest at great speed when coming to feed the offspring.

DIET
Aerial insects, and insects disturbed at grass fires.

BREEDING
SITE: The nest is a basin-shaped chamber with a long entrance tunnel. It is constructed from mud pellets (which the bird collects in its beak) and lined with grass and feathers. It is built under a bridge, a rock overhang or under the eaves of a roof or a porch.
SEASON: August to March.
CLUTCH SIZE: 2-4. INCUBATION PERIOD: Between 18 and 20 days.
FLEDGING PERIOD: About 25 days.

The Greater Striped Swallow is a larger bird than the Lesser Striped Swallow. The underparts are pale and finely streaked.

IN THE GARDEN
HABITAT: The Greater Striped Swallow is often closely associated with buildings and it is not uncommon to have more than one nest under the eaves of the roof of the house. The adults become quite used to human activities. 
FOOD REQUIREMENTS: This bird will respond well to a night light, flying around it to feed on moths and other aerial insects.
NESTING: The Greater Striped Swallow, like its relative the Lesser Striped Swallow, has readily adapted to urbanization and may nest under the eaves of the roof of a house or a porch; they also build their nests under bridges. The same nesting site is used each year. Nest-building begins shortly after the arrival of the swallows in early spring, as soon as an adequate supply of mud is available.

DIRECTORY OF GARDEN BIRDS

Lesser Striped Swallow
Hirundo abyssinica (527) Length: 16 cm

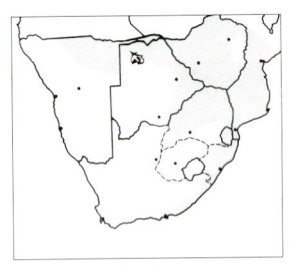

Although smaller than the Greater Striped Swallow, this bird is very similar in appearance, differing only in finer details. It is also an intra-African migrant, arriving in southern Africa in July and leaving in March; some birds remain throughout the year, especially in Zimbabwe. It is found in pairs during the breeding season, otherwise in small flocks, often in association with other swallows and swifts.

This species is similar to the Greater Striped Swallow but has heavier streaking on the underparts.

DIET
Aerial insects, such as gnats, flies and grasshoppers.

BREEDING
SITE: A bowl-shaped nest with a long entrance is built from mud pellets under bridges, overhanging rocks or the eaves of buildings.
SEASON: July to April in South Africa but throughout the year in Zimbabwe, with a peak from August to January; at least two broods per season. CLUTCH SIZE: 2-4. INCUBATION PERIOD: About 14 days. FLEDGING PERIOD: 20-28 days.

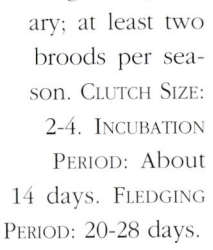

The Lesser Striped Swallow is less migratory than its relative, some birds remaining in the region throughout the winter months.

IN THE GARDEN
HABITAT: This species is exclusively an aerial forager, but will be attracted to the muddy margins of ponds where it collects mud for nest-building. Mud with a high clay content is preferred.
FOOD REQUIREMENTS: This swallow may fly around a light at night, hunting for moths and other insects.
NESTING: Like the Greater Striped Swallow, this species has adapted to an urban lifestyle and will often nest in close association with houses. The Lesser Striped Swallow's nest may be used by the Mocking Chat (see page 144) as a base for its own nest.

The Lesser Striped Swallow favours flying insects, such as butterflies, as food items. Insects will be attracted to a light hung in a tree at night, which may in turn entice this bird into the garden to forage.

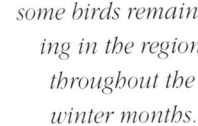

DIRECTORY OF GARDEN BIRDS

Rock Martin

Hirundo fuligula (529) Length: 15 cm

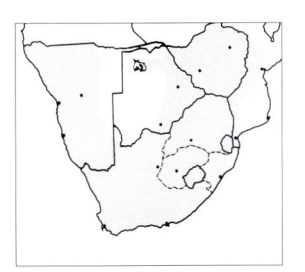

The Rock Martin is a common resident throughout the region, and especially in mountainous areas where there are natural overhangs. In urban areas it is often found around buildings, where it nests. The Rock Martin is seen in pairs during the breeding season but may form small flocks and mix with other swallows and with swifts when not breeding.

Rock Martins have adapted to urban environments and readily nest against the wall of a house.

IN THE GARDEN

Habitat: The Rock Martin is often seen flying around buildings when looking for nest sites.

Food Requirements: This bird will spend time in the garden, hunting in flight and swooping down to drink. A light shining at night may entice the bird out of its nest to hunt for insects.

Nesting: The Rock Martin has adapted well to human habitation and may nest against a wall of the house.

This bird may lay up to six eggs, although three is most common, and chicks fledge about 30 days after hatching.

DIET
Small aerial insects, and spiders.

BREEDING
Site: A half-cup-shaped nest is built from mud pellets against a wall of a building or cliff face.
Season: August to April; at least two broods each season. **Clutch Size:** Up to 6, usually 2-3. **Incubation Period:** About 17 days. **Fledging Period:** 30 days.

The Rock Martin is a common visitor to urban gardens and is often seen around buildings. It hunts aerial insects in flight and will spend time in gardens where there is a rich supply of its prey. It may swoop down to drink at garden water features.

DIRECTORY OF GARDEN BIRDS

FORKTAILED DRONGO
Dicrurus adsimilis (541) Length: 25 cm

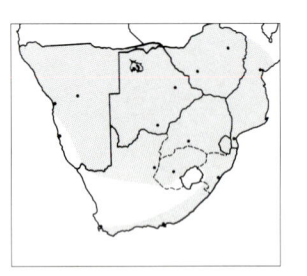

The Forktailed Drongo is a common resident in urban gardens, and is usually seen singly or in pairs. A conspicuous bird, it normally perches on a branch or fence post from which it dives downwards to catch its insect prey. It is a fearless bird and will even chase eagles. An accomplished mimic, this bird can give excellent renditions of cat calls or the flutey calls of the Pearlspotted Owl. Its variable call is regularly heard in the early morning in urban areas.

The Forktailed Drongo is one of many birds parasitized by the African Cuckoo. Here, it attempts to satisfy the voracious appetite of an African Cuckoo chick.

DIET
Mainly insects, but also small birds, fish and nectar.

BREEDING
SITE: A saucer-shaped nest, made of roots and twigs and bound by spider web, is usually constructed in the horizontal fork of a tree.
SEASON: August to January. CLUTCH SIZE: 2-4. INCUBATION PERIOD: 17 days. FLEDGING PERIOD: 18 days.

The Forktailed Drongo is a bold and aggressive garden resident, perching in the open to hunt. It has a glossy sheen to its plumage. When this bird sits upright on a conspicuous perch its forked tail is easily visible from below.

IN THE GARDEN
HABITAT: Any trees or bushes which serve as lookouts will attract these birds.
FOOD REQUIREMENTS: The Forktailed Drongo takes insects from the air, and may be enticed to hunt at night around a lamp that has been suspended from a tree in the garden. It readily visits feeding tables, and will also feed from feeding logs (*see page 30*) filled with bonemeal, suet, mealworms, insects or strips of meat.
NESTING: The provision of nest-lining material may encourage this species to breed in the garden. When breeding, this species is noisy and aggressive and will harry birds much larger than itself.

To encourage this bird to breed in the garden, it is a good idea to provide scraps of fabric and other materials that can be used for lining the nest.

DIRECTORY OF GARDEN BIRDS

Blackheaded Oriole
Oriolus larvatus (545) Length: 24 cm

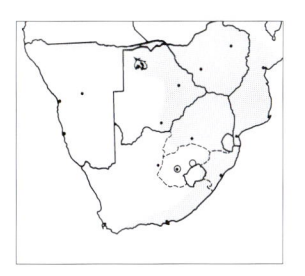

The Blackheaded Oriole can often be heard calling from the top of a tall tree in the garden. Its liquid, whistling call is one of the most melodious heard in the garden. The bird is seen singly or in pairs, often flying between trees.

The Blackheaded Oriole eats fruit and nectar and is particularly fond of feeding at Aloe *species.*

IN THE GARDEN

HABITAT: The canopy habitat, especially the taller trees within this, will appeal to this bird. It is fairly shy, but will become tame with regular visits to the garden.

FOOD REQUIREMENTS: The Blackheaded Oriole is not a common bird at the feeding table but will utilize nectar plants, such as the various *Aloe* species. It may feed on bone-meal and suet placed in a feeding log and hung high up in the exclusion area.

NESTING: The nest is usually placed in a tall tree, typically eight to ten metres above the ground.

The black head, yellow body and coral-red bill are diagnostic features of this species.

DIET
Mostly fruit; also pollen, nectar and insects.

BREEDING
SITE: An unusual, cup-shaped nest is constructed from lichens, moss, spider web and grass, and is suspended from under a thin branch some distance from the main trunk of a tree.
SEASON: September to February, although not normally beyond the end of the year in the south of its range.
CLUTCH SIZE: 2-3, usually 2. INCUBATION PERIOD: About 14 days. FLEDGING PERIOD: About 15 days.

This bird shows a preference for taller trees, calling from high perches and hunting for food in the canopy.

135

DIRECTORY OF GARDEN BIRDS

Pied Crow
Corvus albus (548) Length: 50 cm

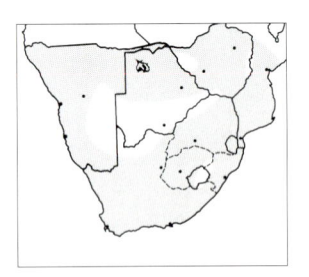

The Pied Crow is a familiar bird in towns and cities throughout most of the region. Although not a common garden visitor, it is frequently seen around rubbish dumps, abattoirs and open parks. The bird's arrogance, playfulness and comical behaviour makes it a great source of entertainment.

DIET
Almost anything organic: seeds, fruit, roots, insects, rodents and birds (including eggs and chicks).

BREEDING
Site: A large nest, comprising sticks and often wire, is built in a fork of a tall tree; also uses man-made structures such as telegraph poles.
Season: August to January. **Clutch Size:** Usually 4 or 5. **Incubation Period:** About 19 days. **Fledging Period:** About 40 days.

IN THE GARDEN
Habitat: Most people would rather not encourage the Pied Crow to the garden, but if it does visit it will generally be seen in open areas, where it will probe the lawn for invertebrates. Birds that grow accustomed to the garden will investigate every part of it, and will be quick to steal unguarded food.
Food Requirements: Most gardeners will be reluctant to attract these birds as they can become a nuisance, removing newly planted seedlings, chasing other birds and generally making pests of themselves. Try throwing food on the roof of the house where they will be less bother to other visiting species.
Nesting: These birds are unlikely to breed in urban gardens, and are inclined to seek out trees in plantations and on farms. Tall trees, such as Bluegums (*Eucalyptus* species), are especially favoured for nesting. In the author's garden, a Pied Crow's nest was built in a Jacaranda tree, about four metres from the ground.

The Pied Crow places its nest high up in tall trees, and seems to favour Bluegums (Eucalyptus species).

This striking black and white bird is the only white-bellied crow in the region. It is closely associated with human habitation, sometimes becoming a pest.

DIRECTORY OF GARDEN BIRDS

Cape Bulbul

Pycnonotus capensis (566) Length: 21 cm

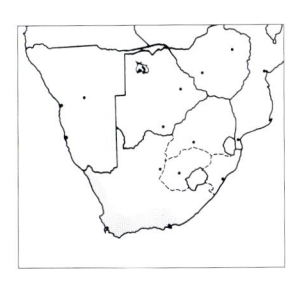

A common resident in gardens and parks of the southern Cape coastal areas, the Cape Bulbul is known by most urban gardeners there. It is very active and conspicuous, and is generally seen in pairs or small groups. This bulbul is responsible for aiding the spread of the alien Rooikrans tree (Acacia cyclops) in the Cape, by eating the seed and passing it undigested.

Above: *Newly-hatched chicks of the Cape Bulbul.*
Below: *This bird is attracted by fynbos plants.*

IN THE GARDEN

HABITAT: This bird prefers dense vegetation and will be attracted by such plants as fynbos and coastal and riverine scrub. It also readily feeds on the fruits of ornamental and other vines, as well as on the fruit of the alien Brazilian Pepper (*Schinus terebinthifolius*).

FOOD REQUIREMENTS: The Cape Bulbul is a regular visitor to the feeding table, especially when fruit such as paw-paw or apple is on offer. It will also feed on bone-meal and any insects that are available.

NESTING: The bird will nest in fynbos thickets and leafy trees. Although a bold and cheeky garden inhabitant, it is not tolerant of disturbance during the breeding season, especially when nest-building. The nest is usually sited two to three metres above the ground.

The white eye-ring of this species distinguishes it from other bulbuls in the region.

DIET
Mostly fruit, berries and nectar but also insects.

BREEDING
SITE: A shallow, cup-shaped nest is built from grass, roots and hair in a bush or tree.
SEASON: August to December, but up to March if rains are good. **CLUTCH SIZE:** 2-3, sometimes 4 or 5. **INCUBATION PERIOD:** 12-14 days. **FLEDGING PERIOD:** 11-15 days.

DIRECTORY OF GARDEN BIRDS

BLACKEYED BULBUL

Pycnonotus barbatus (568) Length: 22 cm

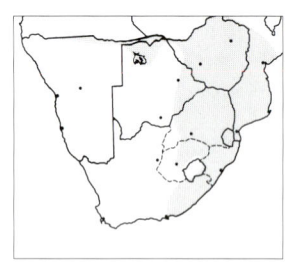

The Blackeyed Bulbul occurs in the eastern half of the region, replacing the other two *Pycnonotus* species here. It is a common resident in urban gardens, often seen in small groups and always active and calling. This bulbul, or 'toppie' as the bulbuls are often known, is very quick to spot an owl or snake and will create such a fuss that other birds will soon be attracted to the commotion. Owls are generally most persecuted by the bulbuls, which never adapt to the owls' presence in the garden and may be seen to mob them in the late afternoon.

Although not strictly a communal species, the Blackeyed Bulbul is often seen in small groups.

BREEDING

Site: A cup-shaped nest is built from grass, roots and hair and is normally situated on an outer branch of a tree or bush.
Season: September to April. **Clutch Size:** 2-3. **Incubation Period:** About 13 days. **Fledging Period:** From 10 to 12 days.

IN THE GARDEN

Habitat: Well known to gardeners, the Blackeyed Bulbul is a friendly and cheerful visitor and will utilize every part of the garden. It is very fond of bird-baths, and eventually becomes very tame.
Food Requirements: Like other bulbuls, this species eats mainly fruit and small berries but will take insects and small lizards. It seems to be particularly fond of termites and can often be found at an active mound feeding on them. The Blackeyed Bulbul will peck at bone-meal and suet from a feeding log and will readily take fruit from the feeding table.
Nesting: The Blackeyed Bulbul willingly nests in urban gardens, usually near the edge of a leafy bush or tree. Some nests are built only two metres from the ground, although most are considerably higher.

The Blackeyed Bulbul lacks the white eye-ring of the Cape Bulbul but has similar yellow under-tail coverts.

DIET

Mainly fruit, but also insects and lizards.

DIRECTORY OF GARDEN BIRDS

Sombre Bulbul
Andropadus importunus (572) Length: 23 cm

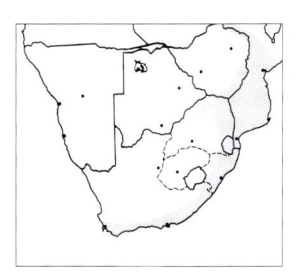

The Sombre Bulbul favours dense vegetation, and prefers even denser thickets than does the Cape Bulbul. It is a common resident of the southern and eastern parts of the region and is seen either singly or in pairs. Although difficult to spot, it is easily recognized by its call, which is rendered as 'willie' and accounts for the bird's colloquial name. The Sombre Bulbul normally perches high up in a tree where it is well concealed, and will call endlessly throughout the day. The best time to see the bird close to the ground is in the early morning.

Above: The nest is usually sited in a sapling and often at the edge of a forest or thicket.
Right: Pine cones with fruit squashed between the scales are an attractant.

SEASON: October to April, with some local variation. CLUTCH SIZE: 1-3. INCUBATION PERIOD: 15-17 days. FLEDGING PERIOD: About 15 days.

IN THE GARDEN
HABITAT: Dense thickets of vegetation in the exclusion area will appeal to this bird.
FOOD REQUIREMENTS: Fruiting trees – the indigenous figs (*Ficus* species), for instance – will encourage this bird to feed in the higher branches. Although shy, the Sombre Bulbul may be attracted to a feeding table placed in the exclusion area and offering fruit items. A pine cone with banana squashed between the scales and suspended high in a tree may also entice it into the garden to feed.
NESTING: The nest is usually placed fairly close to the ground, towards the edge of a bush or thicket. It is likely to breed only in densely vegetated gardens.

The most obvious distinctive feature of the drably coloured Sombre Bulbul is its pale cream eye.

DIET
Mostly fruit and berries; also insects and small snails.

BREEDING
SITE: A flimsy, cup-shaped nest is made using twigs and roots and is lined with fine grass.

DIRECTORY OF GARDEN BIRDS

Kurrichane Thrush

Turdus libonyana (576) Length: 22 cm

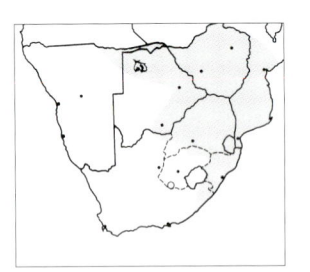

Although quite a timid bird in its natural habitat, the Kurrichane Thrush will be attracted to gardens and parks with shrubs and trees and may become fairly tame. It is seen singly or in pairs, and typically runs in short bursts with its head held low and then stops suddenly to eat. It feeds by scratching in leaf litter and can often be seen foraging under tree canopies for food.

This thrush raises several broods of chicks during its summertime breeding season.

The yellow eye-ring, boldly patterned throat and bright orange bill identify the Kurrichane Thrush.

DIET
Insects, spiders, snails, fruit and berries.

BREEDING
SITE: A nest is built in a sturdy tree fork, using twigs, roots and grass, and often incorporating artificial items such as paper, plastic, string and rags.
SEASON: August to March in Zimbabwe, mostly October and November in South Africa; two to three broods each season. CLUTCH SIZE: 1-4. INCUBATION PERIOD: 13-14 days. FLEDGING PERIOD: About 14 days.

IN THE GARDEN
HABITAT: The Kurrichane Thrush, a very adaptable bird, prefers a mixture of open ground and large trees and shrubs. It is wary of dogs.
FOOD REQUIREMENTS: Gardens with a healthy mulch layer will readily attract this thrush to feed. Artificial feeding should initially be done at ground level in the exclusion area. Bone-meal, suet, fruit and bread can be offered. As the bird becomes tame it may be enticed to the feeding table.
NESTING: This species is only likely to breed in quiet gardens that have large trees.

This species is catholic in its diet, readily taking fruit and berries as well as preying on snails, insects and spiders.

DIRECTORY OF GARDEN BIRDS

Olive Thrush
Turdus olivaceus (577) Length: 24 cm

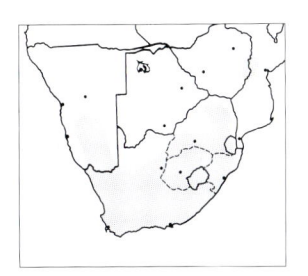

The Olive Thrush is a widespread, common resident throughout most of the region and is commonly seen in urban gardens and parks, most often scratching around in the mulch layer looking for insects. Primarily a ground feeder, it will spend some time in the open grassed areas but only when activity levels in the garden are low. It is usually seen singly or in pairs.

The Olive Thrush may nest in roof gutters but prefers to build its nest in the fork of a sturdy tree.

IN THE GARDEN
Habitat: A quiet, well-developed exclusion area with thickets and the open grassed areas of the garden will be utilized by this bird.

Food Requirements: The exclusion area is where you are most likely to find the Olive Thrush feeding, scratching through the leaf litter in search of food. It is bolder than the Kurrichane Thrush and will venture onto a feeding table if the food offered is appealing to it. Mealworms, bone-meal, suet and fruit will all be eaten. This bird has even been known to catch small fish out of ponds.

Nesting: This species requires a sturdy tree or bush for a nest site. The nest is usually placed two to five metres above the ground.

This species resembles the Kurrichane Thrush but has a yellowish bill, deep yellow legs and a less patterned throat.

DIET
Mainly insects, but also snails, spiders, small lizards and even baby birds.

BREEDING
Site: A fairly large nest of twigs, leaves and moss, and lined with grass and mud, is built in the fork of a tree.
Season: Throughout the year but mainly August to November in the Cape and one to two months later further north. **Clutch Size:** 1-4. **Incubation Period:** About 14 days. **Fledging Period:** About 15 days.

The eggs of the Olive Thrush vary in colour, from pale to dark blue, and are blotched with various shades of brown and lilac. Between one and four eggs are laid.

DIRECTORY OF GARDEN BIRDS

GROUNDSCRAPER THRUSH
Turdus litsitsirupa (580) Length: 22 cm

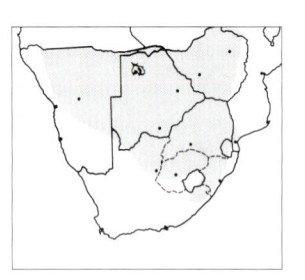

The Groundscraper Thrush is more social than most other thrushes and is sometimes seen in small flocks, although more commonly in pairs or singly. Highly terrestrial, it is often found in open areas such as the lawn, scratching, turning leaves and digging for food, a habit which has given rise to its common name. Its attractive and distinctive colouring makes the bird easy to recognize. It has a habit of flicking one wing at a time while foraging.

Above: *Grassy, open areas of the garden will be utilized by the Groundscraper Thrush but only when human and other activity levels are low.*
Right: *As these thrushes feed on caterpillars, an offer of mealworms may entice them into the garden.*

Teardrop-shaped marks on the breast are conspicuous.

DIET
Mainly insects; also molluscs and other invertebrates.

BREEDING
SITE: A large nest is constructed with twigs, leaves, grass, feathers, and various artificial items if available, and is situated in a fork of a tree.
SEASON: August to January. CLUTCH SIZE: 2-4. INCUBATION PERIOD: Not known. FLEDGING PERIOD: Not known.

IN THE GARDEN
HABITAT: This bird is fairly shy and will be seen only when the garden is quiet. Grassy open areas will attract it, and it may scratch in the mulch layer for food items.
FOOD REQUIREMENTS: Lawn caterpillars and any other insects found in the open area or among the mulch layer will be fed on by the Groundscraper Thrush. Try feeding it at ground level with bone-meal and suet. Although this thrush is not a common visitor at the feeding table, it will become quite tame after regular visits to the garden.
NESTING: This shy but sociable species needs a sturdy tree or bush as a nest site. The nest is placed in a fork between two and six metres above the ground. Very attentive parents, both the adults aggressively defend the nest against predators during the breeding season, even attacking humans who get too close.

DIRECTORY OF GARDEN BIRDS

Familiar Chat

Cercomela familiaris (589) Length: 15 cm

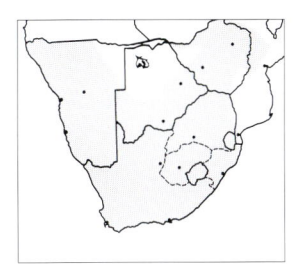

A common resident of the southern African region with a distinctive habit of flicking its wings after every hop or flight, the Familiar Chat becomes very tame in the presence of people and around human settlements. This species was known to eat the grease off wagon-wheel axles which gave rise to the Afrikaans common name of Spekvreter *('fat-eater').*

The Familiar Chat has a rich chestnut rump and outer tail feathers. Like other chats, it flicks its wings on alighting on a perch but this species also 'trembles' its tail when at rest. It is a confiding little bird, and readily makes itself at home in the garden.

DIET

Mainly insects; also fruit and other food scraps.

BREEDING

Site: A cup-like nest is built in a hole in the ground, on a rock face, on or near a building, and often in unused farm machinery. Materials used to build the nest include hair, feathers, wool, plant material and artificial materials like string and paper.

Season: July to April. **Clutch Size:** 2-4. **Incubation Period:** 13-15 days. **Fledging Period:** About 17 days.

This bird places its cup-shaped nest in a hole in a bank or under a stone. It may be successfully lured into breeding in the garden if a hollow-log nesting site is secured in a tree or against a wall. The Familiar Chat is not particularly fussy about where it breeds, however, and even an old paint tin will serve its purposes.

IN THE GARDEN

Habitat: Although this is a common species of rocky hillsides, dongas and rocky outcrops, it is often encountered away from rocks. It is frequently seen in the vicinity of farmhouses. The Familiar Chat may be seen perched on tree tops and, over time, will become tame and trusting in the garden.

Food Requirements: This friendly, confiding, little species may be attracted to suet and bone-meal offered on the feeding table and will also take bread, mealworms and pieces of fruit.

Nesting: These birds frequently make their nests close to human activity, especially on farms and smallholdings, and are very successful at rearing young under such conditions. In the urban garden, hollow logs and nest-boxes (*see* pages 53 and 56) secured to a tree or against a wall may be used by this bird for breeding. They are not particular about nest sites, however, and even an old paint tin placed on its side will suffice.

DIRECTORY OF GARDEN BIRDS

Mocking Chat

Thamnolaea cinnamomeiventris (593) Length: 23 cm

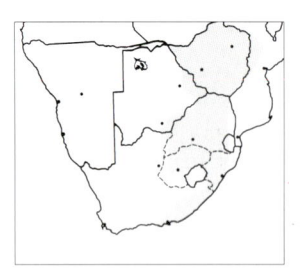

The Mocking Chat is a locally common resident of the region. This remarkable bird is known to imitate the calls of as many as 30 other bird species. It is often found in small groups of up to five birds, and is frequently seen perched on a tree or boulder from which vantage point the male will give a burst of song before moving on to another perch.

Mocking Chats often perch conspicuously, the male giving a short burst of song before flying to another perch.

The female Mocking Chat resembles the male of the species but lacks the white shoulder patches.

DIET
Mainly insects but also fruit.

BREEDING
SITE: Often uses the nest of a Lesser Striped Swallow (expelling the residents if necessary), building a bowl-shaped nest of twigs, leaves and hair within this. Sometimes builds its own, untidy nest, on a rock ledge or a ledge under a roof.
SEASON: August to December. CLUTCH SIZE: 2-4, usually 3. INCUBATION PERIOD: 14-16 days. FLEDGING PERIOD: About 20 days.

IN THE GARDEN
HABITAT: The Mocking Chat prefers a rocky environment but will enter gardens that are close to such areas. The bird may become tame and tolerant of human activity over time.
FOOD REQUIREMENTS: This bird will feed on fruit, mealworms, meat scraps, suet and pieces of fat placed on the feeding table.
NESTING: The presence of a Lesser Striped Swallow's nest in the garden may be an incentive for the Mocking Chat to breed here, although Mocking Chats sometimes construct their own nests.

DIRECTORY OF GARDEN BIRDS

HEUGLIN'S ROBIN
Cossypha heuglini (599) Length: 20 cm

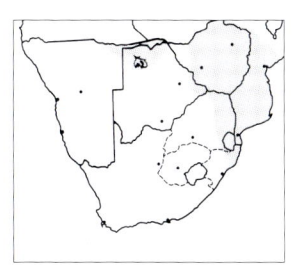

This bird is reputed to be one of the world's best songsters. It has adapted well to urbanization and its song may be heard in many gardens in northern Natal, the Transvaal and Zimbabwe. It is usually seen singly at dawn or in the early evening.

Heuglin's Robin will spend most of its time in dense thickets, moving into the open to feed at quiet times.

BREEDING
SITE: A cup-shaped nest of twigs, leaves and moss is built low down in dense shrubbery, in hollow logs or other cavities. The nest is often parasitized by the Red-chested Cuckoo.
SEASON: September to January. CLUTCH SIZE: 2 or 3. INCUBATION PERIOD: About 15 days. FLEDGING PERIOD: About 17 days.

IN THE GARDEN
HABITAT: Although Heuglin's Robin takes readily to urbanization, it will spend most of its time in the dense thicket of the exclusion area and is heard much more often than it is seen. When all is quiet it will move out into the open area to feed.
FOOD REQUIREMENTS: This bird will feed on insects in the open areas of the garden; although it feeds mostly on the ground, this robin may take termite alates in flight. It will also eat mealworms, bone-meal and suet offered on the ground in the exclusion area, provided there is peace and quiet in which it can feed. Robins are particularly fond of grated cheese!
NESTING: Heuglin's Robin prefers dense thickets to serve as nest sites, and the bird may also be encouraged to breed in a hollow log nest (*see* page 53) provided for it in a low-traffic area of the garden.

The broad, white eyebrow stripe and wholly orange underparts are reliable field characters of Heuglin's Robin.

DIET
Insects, spiders, centipedes, small frogs and reptiles.

DIRECTORY OF GARDEN BIRDS

NATAL ROBIN

Cossypha natalensis (600) Length: 18 cm

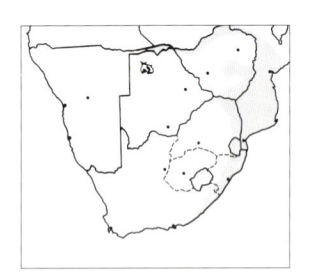

This shy, secretive bird normally ventures out of the dense bush in the early morning or evening to feed, and is usually solitary. Its large eyes probably assist with its low-light feeding schedule. It is well adapted to urban areas and will breed there. This robin is an excellent mimic and is reported to imitate at least 30 bird calls including that of the African Fish Eagle.

This bird-friendly garden would be likely to attract the Natal Robin, which appreciates dense cover.

SEASON: September to January. CLUTCH SIZE: 2-4, usually 3. INCUBATION PERIOD: About 14 days. FLEDGING PERIOD: About 12-15 days.

The Natal Robin differs from other robins in having a powder-blue back and orange head.

DIET
Mainly insects; also fruit including berries.

BREEDING
SITE: A cup-shaped nest is constructed using dead leaves, twigs and tendrils. The nest is lined with finer plant material or hair and is normally located, well hidden, in hollow logs and other cavities, in creepers or on the ground. The nest, as is the case with some other robins, is parasitized by the Redchested Cuckoo.

IN THE GARDEN
HABITAT: This shy, secretive bird is attracted to dense bush and will therefore spend most of its time in the exclusion area.
FOOD REQUIREMENTS: Bone-meal, suet, cheese, mealworms and fruit will all be enjoyed, as long as thick bush is not too far away for cover. Try feeding the bird at ground level in the exclusion area until it becomes used to the garden surroundings.
NESTING: The Natal Robin will readily breed in gardens, using shrubs and hedges as nesting sites. It also regularly breeds in holes in walls, and in hollow logs provided for it (*see* page 53).

DIRECTORY OF GARDEN BIRDS

Cape Robin

Cossypha caffra (601) Length: 18 cm

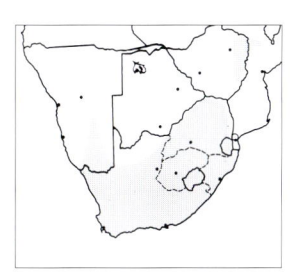

Usually seen singly or in pairs, this bird is a common resident throughout South Africa. Like the other robins, it has a shy nature and typically favours dense bush. It is most often seen in the early morning or evening when it will venture out to feed. The Cape Robin is the most common of all the robins in urban areas.

The Cape Robin lays two or three eggs, which hatch after an incubation period of between two and three weeks. The chicks fledge after a further fortnight.

Although, like Heuglin's Robin, the Cape Robin has a white eyebrow stripe, the grey lower breast will distinguish it from that species.

DIET
Mainly insects; also spiders, worms, frogs and lizards; and fruit including berries.

BREEDING
Site: A nest of leaves and twigs, lined with hair and fine plant material, is built in dense vegetation, tree stumps, hollows in banks, and in garden containers such as flowerpots. Some nests are built on the ground. The nest, as is the case with those of Heuglin's and the Natal robins, is parasitized by the Redchested Cuckoo.
Season: September to December in the summer-rainfall areas and June to December in the winter-rainfall areas; occasionally 2 broods per season. **Clutch Size:** 1-4. **Incubation Period:** 14-18 days. **Fledging Period:** About 16 days.

IN THE GARDEN
Habitat: This robin usually forages close to the ground in dense, shrubby vegetation. A shy bird, it will favour the exclusion area as well as other shady spots in the garden, such as fern gardens.
Food Requirements: The Cape Robin will take bonemeal, suet, cheese, mealworms and even porridge from the feeding table or off the ground in the exclusion area. It becomes tame over time and can, with patience and perseverance, eventually be enticed to take food from the hand.
Nesting: Although secretive by nature, robins will often nest in tool sheds, flower-boxes and garden creepers, and other sites close to human habitation.

DIRECTORY OF GARDEN BIRDS

Willow Warbler
Phylloscopus trochilus (643) Length: 11 cm

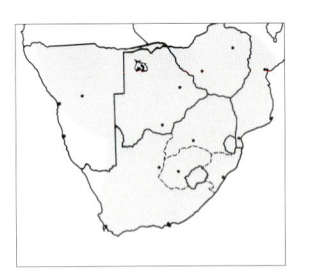

A common non-breeding migrant from Asia and Europe, the Willow Warbler arrives in November and departs in March and April. It may cover a distance of up to 13 000 kilometres twice a year and yet weighs only 10 grams. It is often overlooked due to its small size and inconspicuous colouring. It is always seen foraging among leaves and branches of trees. Three subspecies of the Willow Warbler are found in southern Africa, ranging in colour from greenish-yellow to brown and white.

The tiny Willow Warbler ranges in colour from olive and yellow to brown and white.

DIET
Almost exclusively small insects; known to take berries in its breeding quarters.

BREEDING
This bird does not breed in southern Africa.

The Willow Warbler occurs wherever there are trees, although it avoids forest; it is absent from completely open country. This warbler is found among trees and bushes, keeping to the interior and usually to the canopy, but it does not hide away as do some of the other warblers.

IN THE GARDEN
HABITAT: This bird will spend most of its time in trees, and will therefore keep to the exclusion area and canopy habitat. It seems to favour White Stinkwood (*Celtis africana*) trees.

FOOD REQUIREMENTS: The Willow Warbler is not a common bird at the feeding table but may be enticed by suet and bone-meal offered in a feeding log (*see page 30*). It is a useful bird in the garden as it gleans aphids from leaves and twigs.

NESTING: Breeds outside of the southern African region.

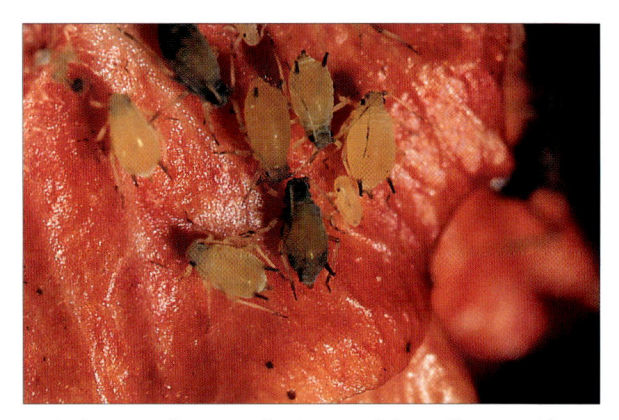

Aphids are a favourite food item of the Willow Warbler, which gleans these little insects from leaves and twigs.

DIRECTORY OF GARDEN BIRDS

Barthroated Apalis

Apalis thoracica (645) Length: 13 cm

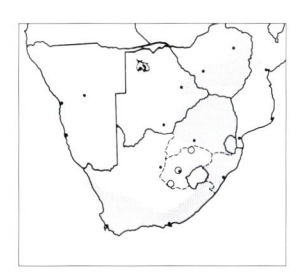

The Barthroated Apalis is a common resident of the region and is normally seen in pairs but sometimes moves in groups of mixed birds. It is well known in many urban gardens which offer evergreen thickets and dense bush. The loud, repetitive, characteristic call of this bird usually discloses its presence.

The Barthroated Apalis has a particular liking for caterpillars, gleaning these off tree trunks.

IN THE GARDEN

HABITAT: The Barthroated Apalis will spend most of its time in the exclusion area and canopy habitat. All the strata of vegetation are utilized, from ground level up to the tree canopies.

FOOD REQUIREMENTS: Acacia trees, particularly *Acacia sieberiana*, attract these birds. Insects are gleaned from flowers, leaves and tree trunks. The Barthroated Apalis may visit a feeding table situated near or in the exclusion area, especially if mealworms, bone-meal and suet are on offer.

NESTING: The nest, oval and with a side entrance, is usually built close to the ground, favoured sites being tall, rank grass and creeper-covered bushes.

Various colour forms of the Barthroated Apalis occur, and it is best to identify this species by its black collar (less well defined in females), white outer tail feathers and pale eye.

Acacia trees attract the Barthroated Apalis.

DIET
Insects, particularly favouring caterpillars.

BREEDING
SITE: An enclosed, upright nest is built in a bush or creeper from grass, moss, various other plant material, and spider web.
SEASON: Mostly August to January in the south of its range, extending to March further north, in Zimbabwe.
CLUTCH SIZE: 2-4. INCUBATION PERIOD: 17-18 days. FLEDGING PERIOD: About 18 days.

DIRECTORY OF GARDEN BIRDS

Tawnyflanked Prinia

Prinia subflava (683) Length: 11 cm

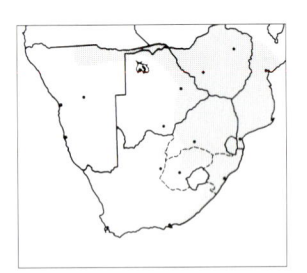

This common resident of the eastern and northern parts of the region is found in areas of rank grass, weeds and bushes near streams and watercourses. It is often seen in urban gardens, and is usually in pairs. The bird is fairly bold and always on the move.

Although found in a variety of habitats, the Tawny-flanked Prinia tends to favour wetlands.

DIET
Mainly insects but also nectar.

BREEDING
SITE: An upright, woven nest, usually attached to the stems of reeds or grass or built in low bushes, is made from green blades of grass and is sometimes lined with soft grass flowers. The bird may take over the nest of a Red Bishop. This prinia's nest is parasitized by the Cuckoo Finch.
SEASON: August to April. CLUTCH SIZE: 3-4. INCUBATION PERIOD: 13-14 days. FLEDGING PERIOD: About 15 days.

IN THE GARDEN
HABITAT: A frequent visitor to gardens, the Tawny-flanked Prinia will be further encouraged by the presence of a water feature and a wetland area.
FOOD REQUIREMENTS: Insects will be gleaned from vegetation near the ground. You may be able to lure the bird to the feeding table with bone-meal and juicy pieces of orange.
NESTING: Areas of rank vegetation and scrubby bush will encourage this bird to breed. The distinctive, upright, oval nest is usually placed about one metre above the ground, and often attached to the stems of weeds, reeds or grass.

The most distinctive feature of this 'little brown job' is its long, graduated tail, which is often held cocked.

DIRECTORY OF GARDEN BIRDS

Fiscal Flycatcher
Sigelus silens (698) Length: 17-20 cm

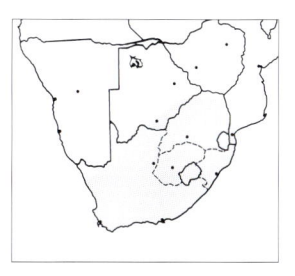

A bold bird, the Fiscal Flycatcher is often confused with the Fiscal Shrike. It does not have the hooked beak of the shrike, however, but displays a similar behaviour in 'hawking' for insects from a perch. This bird is a common resident of South Africa and extreme southern Botswana and is often seen in the garden, either singly or in pairs.

The Fiscal Flycatcher closely resembles the Fiscal Shrike but lacks the stubby, hooked bill of that species.

This species will build its nest, up to six metres above the ground, in a tree anywhere in the garden.

DIET
Mostly insects but also fruit and nectar.

BREEDING
Site: A large, shallow nest is built in a fork of a tree, and comprises grass and various other plant material; it is lined with plant down and rootlets.
Season: Throughout summer but mostly September to December. **Clutch Size:** 2-4, usually 3. **Incubation Period:** 13-15 days. **Fledging Period:** Not known.

IN THE GARDEN
Habitat: The Fiscal Flycatcher is commonly seen in gardens, perching on the tops and edges of trees and bushes, and is to be welcomed as it will help to remove many unwanted insect pests.
Food Requirements: This bird will sometimes eat fruit from a feeding table but will prefer offerings of bonemeal. A post erected in the open area will provide it with a hunting perch. It becomes fairly tame and will feed in close proximity to people.
Nesting: The Fiscal Flycatcher may nest anywhere in the garden, often about five or six metres above the ground in a fork of a tree. A favoured nest site is at the base of an aloe leaf.

DIRECTORY OF GARDEN BIRDS

Paradise Flycatcher

Terpsiphone viridis (710) Length: male 40 cm, female 23 cm

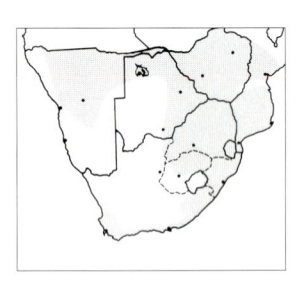

This common intra-African migrant arrives in the country in September and leaves again mostly in April and May. Some birds remain through the winter in the eastern lowlands. The long, graceful tail of the male makes it an easy bird to identify. The Paradise Flycatcher is often found in well-wooded gardens where it may nest surprisingly close to human structures and activities.

Both sexes feed the young. The male is immediately recognizable by its long, chestnut central tail feathers.

DIET
Almost entirely small insects, captured in flight.

BREEDING
SITE: A small, cup-shaped nest is built in a fork of a tree using bark and fine plant material bound with spider web; the outside of the nest is generally decorated with lichens, which aids in camouflage.
SEASON: September to March; produces 2-3 broods each season. CLUTCH SIZE: 2-3. INCUBATION PERIOD: About 14 days. FLEDGING PERIOD: About 12 days.

IN THE GARDEN
HABITAT: This bird will readily visit a bird-bath or pond in the garden where it will plunge bath. It does not feel threatened by human proximity but will spend most of its time in the more densely vegetated parts of the garden, such as the exclusion area.

Both the male and the female (shown left) of this species are beautiful birds, but only at close range can the bright blue bill and eye wattle and the glossy crest be seen.

FOOD REQUIREMENTS: Although not a common visitor to the feeding table it may be possible to entice this flycatcher to feed from a feeding log (*see* page 30) containing suet and bone-meal.
NESTING: The Paradise Flycatcher often nests in gardens, sometimes suprisingly close to areas of human activity. The very neat nest is usually placed about three metres above the ground in a fork of a slender, downward-hanging branch. Although the nest is generally well camouflaged, it is seldom completely hidden and the long tail feathers of the incubating male Paradise Flycatcher, drooping gracefully over the edge, may reveal its presence.

DIRECTORY OF GARDEN BIRDS

Cape Wagtail

Motacilla capensis (713) Length: 18 cm

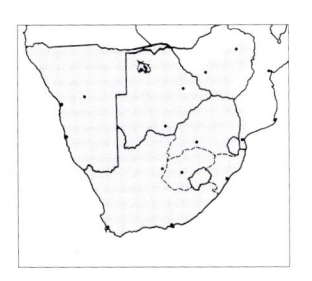

Once a very common garden bird, this species has been severely affected by the use of garden chemicals and is often locally absent from urban gardens. Its characteristic habit of bobbing its tail as it patrols the mowed lawn, looking for insects, makes it unmistakable. It is seen either singly or in pairs and rapidly becomes tame in the garden environment.

Away from human habitation, the favoured nest site of this bird is a hollow in a river bank. In urban situations, however, it may nest in creepers on house walls, and in hedges and in the stumps of trees.

In common with some other wagtails, this comparatively dull species shows white outer tail feathers.

DIET

Mainly insects, but this bird also takes small crustaceans, fish and tadpoles.

BREEDING

SITE: A nest is built in creepers, but also often in tool sheds and other artificial facilities. Grass and various plant material forms the base of a cup-shaped structure made of fine hair, roots and feathers. This bird may be parasitized by the Diederik Cuckoo.
SEASON: All months of the year, but mostly in spring and early summer. CLUTCH SIZE: Usually 3. INCUBATION PERIOD: 14 days. FLEDGING PERIOD: About 14 days.

IN THE GARDEN

HABITAT: The Cape Wagtail will utilize most areas in the garden, from the open areas to the canopies, and also ponds and wetlands.
FOOD REQUIREMENTS: A true friend of the gardener, the Cape Wagtail feeds on many common garden pests, particularly those found in the lawn. It will readily take food from a feeding table where mealworms, bone-meal and suet will all be enjoyed.
NESTING: This bird may build its nest in creepers or bushes, but will just as readily use a plant-box or a nook or cavity in a wall for a nest site. It is one of relatively few species in the region which comfortably nest on or very close to houses.

DIRECTORY OF GARDEN BIRDS

Fiscal Shrike
Lanius collaris (732) Length: 23 cm

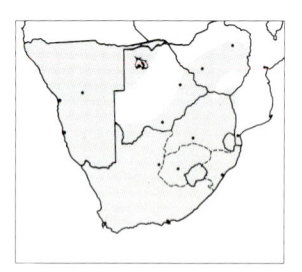

This is a very common resident of the region and a species that is well known in urban gardens. The Fiscal Shrike normally occurs singly and is often seen sitting on a prominent perch from which it is able to survey the garden for insects. It typically swoops down off its perch to catch these, frequently taking them in flight. Prey is sometimes carried off in its feet.

Fiscal Shrikes are territorial, scaring other birds out of the garden and occasionally becoming a nuisance.

DIET
Large insects, small rodents, reptiles and birds. It is known occasionally to kill birds as large as a Laughing Dove.

The Fiscal Shrike is a trim, black and white bird.

BREEDING
SITE: The cup-shaped nest is constructed in a fork of a tree or bush and consists of grass and twigs, lined with soft plant material.
SEASON: All months of the year except February. CLUTCH SIZE: 1-5. INCUBATION PERIOD: About 16 days. FLEDGING PERIOD: About 20 days.

IN THE GARDEN
HABITAT: This common garden visitor will be seen sitting on prominent perches in the open area of the garden. It rapidly becomes tame but is aggressive and may often chase birds away from its territory.
FOOD REQUIREMENTS: The Fiscal Shrike will hawk insects in the garden from a perch. The hooked bill is used to first kill and then dismember prey while the bird holds it in its feet. Prey that is captured but not eaten may be impaled on barbed wire fences or on the thorns of *Acacia* species. Pellets consisting of undigested material are regurgitated; this behaviour is similar to that shown by raptors such as owls. This shrike will readily visit the feeding table or a feeding log, where it will enjoy mealworms, bone-meal and suet.
NESTING: The nest is usually placed about three metres above the ground in a thorn tree, but other nest sites, such as a covered verandah, are also used. The same nest is regularly re-used in successive years.

This species, like many of its relatives, may impale its prey on a sharp object. It is not known if the bird returns later to eat the victim.

SOUTHERN BOUBOU
Laniarius ferrugineus (736) Length: 23 cm

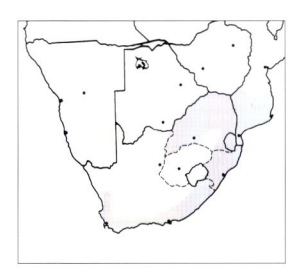

This attractive bird is often confused with the Fiscal Shrike but has extensive rufous colouring on the underparts and quite different habits, which helps to distinguish it. It is a common resident of the region but has a secretive nature and tends to skulk in thick vegetation. However, it occurs frequently in urban gardens and will visit either singly or in pairs.

The Southern Boubou resembles the Fiscal Shrike but is larger than that species and has a shorter tail.

This species requires undisturbed and well-concealed surroundings in which to breed.

DIET
Insects, fledging birds, and occasionally fruit and eggs.

BREEDING
Site: The nest is a shallow construction of rootlets and twigs, bound together with spider web and lined with fine plant material. It is usually well concealed in a bush, tree or creeper about two metres off the ground.
Season: August to March, but mainly September to November. **Clutch Size:** 1-3. **Incubation Period:** About 17 days. **Fledging Period:** About 17 days.

IN THE GARDEN
Habitat: Although generally a shy bird, the Southern Boubou will tame in a garden environment. It will spend most of its time in the exclusion area hopping around the lower branches, or in the mulch layer.
Food Requirements: A well-matured mulch layer will attract this bird to feed. It will also visit the feeding table or a feeding log (*see* page 30) and can be offered bone-meal, suet and mealworms, but start by feeding it in the exclusion area until it becomes used to the more open expanses of the garden.
Nesting: This species will breed only among dense foliage where it can hide its nest. The nest is usually sited about two metres above the ground near the end of a branch. The Southern Boubou is susceptible to disturbance when breeding. If this occurs it may abandon the nest. The chicks are dependent on the parents until they are about seven weeks old.

DIRECTORY OF GARDEN BIRDS

Puffback
Dryoscopus cubla (740) Length: 18 cm

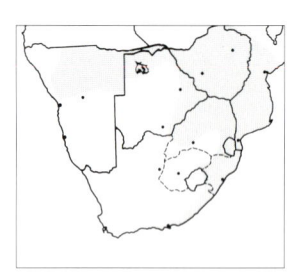

One of the smaller shrikes, the Puffback is a common resident of the region, and tends to keep to the tree canopies. The common name is derived from the male bird's habit of puffing up the feathers of the rump during courtship displays. The bird is usually seen in pairs but sometimes occurs in mixed bird groups.

Both the male and the female (above) Puffback have a red eye but the male has a wholly black cap.

DIET
Insects and spiders; occasionally small lizards.

BREEDING
SITE: A neat, cup-shaped nest is built in a fork of a tree, between three and ten metres above the ground and consists of twigs, rootlets, grass and bark, bound together with spider web. This little bird may decorate the outside of the nest with lichens and dry leaves.
SEASON: September to January. CLUTCH SIZE: 2-3. INCUBATION PERIOD: 13 days. FLEDGING PERIOD: About 17 days.

Puffbacks search for their predominantly insect prey on leaves, twigs and the bark of trees. Woodborers (above) are among those that may be taken.

IN THE GARDEN
HABITAT: The characteristic click-and-whistle call of this bird generally announces its presence in the garden before it is seen. It is a fairly shy bird and does not often venture out of the tree canopies.
FOOD REQUIREMENTS: The Puffback will eat insects from within the tree canopies and from the bark of trees. It is not a regular visitor to the feeding table but may be enticed to take bone-meal, suet and mealworms from a feeding log or feeding table situated within easy reach of the exclusion area.
NESTING: The Puffback favours well-wooded habitats, in the wild preferring forest edges, and is likely to breed only in a mature exclusion area which contains large trees. The nestlings are fed by both adults, and the male also feeds the female on the nest. Fledglings remain within the parents' territory for up to a year. The Puffback is parasitized by the Emerald Cuckoo.

DIRECTORY OF GARDEN BIRDS

Bokmakierie

Telophorus zeylonus (746) Length: 23 cm

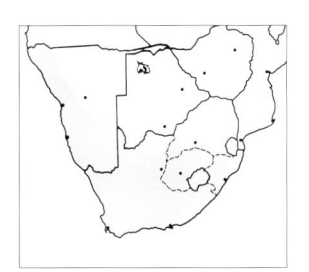

The Bokmakierie is one of the bush shrikes, and is a common resident, widespread throughout most of South Africa and southern and western Namibia. It is well known for its ringing duets, delivered from the tops of trees, posts or roof tops. This species may be seen singly or in pairs. It is a highly attractive bird which readily becomes tame in urban areas.

The Bokmakierie is an unmistakable bush shrike with its yellow front and broad, black bib.

The nest of the Bokmakierie is always well concealed in foliage. Both sexes incubate and feed the young, and they are often seen in pairs with fledged young.

DIET
Insects, small reptiles, frogs and small birds, and occasionally seeds and small fruits.

BREEDING
SITE: A fairly large, cup-shaped nest of twigs, grass and small roots is well hidden in a bush, tree, hedge or creeper, usually one to four metres above the ground.
SEASON: The Bokmakierie has been recorded breeding throughout the year, but generally peaks between late winter and early summer. CLUTCH SIZE: 2-6, usually 3. INCUBATION PERIOD: About 16 days. FLEDGING PERIOD: About 18 days.

IN THE GARDEN
HABITAT: This bird is usually located by its attractive call before it is seen. It will spend most of its time in the well-concealed parts of the garden but will also enter more open areas to feed.
FOOD REQUIREMENTS: A rich mulch layer will be an attraction, as this bird prefers to search for its invertebrate prey on the ground under shrubbery and leaves. Mealworms, suet and bone-meal offered at a feeding table will encourage it to come out of the undergrowth.
NESTING: Areas of dense growth in the garden may encourage breeding. The nest is usually built within two metres of the ground. The Bokmakierie typically returns to breed in the same area each year and sometimes builds a new nest on top of an old one. Both sexes incubate, brood and feed the young, which learn to fly within about three weeks of hatching.

DIRECTORY OF GARDEN BIRDS

Orangebreasted Bush Shrike

Telophorus sulfureopectus (748) Length: 19 cm

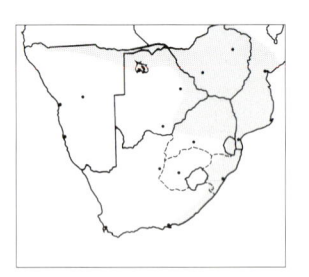

One of the more brightly coloured shrikes, this bird is a fairly common resident in the east and north of the region and is usually seen singly or in pairs. It is a very vocal bird but is often difficult to locate due to its habit of perching high up in tree canopies.

This bird takes its name from the rather ill-defined orange flush over its yellow underparts. The upperparts are green, and it has a grey cap.

DIET
Small invertebrates, especially bees and wasps but also beetles, caterpillars and a variety of other insects.

BREEDING
SITE: The untidy, flimsy nest is located on a horizontal branch or among creepers. It is constructed from small twigs and roots, and is lined with finer plant material.
SEASON: Mostly September to December. CLUTCH SIZE: 1-3. INCUBATION PERIOD: Not known, probably about 14 days. FLEDGING PERIOD: About 12 days.

IN THE GARDEN
HABITAT: The canopy habitat will attract this bird which occurs on the edges of forests, although it does not inhabit forest interiors. It is a regular member of mixed bird parties.
FOOD REQUIREMENTS: The Orangebreasted Bush Shrike may be seen gleaning its insect prey from within the canopy in the exclusion area, hopping and peering about as it moves up the trees. This bird occasionally takes aerial insects. This species is not a common visitor to the feeding table because of its shy nature. Mealworms, bone-meal and suet can be offered near the exclusion area and as high up as possible. The bird may also feed from a feeding log (*see* page 30), hung in a well-covered part of the garden.
NESTING: The presence of thorn trees in the garden may encourage the bird to nest as it favours thick thorn scrub in the wild. The nest is built about four metres above the ground.

The Orangebreasted Bush Shrike typically lays two or three eggs which hatch in about two weeks.

DIRECTORY OF GARDEN BIRDS

GREYHEADED BUSH SHRIKE
Malaconotus blanchoti (751) Length: 26 cm

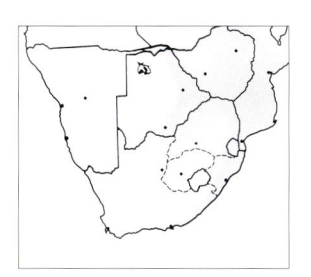

This is the largest of the shrikes in the region and is usually seen singly or in pairs. It is not a common visitor to the urban garden but will enter those bordering on areas of natural bush, particularly if they offer good vegetation cover. It is mostly seen in gardens during local migrations. The bird's call is a haunting, hooting whistle with an upward inflection at the end that has earned it the Afrikaans common name of Spookvoël *(Ghost bird)*.

Insects make up the bulk of this bird's diet.

This is the largest African shrike and both its size and its formidable bill make it unmistakable.

DIET
Mainly large insects, but also small reptiles, frogs, rodents, bats, birds, nestlings and eggs.

BREEDING
SITE: The nest is a shallow structure, built in a fork of a tree, and made from twigs, roots, leaves and grass.
SEASON: Mostly the months September to November.
CLUTCH SIZE: 2-4. INCUBATION PERIOD: About 17 days.
FLEDGING PERIOD: About 21 days.

IN THE GARDEN
HABITAT: The bird will enter gardens which offer sufficient cover and protection, and will therefore keep to the exclusion area.
FOOD REQUIREMENTS: The Greyheaded Bush Shrike forages at all levels of vegetation. It may be enticed to visit a feeding table if mealworms, bone-meal and suet are on offer. Any food offered, however, should be placed near or within the exclusion area.
NESTING: This species may nest in the exclusion area. Nests are usually about four metres above the ground and placed in deciduous trees that lack thorns.

The bill is an efficient tool for dismembering prey.

DIRECTORY OF GARDEN BIRDS

European Starling
Sturnus vulgaris (757) Length: 21 cm

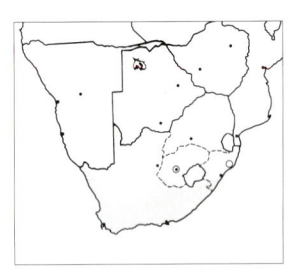

The European Starling was introduced to the south-western Cape (now abundant there) from Europe by Cecil John Rhodes in 1899. It has since spread northwards and eastwards, and now occurs as far east as Durban. It is found only in close association with human settlements. This bird often occurs in flocks of hundreds, even thousands, and is responsible for fouling buildings with its droppings where it roosts. It typically forages on lawns and probes the grass for invertebrates.

DIET
Insects, fruit, seeds, snails and small reptiles.

BREEDING
SITE: The nest is a loose bowl consisting of grass, pine needles and twigs and is lined with feathers, moss and wool if available. It is placed in any convenient cavity, often under roofs and on the tops of buildings.
SEASON: September to December.

The male European Starling has a glossy black plumage with a green and purple sheen and is speckled with white.

This bird lays between three and six pale blue eggs in an untidy nest made with grass and twigs.

CLUTCH SIZE: 3-6. INCUBATION PERIOD: 12-13 days. FLEDGING PERIOD: About 20 days.

IN THE GARDEN
HABITAT: The European Starling is not a popular bird in the garden as it displaces other species. It will be seen most often in open areas, usually in small flocks, probing the lawns for food.
FOOD REQUIREMENTS: This bird tends to take over at the feeding table, devouring anything offered. It is difficult to discourage it from entering the garden, however, due to its abundance in urban areas and its boldness.
NESTING: The bird may nest in the garden without any encouragement to do so, often selecting eaves, pipes or gutters as nesting sites. The birds carry lice which also occur in the nests. Hollow nesting logs (*see* page 53) will be utilized for breeding if the entrance hole is large enough.

This bird may imitate other birds' calls. It sings with its bill pointed up and wings quivering.

DIRECTORY OF GARDEN BIRDS

Indian Myna

Acridotheres tristis (758) Length: 25 cm

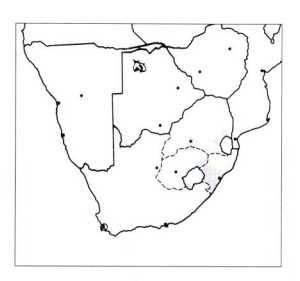

An abundant resident, the Indian Myna was introduced from India to Durban in the late nineteenth century. It has since spread to the Witwatersrand and other urban areas, mainly in Natal and the Transvaal. It associates only with human settlements and in this context is very adaptable. Birds pair for life and can be highly territorial; outside of the breeding season, however, they may be seen in large groups. These aggressive birds form large communal roosts at night, often in palm trees.

Insects form a large part of the Indian Myna's diet.

This common bird is easily identified by the bare yellow skin around its eyes, and by its yellow bill and legs.

DIET
Invertebrates, fruit and seeds, small reptiles, amphibians, mammals and the eggs of other birds.

BREEDING
SITE: A large nest, located in a hole in a tree or building, under eaves or in a pipe, is made from a variety of plant components, but plastic, rags, string and other artificial items may be included if available.
SEASON: September to December. CLUTCH SIZE: 2-5. INCUBATION PERIOD: About 18 days. FLEDGING PERIOD: About 23 days.

IN THE GARDEN
HABITAT: The Indian Myna is commonly seen foraging in mown grass areas for invertebrates. It is aggressive towards other birds, particularly when breeding. Many gardeners and conservationists shoot these birds, but the large numbers of this species already present in urban areas makes this a futile exercise.
FOOD REQUIREMENTS: This bird will forage for insects on the lawn. It will consume anything edible at the feeding table generally to the exclusion of other birds.
NESTING: The bird may nest under the eaves of a roof, in a hole in a wall or in a tree. A hollow nesting log (*see* page 53) will readily be used. A breeding pair in the garden will prevent other Indian Mynas from entering their territory. The eggs can be pricked with a pin to prevent a 'large family' but adequate protection should be worn when approaching the nest as these birds can be highly aggressive.

DIRECTORY OF GARDEN BIRDS

Plumcoloured Starling
Cinnyricinclus leucogaster (761) Length: 19 cm

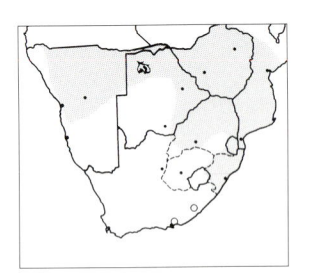

The striking purple back, chest and throat of the male Plumcoloured Starling and the heavily streaked chest of the female distinguish this species from other starlings likely to visit the garden. This bird is a migrant from central Africa, arriving in southern Africa in October and departing again in April. Some birds remain in the northern Transvaal and in Zimbabwe throughout the year. The Plumcoloured Starling may often be seen in gardens on the fringes of suburbs but seldom ventures into more densely populated areas.

The female has a mottled appearance above and is white below, streaked with brown. The birds nest in cavities in trees and may take over old nests of other species.

DIET
Mainly fruit, particularly figs, but also insects.

BREEDING
SITE: A pad of fresh leaves and grass is placed in a suitable cavity in a fence post or hollow tree. Fresh leaves are continually added to the nest lining throughout the incubation period.
SEASON: Mainly in summer, October to February.
CLUTCH SIZE: 2-4. INCUBATION PERIOD: About 12 days.
FLEDGING PERIOD: About 21 days.

IN THE GARDEN
HABITAT: This is a bird of savanna and woodland. Only gardens containing large, open trees, such as Acacias, are likely to attract the Plumcoloured Starling.
FOOD REQUIREMENTS: Fruit trees in the garden will attract this bird. Bone-meal, suet, mealworms and fruit offered near the exclusion area will also be taken.
NESTING: The bird will breed in a hollow log (*see* page 53) placed in the garden and may take over the nest of a barbet once the barbet chicks have fledged.

The male and female Plumcoloured Starlings differ markedly in appearance during the breeding season. The breeding male (above) *is a brilliant, glossy purple on the upperparts, head and throat.*

DIRECTORY OF GARDEN BIRDS

Glossy Starling

Lamprotornis nitens (764) Length: 25 cm

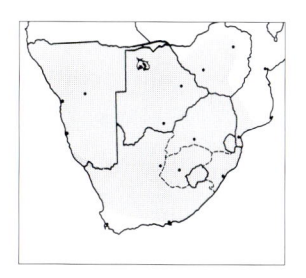

A species that is widely distributed throughout southern Africa, the Glossy Starling is locally common. It is very often seen in the Kruger National Park rest camps where it has become so tame that it may even be a nuisance, stealing food off tables while people are eating. In the north and east of its range it may be confused with one of the other glossy-plumaged starlings, particularly the Greater Blue-eared Starling. It is seen in pairs during the breeding season, and at other times in small flocks of up to ten birds.

This bird has a varied diet and will feed on natural supplies of fruit or nectar, but will also frequent the feeding table to eat whatever is on offer there.

DIET
Omnivorous and opportunistic, taking mainly insects, fruit and nectar, but gathering at any abundant, localized food source.

BREEDING
SITE: Hollows in trees and fence posts are used as nest sites, although the abandoned holes of primary hole-nesting species may be taken over. The nesting sites are lined with grass and green leaves.

The Glossy Starling has an iridescent plumage and a bright yellow eye.

SEASON: Mostly October to December, but as early as September in the Transvaal and Zimbabwe. CLUTCH SIZE: 2-3, sometimes more. INCUBATION PERIOD: Not known. FLEDGING PERIOD: About 20 days.

IN THE GARDEN
HABITAT: This common, bold species is not particularly fussy about its habitat, but tends to avoid densely vegetated areas.
FOOD REQUIREMENTS: Glossy Starlings are opportunistic feeders, taking insects such as harvester termites and flying ants, and eating the fruits of indigenous plant species. They are quick to take advantage of any sudden abundance of food, and are therefore easy to attract into the garden. In areas where this bird is resident, it rapidly becomes tame and will readily visit the feeding table for fruit, bone-meal, suet and any other scraps. Nectar plants, such as aloes, will also attract it.
NESTING: Because the preferred nest sites of this bird are often in short supply and it has to compete with various other hole-nesting species, the Glossy Starling may easily be persuaded to nest in a hollow log or nest-box (*see* pages 53 and 56).

DIRECTORY OF GARDEN BIRDS

Redwinged Starling
Onychognathus morio (769) Length: 27 cm

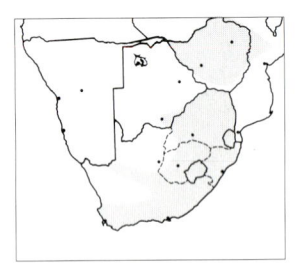

This is one of the largest starlings in the region. It will readily enter gardens, especially those near its natural mountainous habitat, and has started breeding and roosting on buildings. It is seen in pairs during the breeding cycle, but thereafter in flocks of up to several thousand birds. The Redwinged Starling is skilled at flying in mountainous areas at great speeds and amazingly close to the rock faces. The sexes are similar but the female has a grey head and the male a black head.

The Redwinged Starling is not considered to be one of the glossy starlings although its plumage is shiny. In coloration it is predominantly bluish-black but the bird's flight feathers are chestnut coloured, tipped with black. It has adapted to breeding on buildings, even in cities.

Redwinged Starlings may strip cultivated fruit trees and vines, so it is a good idea to put out fruit for them.

DIET
Mainly fruit, but also insects, small reptiles and nectar.

BREEDING
Site: A nest is built in a crevice, usually beneath an overhang of rock or a building, sometimes at the base of a palm frond. It consists of plant material bound with mud and is lined with hair, pine needles or roots.
Season: October to March; usually two clutches each season. **Clutch Size:** 2-4. **Incubation Period:** Variable, averaging 16 days. **Fledging Period:** About 26 days.

IN THE GARDEN
Habitat: This bird is attracted by plants which produce fleshy fruits. In most gardens it is a seasonal visitor, arriving when vines or fruit trees have a large crop.
Food Requirements: The Redwinged Starling feeds at all levels of vegetation and can be encouraged to take fruit, bone-meal, suet and mealworms from the feeding table or a feeding log. Fruiting trees and vines frequently come under attack from this bird.
Nesting: This starling is most likely to nest on buildings or walls covered in creepers. Occasionally, it nests inside buildings. Unusual among birds, the fledged young resemble adult males, not females.

DIRECTORY OF GARDEN BIRDS

Cape Sugarbird

Promerops cafer (773) Length: male 34-44 cm, female 25-29 cm

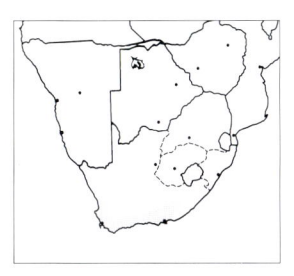

This conspicuous, loud resident of the southern and south-western Cape is found mainly among fynbos in association with proteas. The Cape Sugarbird has a habit of perching in exposed and prominent positions.

The female does most of the nest-building, weaving a cup-shaped structure which is often placed in a protea bush.

The Cape Sugarbird, here perched on a Pincushion, is easily recognized by its extremely long, flowing tail.

DIET
Nectar of indigenous plant species, insects and spiders.

BREEDING
Site: A cup-shaped nest is constructed from twigs, roots, pine needles and grass, and is lined with brown protea down which is held in place by fine plant fibres. It is most often situated in a protea bush.
Season: February to August. **Clutch Size:** 2. **Incubation Period:** 17 days. **Fledging Period:** About 20 days.

IN THE GARDEN
Habitat: The Cape Sugarbird has adapted to urban areas and will readily enter gardens, particularly if nectar plants are available there. It usually visits gardens during the winter, moving higher up into the mountains in the summer.
Food Requirements: Proteas, ericas, Cape Honeysuckle, Red-hot Pokers and other nectar-producing plants cultivated in the garden will attract the Cape Sugarbird. It may then be encouraged to take sugar water from artificial feeders.
Nesting: The presence of proteas in the garden will be an incentive for this bird to nest here. It will, however, also nest in other plants, including ericas, bracken, bramble and *Rhus* species.

The Cape Sugarbird will visit the garden to feed on nectar-producing plants such as Agapanthus.

DIRECTORY OF GARDEN BIRDS

Malachite Sunbird

Nectarinia famosa (775) Length: male 25 cm, female 15 cm

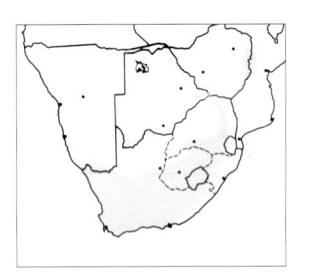

A resident of the region, this bird displays some seasonal movements in winter, from highlands, such as Lesotho, to lower-lying areas like the eastern Orange Free State and Natal midlands. It may be found in a variety of habitats and, although it is usually seen singly outside the breeding season, large aggregations sometimes occur at concentrated nectar sources.

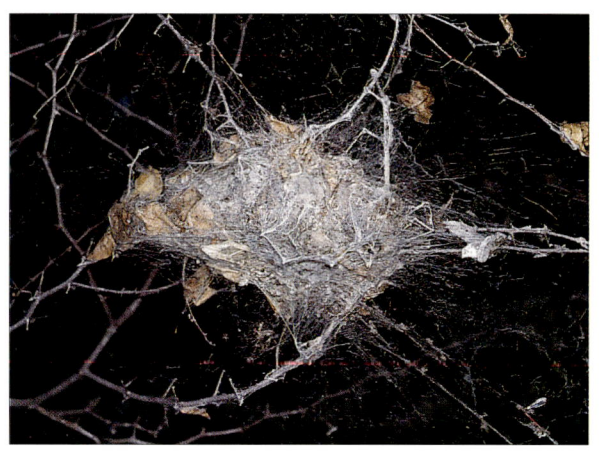

Most sunbirds use spider web to bind together a variety of plant material when building their nests.

DIET
Nectar, small insects and spiders.

BREEDING
SITE: Spider web is used to bind an oval nest made of plant material, with a side-top entrance and usually a porch; the nest is lined with fine plant material, hair and feathers, and is suspended from a branch or among grass or weeds.

SEASON: Winter and spring in the south-western Cape; mostly early to mid-summer elsewhere. CLUTCH SIZE: 1-3. INCUBATION PERIOD: 13 days. FLEDGING PERIOD: About 20 days.

The female (left) is a drab, grey-brown colour above with a yellowish wash on the underparts. The male is the only sunbird in the region with all-over metallic green colouring and long central tail feathers. Although not particularly territorial, these birds may be surprisingly aggressive.

IN THE GARDEN
HABITAT: This species favours scrubby and weedy habitats and will be seen most often in the exclusion area of the garden. Acacia trees, particularly *Acacia sieberiana*, attract sunbirds, while the Tree Fuchsia (*Halleria lucida*) is a good shrub to have. This bird will bath in the spray of sprinklers.

FOOD REQUIREMENTS: Nectar-producing plants such as Wild Dagga (*Leonotis leonurus*), aloes, proteas, Red-hot Pokers (*Kniphofia* species) and *Watsonia* species will help to attract this bird to the garden. It may be possible, over time, to introduce the bird to sugar water offered in an artificial feeder.

NESTING: The nest is built close to the ground, usually among weeds, grasses or small, spiky bushes. Hanging fern baskets with coconut fibre or coir as a base, may attract the Malachite Sunbird, which will collect the fibres for nest-building.

DIRECTORY OF GARDEN BIRDS

LESSER DOUBLECOLLARED SUNBIRD
Nectarinia chalybea (783) Length: 12 cm

Locally common in the region, and one of the most common sunbirds where it occurs, this resident species is a frequent visitor to urban gardens and will become tame over time and allow close contact. It may be seen singly, in pairs or in groups of up to six birds. The Lesser Doublecollared Sunbird forages both in tree canopies and in lower vegetation.

These birds take nectar from flowers like Strelitzia, *by inserting the long tongue or by piercing the flower's base.*

DIET
Mainly nectar, spiders and small insects.

BREEDING
SITE: A nest of plant material, including lichens, is bound with spider web and lined with plant down, feathers and even wool if available. The nest has a side-top entrance, with or without a porch, and is commonly situated in a shrub or bush.
SEASON: Throughout the rainy season in the winter-rainfall region. In the summer-rainfall region, generally breeds before the onset of the main rains.
CLUTCH SIZE: 2-3. INCUBATION PERIOD: 13-15 days. FLEDGING PERIOD: About 17 days.

The strikingly coloured Lesser Doublecollared Sunbird, here seen taking nectar from an erica, very closely resembles its larger relative, the Greater Doublecollared Sunbird.

IN THE GARDEN
HABITAT: A common urban visitor, this bird will utilize nectar plants, including the Cape Honeysuckle (*Tecomaria capensis*) and *Aloe* species.
FOOD REQUIREMENTS: Indigenous and exotic flowers will attract this bird to feed in the garden. It may also be possible to encourage it to drink sugar water from an artificial feeder, by first placing the feeder between the nectar plants and then, as the bird becomes used to the idea, moving it to a more open site. Ripe fruit offered on the table will also provide the bird with much-loved fruit juice.
NESTING: In the southern and south-western Cape the nest is usually placed close to the ground in a bush or shrub, although in the summer-rainfall region the nests are more typically two to ten metres above the ground. This species is most likely to breed in the exclusion area of the garden.

DIRECTORY OF GARDEN BIRDS

Greater Doublecollared Sunbird

Nectarinia afra (785) Length: 14 cm

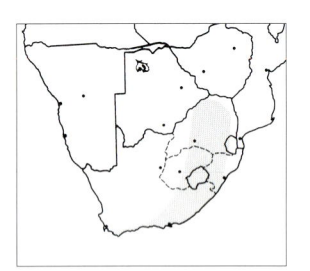

Although similar to the Lesser Doublecollared Sunbird, this species is larger, has a longer bill and a broader red breast band, and is more daring. It may be seen singly, in pairs or in small groups at a good food source.

The male Greater Doublecollared Sunbird, with its glossy green head, throat and upperparts and red breast band, is difficult to distinguish from the Lesser Doublecollared Sunbird, but is a larger bird with a heavier bill and a broader breast band.

The female bird is far less striking than the male of the species, being dark olive above and having a dull yellow wash on the belly.

INCUBATION PERIOD: 15-16 days, by female bird only.
FLEDGING PERIOD: Not known, probably about 20 days.

DIET
Nectar, small insects and spiders.

BREEDING
SITE: An oval nest is constructed from plant material, including lichens, and may also comprise wool, rags and dried fruit, all bound together with spider web and lined with feathers. A side-top entrance is present and is covered with a porch.
SEASON: Throughout the year, with a peak in the months of October and November. CLUTCH SIZE: 1-2.

IN THE GARDEN
HABITAT: Like the Lesser Doublecollared Sunbird, this bird is attracted to gardens with nectar-producing plants, especially *Erythrina* species, proteas, ericas, and the Cape Leadwort (*Plumbago auriculata*). Acacia trees, particularly *Acacia sieberiana*, attract sunbirds, while the Tree Fuchsia (*Halleria lucida*) is worth growing too if you want these birds in your garden. Sunbirds will bath in the spray of garden sprinklers.
FOOD REQUIREMENTS: The presence of both indigenous and exotic nectar-producing plants (*see* above) will encourage the bird to visit the garden to feed. It may also take sugar water offered in a feeder near or placed among nectar plants.
NESTING: The nest is usually sited near the top of a tree or shrub, two or three metres above the ground. Preferred nesting sites include *Euclea*, *Acacia* and *Schotia* species. This bird will often breed in the same tree year after year. Hanging fern baskets with coconut fibre or coir as a base will attract the bird, which collects the fibres for nest-building.

DIRECTORY OF GARDEN BIRDS

Whitebellied Sunbird

Nectarinia talatala (787) Length: 11 cm

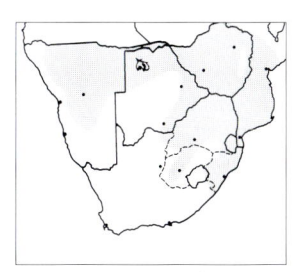

The Whitebellied Sunbird is one of the commonest sunbirds in the north and east of the region and is a frequent visitor to urban gardens. It is usually seen singly or in pairs although groups may be found at a good food source. It is always active, moving from plant to plant or chasing other sunbirds.

The exotic Bottlebrush is a rich source of nectar and will be readily utilized by a host of sunbird species.

The male of this species is easily identified by virtue of its white belly and metallic green head, breast and back.

DIET
Nectar; insects such as aphids and moths; and spiders.

BREEDING
Site: This bird chooses varied and interesting nesting sites, some having been found within spiders' nests, others against cactus leaves and still others alongside wasps' nests. The nest is constructed from plant material, bound with spider web and lined with plant down and feathers. A side-top entrance is created, and is covered by a small porch. The nest, usually suspended from twigs on a small shrub, is often built nearer the ground than is the case with other woodland sunbirds, but occasionally some are constructed as high as six metres above the ground.

Season: July to February, with a peak from August to December. **Clutch Size:** 1-3. **Incubation Period:** About 13 days. **Fledging Period:** About 15 days.

IN THE GARDEN
Habitat: This sunbird is attracted by nectar plants, such as aloes, and even exotics, such as the Weeping Bottlebrush (*Callistemon viminalis*). Acacia trees, particularly *Acacia sieberiana*, also attract it, and the Tree Fuchsia (*Halleria lucida*) is a good shrub to plant if you want sunbirds to frequent your garden. This bird will bath in the spray of sprinklers.

Food Requirements: Indigenous and also exotic nectar-producing plants will attract the bird to feed in the garden. It may be possible to coax it to drink from an artificial feeder filled with sugar water.

Nesting: The Whitebellied Sunbird becomes quite tame in the garden and may breed if sufficient food is available. The nest is usually built a metre or less above the ground in a small tree or thorny shrub. It is often built among dense cobwebs. Hanging fern baskets with coconut fibre or coir as a base will attract the bird, which will collect the fibres for nest-building.

DIRECTORY OF GARDEN BIRDS

SCARLETCHESTED SUNBIRD

Nectarinia senegalensis (791) Length: 15 cm

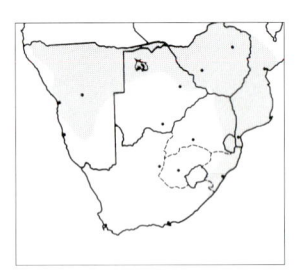

This sunbird is confined to the northern reaches of the region where it is a common resident. It is usually seen singly or in pairs. Male birds are quite aggressive and will chase other sunbirds from a food source and nesting area. The Scarletchested Sunbird is often seen singing from a high, conspicuous perch.

Sunbirds are attracted to a variety of Acacia trees.

The black body and bright scarlet chest of the male Scarletchested Sunbird make this an easy bird to identify. In the non-breeding season these fairly aggressive sunbirds may hold 'feeding' territories to protect a much-prized food source such as a nectar-producing plant that is in flower.

DIET
Mainly nectar, but also spiders and insects.

BREEDING
SITE: A nest is constructed with plant material, wool and feathers, and is bound with spider web. The nest includes a side-top entrance and porch, and is usually suspended from a branch of a tree or bush.
SEASON: Mostly August to December. CLUTCH SIZE: 1-3. INCUBATION PERIOD: About 14 days. FLEDGING PERIOD: About 18 days.

IN THE GARDEN
HABITAT: This sunbird will readily enter the garden, especially if there are nectar-producing plants on which to feed. Most Acacia trees, particularly *Acacia sieberiana*, attract sunbirds, and the Tree Fuchsia (*Halleria lucida*) is a good shrub to plant for this purpose. This bird will bath in the spray of sprinklers.
FOOD REQUIREMENTS: *Aloe* and *Erythrina* species are particular favourites of this sunbird. It may be enticed to feed on sugar water from a feeding bottle placed between nectar plants.
NESTING: The nest site is highly variable, both in terms of its height and the choice of plant species. It may breed in large Acacias and Jacarandas, in small thorny trees, or in exotic Bluegums (*Eucalyptus* species), among others. Most nests are sited between five and ten metres above the ground, but some are less than two metres up. These sunbirds sometimes nest in or on man-made structures, including thatched roofs and electric cables. Hanging fern baskets with coconut fibre or coir as a base will attract this bird, which will collect the fibres for nest-building.

DIRECTORY OF GARDEN BIRDS

BLACK SUNBIRD

Nectarinia amethystina (792) Length: 15 cm

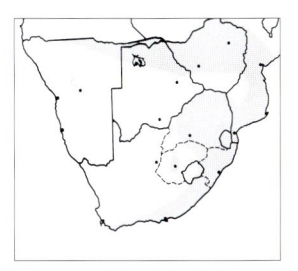

This sunbird is a fairly common garden visitor and is quite noisy and conspicuous. It is usually seen singly or in pairs, although it may occur in the company of other sunbird species. The Black Sunbird typically hovers while feeding on nectar and is continually active, moving from plant to plant in search of food.

Nectar-feeding birds are particularly fond of the bright red flowers of the Common Coral Tree.

suspended from a thin branch of a tree or bush. A side-top entrance and porch made with grass seed heads form part of the structure.

SEASON: Mainly September to November in the north of its range, and between July and April in the eastern Cape. CLUTCH SIZE: 1-3. INCUBATION PERIOD: 13-18 days. FLEDGING PERIOD: 14-18 days.

IN THE GARDEN

HABITAT: As with other sunbirds, any nectar-producing plants, especially *Aloes* and *Strelitzia* species, will attract this bird to the garden. Acacia trees, particularly *Acacia sieberiana*, attract sunbirds, while the Tree Fuchsia (*Halleria lucida*) is a good shrub to have for this purpose. All sunbirds visiting the garden will bath in the spray of a garden sprinkler.

FOOD REQUIREMENTS: This bird will feed from both indigenous and exotic flowers. It may also be enticed, over time, to take sugar water from a feeder placed between the nectar plants.

NESTING: This species frequently nests in garden trees and may also select a hanging plant basket, light fitting or clothes line in the garden as a nesting site. Coconut fibre or coir in the base of a fern basket will be taken by the bird for nest-building.

The male Black Sunbird has a violet throat patch and rump, which are visible in good light.

DIET
Nectar, and also spiders and aerial insects.

BREEDING
SITE: A nest made with a variety of plant material, lined with plant down and bound with spider web, is

171

COLLARED SUNBIRD

Anthreptes collaris (793) Length: 10 cm

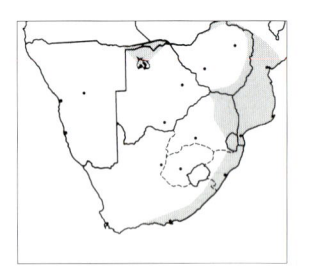

The Collared Sunbird is one of the smaller sunbirds and has a short, sharp bill. It is locally common in forests and coastal bush and is almost always seen in pairs, although it may occasionally join mixed bird parties.

DIET
Mostly insects; but also nectar, spiders, snails, berries and other small fruits, and seed.

BREEDING
SITE: An oval nest is built from a hanging branch of a tree or shrub and consists of various plant materials (small twigs, leaves and grasses), bound with spider web and lined with hair, feathers and plant fibres. The nest incorporates a side-top entrance with a porch.
SEASON: Mostly September to January.
CLUTCH SIZE: 1-4.
INCUBATION PERIOD: About 14 days.
FLEDGING PERIOD: About 17 days.

The male and female of this species are similar.

The nest of the Collared Sunbird is a small, oval structure with a well-formed porch over the entrance.

IN THE GARDEN
HABITAT: This species is likely to be attracted only to gardens close to tracts of its natural habitat. It prefers dense tangles of vegetation, which may be present in the exclusion area. The Collared Sunbird shows little fear of man and will sometimes enter houses to sip nectar from vases of cut flowers. Acacia trees, particularly *Acacia sieberiana*, attract sunbirds. Like the other sunbirds, this bird will bath in the spray of sprinklers.
FOOD REQUIREMENTS: Nectar plants, especially *Hibiscus* and *Erythrina* species, the Tree Fuchsia (*Halleria lucida*) and the Wild Pomegranate (*Burchellia bubalina*) will attract this bird. Its bill is shorter than those of most other sunbirds and it therefore will often split flowers to reach the nectar.
NESTING: The nest of this sunbird will typically be sited at the edge of dense vegetation, against a dark background. This species will also breed in tangled creepers on the walls of buildings. Coconut fibre or coir in the base of a fern basket will be utilized by these birds, which will take the fibres for nest-building.

DIRECTORY OF GARDEN BIRDS

CAPE WHITE-EYE
Zosterops pallidus (796) Length: 12 cm

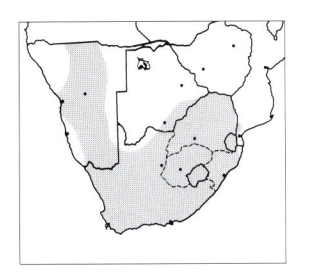

In South Africa the Cape White-eye is one of the best known garden birds, often being highly vocal. Its colouring varies locally, from a greenish colour in Natal and the Cape to a more yellowish colour in the Transvaal Highveld. Outside of the breeding season, it moves in loose groups and frequents thickets, trees or vines, sometimes hanging upside down, and hopping from branch to branch in search of food.

The conspicuous white eye-ring is the best distinguishing feature of this bird, which varies regionally in colour.

DIET
Spiders, insects, nectar, fruit and some seeds.

BREEDING
SITE: A cup-shaped nest is constructed in a tree or shrub using grass and other plant material, and is bound with spider web. The nest is covered with moss and lined with plant down and feathers.

A Cape White-eye attends to its chicks. The male and the female share the responsibilities of breeding, with both sexes taking part in nest-building, incubation and the feeding of the young.

SEASON: August to December in the western Cape, extending to February and March further east and north. **CLUTCH SIZE:** 2-4. **INCUBATION PERIOD:** About 11 days. **FLEDGING PERIOD:** About 13 days.

IN THE GARDEN
HABITAT: Initially, this bird will stay in the exclusion area but once tame will investigate the bird-bath and other parts of the garden. Acacia trees and the Tree Fuchsia (*Halleria lucida*) will attract this bird.

FOOD REQUIREMENTS: The Cape White-eye feeds on aphids, scale insects and other garden pests. Fruit offered on a feeding table will be an attraction, as will sugar water offered in a bird feeder. Nectar- and berry-producing plants, such as the Virginia Creeper (*Parthenocissus quinquefolia*) and Tassel Berry (*Antidesma venosum*), will also be utilized.

NESTING: Nests are usually built one to six metres above the ground in a wide variety of tree and bush species, such as ericas, the White Bristle Bush (*Metalasia muricata*), the Ginger Bush (*Tetradenia riparia*) and the bone-apples (*Xeromphis* species). These birds will collect fibres for nest-building from hanging fern baskets with coconut fibre or coir bases.

DIRECTORY OF GARDEN BIRDS

House Sparrow

Passer domesticus (801) Length: 14 cm

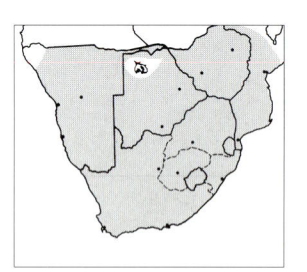

The House Sparrow needs no introduction to gardeners throughout the region and is often an unwelcome boarder because of the untidy nests it constructs under the eaves of the roof. It was first introduced from Asia to Durban in the 1890s and quickly spread throughout southern Africa to areas of human settlement.

A nest-box secured under the eaves of the house may attract the House Sparrow to breed, although not all home-owners encourage it because of the mess it makes.

The House Sparrow may be recognized by its reddish-brown back, grey crown, black bib and white cheeks.

DIET
Seed, fruit, spiders and insects; also household refuse.

BREEDING
SITE: An untidy nest of grass, feathers, string and any other soft material available is usually placed against a building under the eaves, or in a cavity in a building.
SEASON: Throughout the year with a peak in the first half of summer. CLUTCH SIZE: 4-6. INCUBATION PERIOD: 12-14 days. FLEDGING PERIOD: About 15 days.

IN THE GARDEN
HABITAT: Closely tied to human habitation, this bird will most often be seen close to the house, searching for scraps, and around outbuildings on smallholdings.
FOOD REQUIREMENTS: The House Sparrow needs no encouragement to enter the garden and will probably be the most frequent visitor to the feeding table. Almost any food placed on the table will be devoured, although seed makes up the main part of the diet of this cosmopolitan little bird. The House Sparrow tends to congregate in large numbers at the table, often discouraging other birds from feeding there.
NESTING: The House Sparrow may be tempted to nest in a box (*see* page 56) placed for this purpose under the eaves of a roof, and this may discourage it from building its own large, untidy nest there.

DIRECTORY OF GARDEN BIRDS

CAPE SPARROW

Passer melanurus (803) Length: 15 cm

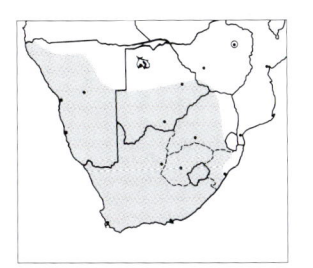

Like the House Sparrow, this bird is well known to gardeners throughout most of the region. The Cape Sparrow rapidly becomes tame in the garden, where it will feed and breed. It does not compete with the House Sparrow, although it is dominant over its smaller relative. Outside of the breeding season the Cape Sparrow may form large groups.

DIET

Seeds, fruit (both fallen and on the tree) and insects.

BREEDING

SITE: A large, untidy nest is built using grass, feathers, wool and other cloth fabrics if available. The nest is usually located in a thorn tree but may also be built among trellised vines, on fences, telephone poles and in hollow pipes.
SEASON: Throughout the year, but mostly in spring and summer.
CLUTCH SIZE: 2-5.
INCUBATION PERIOD: 12-14 days. FLEDGING PERIOD: 16-25 days.
The Cape Sparrow may be parasitized by the Diederik Cuckoo.

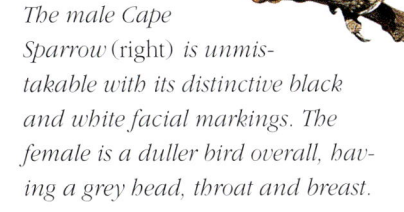

The male Cape Sparrow (right) *is unmistakable with its distinctive black and white facial markings. The female is a duller bird overall, having a grey head, throat and breast.*

The Cape Sparrow builds its large, untidy nest in a variety of places, including indigenous and exotic trees.

IN THE GARDEN

HABITAT: This bird typically forages in trees with little leaf cover or on the lawn.
FOOD REQUIREMENTS: The Cape Sparrow will be a regular visitor to the feeding table and will eat almost anything offered there. It is a voracious consumer of seed, which can be dispersed on the lawn to reduce competition at the table.
NESTING: Thorn trees in the exclusion area will be used for nesting. A variety of nesting material can be provided in a mesh bag suspended from a branch.

Sunflower seeds, and other wild seed varieties, will be relished by the Cape Sparrow. This little bird will also take a wide range of fruit and insects.

175

DIRECTORY OF GARDEN BIRDS

GREYHEADED SPARROW

Passer griseus (804) Length: 15 cm

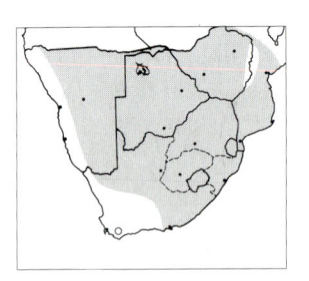

This bird is gregarious outside of the breeding season, forming small flocks in winter. It is not as commonly seen as the Cape Sparrow or the House Sparrow and, although it is a regular visitor, it is not as well adapted to garden conditions as those species. It often frequents larger trees, but always feeds on the ground. Unlike the other two sparrows, the sexes are similar.

These birds are attracted to seed offered in a home-made seed holder and may dominate at a feeding site.

SEASON: Mostly November to March. CLUTCH SIZE: 2-5, usually 3. INCUBATION PERIOD: Not known. FLEDGING PERIOD: Not known.

This sparrow can be told apart from others in the region by its grey head and underparts, and chestnut back.

DIET
Seeds and insects, taken on the ground.

BREEDING
SITE: A nest pad of grass, feathers and hair is made in any convenient niche: a hollow of a tree or fence post, or under the eaves of house roofs. The abandoned nest of a swallow or a swift may also be used.

IN THE GARDEN
HABITAT: A combination of large trees and open ground in the garden will attract this bird.
FOOD REQUIREMENTS: This bird is not generally a common visitor to the feeding table and prefers to take seed spread around in the open area of the garden.
NESTING: The Greyheaded Sparrow may make use of a nest-box (*see* page 56) provided for it.

The Greyheaded Sparrow forages for seeds on bare-earth areas, and will readily take seed scattered in the garden.

176

DIRECTORY OF GARDEN BIRDS

THICKBILLED WEAVER
Amblyospiza albifrons (807) Length: 18 cm

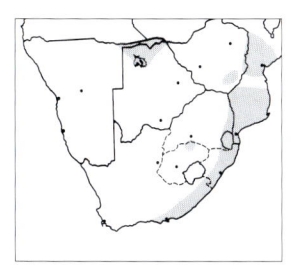

A common bird in coastal areas in the east of the region, this weaver makes use of reedbeds for breeding; otherwise, it is found in forests or thickets of the exotic invader Bugweed (Solanum mauritianum). *It is usually seen in groups which contain up to 50 birds. The bird's powerful bill enables it to feed with ease on seeds that have hard outer coats.*

This weaver builds its nest among reeds near water.

DIET
Seeds, fruit and insects; small water snails are sometimes fed to the nestlings.

BREEDING
SITE: Reeds close to water. The nest is woven around the stems of indigenous reeds and is neatly fashioned out of strips of grass, palms and wetland plant leaves.
SEASON: September to March. CLUTCH SIZE: 2-4, usually 3. INCUBATION PERIOD: 14-16 days. FLEDGING PERIOD: About 20 days.

IN THE GARDEN
HABITAT: This weaver prefers dense vegetation and may be found in the exclusion area. It will normally forage in open areas only when food is provided.
FOOD REQUIREMENTS: This bird is partial to the fruit of the White Stinkwood (*Celtis africana*). Seed, especially sunflower seed, offered in the open area or on the feeding table will also attract it to feed in the garden.
NESTING: This bird may visit the garden but is unlikely to nest there unless a fairly extensive wetland area is present, as it prefers to build its nest among reeds.

This is a predominantly dark bird, except for the white patch on the forehead and the white wing patches. Its thick bill should rule out confusion with other dark birds.

DIRECTORY OF GARDEN BIRDS

Spottedbacked Weaver

Ploceus cucullatus (811) Length: 17 cm

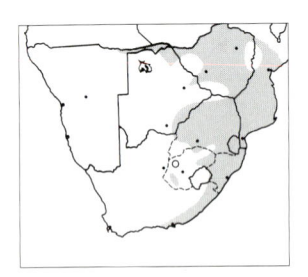

This weaver is often associated with urban settlements and is frequently seen near water. The male can be distinguished from the male Masked Weaver by its heavily spotted back and by the fact that its mask does not extend above the bill on the forehead.

Many weavers favour thorn trees as nesting sites. Here, a Spottedbacked Weaver colony has monopolized a site.

The breeding male of this species has a yellow-speckled black back and a yellow breast and belly.

DIET

Fruits, seeds and insects, and sometimes nectar.

BREEDING

SITE: The male weaves several nests from palm leaves, grass and other strips torn from the leaves of wetland plants, especially reeds. The nests have an entrance on the underside, and sometimes a short entrance tunnel, and are usually suspended from hanging palm or bamboo branches or between reeds. Nests which are not subsequently occupied by a female are often destroyed. This species nests in colonies.

SEASON: September to February. CLUTCH SIZE: 2-5. INCUBATION PERIOD: About 12 days. FLEDGING PERIOD: About 19 days.

IN THE GARDEN

HABITAT: This weaver is closely associated with human settlements and is a frequent visitor to urban gardens. It may be seen anywhere in the garden.

FOOD REQUIREMENTS: The Spottedbacked Weaver eats seeds, taken either while clinging to plants or while scuffling among dead leaves on the ground; and it also consumes insects, taken from the bark or in the air, and sometimes feeds on flowers or nectar. It is not a fussy feeder and will devour a variety of food items offered on the feeding table.

NESTING: A large wetland area will attract this bird to breed in the garden, especially if it includes *Phragmites* reeds and Bulrushes, which the bird will use for nest-building. A Fever Tree (*Acacia xanthophloea*) will be a further attraction to this weaver.

DIRECTORY OF GARDEN BIRDS

CAPE WEAVER

Ploceus capensis (813) Length: 17 cm

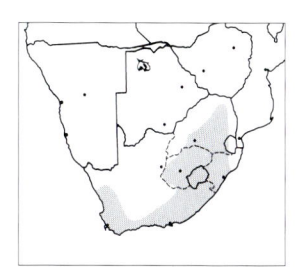

A fairly large weaver, the Cape Weaver is normally seen in small flocks and may form large roosts at night. It is aggressive, and often chases other birds away from feeding sites.

The female Cape Weaver is unremarkable compared to the male, being dull olive-brown above and pale below.

The male Cape Weaver in full breeding plumage guards the nest. The male builds several nests at which he displays in an effort to impress his mate.

DIET
Seeds, insects, fruit, nectar and flowers.

BREEDING
SITE: The male builds several kidney-shaped nests from strips of grass and palm leaves, with an entrance at the bottom. The nests are usually suspended from hanging tree branches or between reed stems. Once a female has accepted a nest and mated, she lines the egg chamber with grass and other soft material. This weaver nests in large colonies.
SEASON: During winter and spring in the western Cape, and in the spring and summer months further north.
CLUTCH SIZE: 2-4. **INCUBATION PERIOD:** About 13 days.
FLEDGING PERIOD: About 17 days.

IN THE GARDEN
HABITAT: This bird will be attracted to a wetland area in the garden.
FOOD REQUIREMENTS: It will visit the feeding table and will devour almost anything offered. Partial to nectar, it will be attracted to flowering plants, especially *Aloe* species. It is often seen with its face full of pollen after having probed for nectar in the flowers.
NESTING: This bird will nest only in a large wetland area with tall reeds and other wetland plants. A Fever Tree (*Acacia xanthophloea*) overhanging water may encourage it to build its nest in your garden.

DIRECTORY OF GARDEN BIRDS

Masked Weaver

Ploceus velatus (814) Length: 15 cm

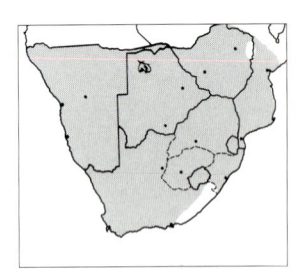

The Masked Weaver is a common resident throughout the southern African region. It visits a great many urban gardens and also breeds there. It is often an unpopular bird because of its habit of stripping palms for nesting material. It also tends to strip large trees, such as the Pin Oak, of their leaves, presumably to gain an unobstructed view of potential predators.

The male Masked Weaver is an attractive and striking bird, with its bright yellow underparts and distinctive black mask.

DIET

Seeds, nectar, flowers, berries and fruit. Chicks are fed largely on insects.

BREEDING

SITE: The male constructs a nest using strips of leaves from palms, reeds or grass, and lines it with grass seed heads. The nest is suspended from hanging branches or between reeds and is commonly sited above water. The nest is often parasitized by the Diederik Cuckoo.
SEASON: July to April; up to eight broods per season.
CLUTCH SIZE: 2-4, usually 2 or 3. INCUBATION PERIOD: About 14 days. FLEDGING PERIOD: About 15 days.

Masked Weavers eat insects and vegetable matter including the seeds, flowers, shoots and berries of plants.

IN THE GARDEN

HABITAT: This weaver will utilize a wetland area and pond, as well as any open areas in the garden.
FOOD REQUIREMENTS: The Masked Weaver will readily visit (and may often dominate) the feeding table, and will consume almost anything offered there. The planting of pasture grass, oats or millet in the open area will be an added attraction.
NESTING: This is a common nesting bird in urban gardens, particularly if water is present. The male bird builds several nests for its partner, and then destroys any which are rejected after careful scrutiny by the female. A Fever Tree (*Acacia xanthophloea*) may provide a suitable site in which this weaver can construct its nests. Single palms in the garden are often destroyed by these weavers in the nest-building process, as the area around each nest is defoliated by the hardworking male. So, if you are thinking of planting palms, group them so as to diminish the visible damage. The spraying of young palms with Aloe extract (available from chemists) is said to stop the weavers from stripping these plants. A section of Kikuyu lawn left to grow long will almost certainly be visited by the birds to collect nest material.

DIRECTORY OF GARDEN BIRDS

Golden Weaver
Ploceus xanthops (816) Length: 18 cm

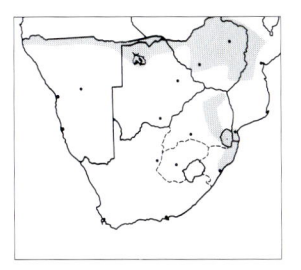

A large bird for a weaver, the Golden Weaver is shy and less obtrusive, often solitary and seen less frequently than many other weaver species. It may move in small groups but is seen in pairs when breeding.

A garden such as this one, which incorporates a large water feature and wetland plants, will attract this bird to visit and possibly to breed.

The Golden Weaver is distinguished from other yellow weavers by its lack of head markings, pale eye and heavy, black bill. The female resembles the male but is paler. Neither sex has any black about the head plumage.

DIET
This weaver has a fairly catholic diet, taking insects, fruit and seeds, its strong bill enabling it to deal with seeds with hard outer coatings.

BREEDING
SITE: The Golden Weaver is, unlike many other weavers, not a colonial breeder. A large, roughly woven nest is constructed from strips of palm, grass and various wetland plant leaves. Characteristic of the nest are the grass seed heads which form part of the lining and protrude through the nest wall. Nests are tied to hanging branches or between reeds. The weight of the nest often causes the supporting branch or reed to bend so that the opening is underneath, as is the case with the nests of other weaver species.
SEASON: Mostly September to February. CLUTCH SIZE: 2-3. INCUBATION PERIOD: Not known. FLEDGING PERIOD: About 20 days.

IN THE GARDEN
HABITAT: The normal habitat of this large, shy bird is one of reedbeds and rank growth alongside streams, so a large wetland area or stream with appropriate waterside growth will attract the bird to the garden where it may be encouraged to breed.
FOOD REQUIREMENTS: The Golden Weaver has a fairly varied diet, taking seeds and fruits directly from bushes, trees or grassheads. It will occasionally visit feeding tables in the garden and will feed on most of the items that are on offer there.
NESTING: This weaver will probably not breed in the urban garden unless a large wetland area is present in a remote part and with a suitable tree, a Fever Tree (*Acacia xanthophloea*) for example, overhanging the water, where it might choose to build its nest.

DIRECTORY OF GARDEN BIRDS

Red Bishop

Euplectes orix (824) Length: 14 cm

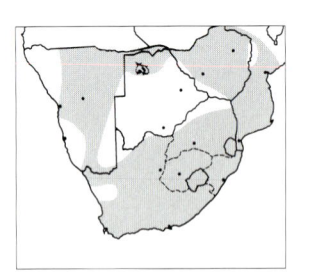

This is a well-known and common resident of the region, being particularly abundant where wetlands and croplands adjoin. It is also found in urban gardens. The Red Bishop is a gregarious bird and forms large colonies in reedbeds. This bird is known to cause crop damage in agricultural areas. The breeding male is easily recognized by its bright red and black plumage which is puffed up during displays.

A well-developed wetland area with reedbeds, as shown in this bird-friendly garden (above), will almost certainly attract the Red Bishop to breed.

DIET
Mainly seeds but also insects.

BREEDING
SITE: A woven nest is produced using strips of leaves from grass and reeds. The nest is placed between the stems of reeds or other wetland plants, and very rarely in trees, and has a side-top entrance with a porch. These birds often form dense colonies in reedbeds and males may build a dozen nests or more within their territories, acquiring up to seven mates during the course of the breeding season. The nests of this bird may be parasitized by the Diederik Cuckoo.

SEASON: Synchronized with the rainfall period in each region; from July to December in the south-western Cape, and mostly from December to March elsewhere. CLUTCH SIZE: 2-5, usually 3. INCUBATION PERIOD: 12-13 days. FLEDGING PERIOD: About 14 days.

IN THE GARDEN
HABITAT: The Red Bishop grows fairly tame in the urban garden and may become a regular visitor if there is a wetland area.

FOOD REQUIREMENTS: This mainly seed-eating species will readily feed from a feeding table or seed-feeder and will devour large quantities of grain and other seeds. The young chicks are fed on insects and regurgitated seed. It is a good idea to spread the seed in the open area of the garden so as to lower competition with the other birds at the feeding table.

NESTING: The Red Bishop will nest and raise its young in gardens as long as there is a wetland (even a small one) which incorporates Bulrushes and reeds. The striking colours of the male in the breeding season will be a welcome addition to the garden.

The breeding male Red Bishop with its bright red and black colouring is unlikely to be confused with any other bird visiting the garden.

DIRECTORY OF GARDEN BIRDS

Common Waxbill
Estrilda astrild (846) Length: 13 cm

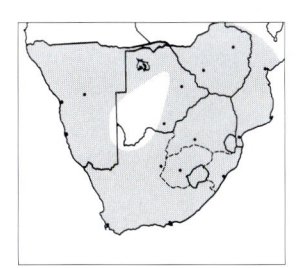

The Common Waxbill is widely distributed throughout the region and can be found in a range of habitats, although it is most often seen near water amid reeds and other low-growing vegetation. It congregates in flocks of up to 30 birds outside of the breeding season, but otherwise occurs in pairs or family groups. The bird may roost in very large numbers in reedbeds.

This bird is predominantly a seed eater, taking grass seeds from the seed heads while they are still green.

The Common Waxbill is easily identified by its red bill, red eye-stripe and the pink streak on its belly.

the base of grass or shrubs. The nest is lined with feathers and grass seed heads. A smaller chamber is often built above the main nest and is known as the 'cock's nest'. The Common Waxbill is the main host species to the Pintailed Whydah.
SEASON: Between September and January in the winter-rainfall area, but in mid-summer elsewhere. CLUTCH SIZE: 3-9. INCUBATION PERIOD: About 12 days. FLEDGING PERIOD: About 19 days.

DIET
Mostly seeds, but also insects and fruit.

BREEDING
SITE: A spherical nest is constructed from dry grass stems and is usually situated on or near the ground at

IN THE GARDEN
HABITAT: A wetland area in the garden will attract the Common Waxbill, as will any sections of veld grass in the open area.
FOOD REQUIREMENTS: Seeds from pasture grasses, millet and other seed-producing grasses will be relished, and the bird will also visit the feeding table to take seed, fruit and other scraps.
NESTING: This species is likely to breed only among bushes and grasses in the exclusion area.

DIRECTORY OF GARDEN BIRDS

BRONZE MANNIKIN

Spermestes cucullatus (857) Length: 9 cm

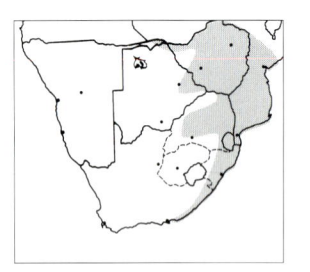

This little bird of open woodland has adapted remarkably well to urban areas and spends a great deal of time in gardens. It congregates in small flocks of up to 30 birds outside of the breeding season, but otherwise may be seen in pairs or family groups.

The Bronze Mannikin is a seed-eating bird.

DIET

Seeds (mainly grass seeds), nectar and insects.

BREEDING

SITE: An untidy ball nest is built from dried grass and has a side entrance. The nest is usually placed in a shrub, tree or creeper. This bird sometimes uses the nest of a bishop, weaver or waxbill. The Bronze Mannikin is often parasitized by the Pintailed Whydah.
SEASON: August to April. CLUTCH SIZE: 2-8. INCUBATION PERIOD: 14-16 days. FLEDGING PERIOD: 17-23 days.

The Bronze Mannikin has adapted so well to gardens that it will readily nest in creepers on buildings, often preferring the urban environment to surrounding woodlands.

IN THE GARDEN

HABITAT: This bird will be attracted to open areas, especially those incorporating wild grasses.
FOOD REQUIREMENTS: The Bronze Mannikin is a regular visitor to bird-baths and feeders. Up to 30 birds may descend on a feeding table at once and they will eat most items offered, but particularly any type of seed.
NESTING: The Bronze Mannikin will readily breed in creepers and bushes and may nest close to or on buildings.

A bird-bath in the garden will be an attraction to this little bird which makes frequent use of water, sunbathing and preening after each visit to a bath.

DIRECTORY OF GARDEN BIRDS

Pintailed Whydah

Vidua macroura (860) Length: male 26-34 cm, female 12 cm

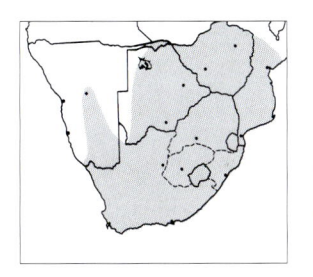

A locally common resident, this bird may well be overlooked until the male appears in its attractive breeding plumage. This is a gregarious species and may be found in groups of up to 30 birds. In the breeding season a single male will normally be accompanied by a 'harem' of up to six females and immature males. The male can often be seen displaying to the females by hovering and bobbing above them in the air.

DIET
Mostly seed; also some insects.

BREEDING
Site: A parasitic nesting bird in southern Africa, it lays its eggs in the nests of several species including the Bronze Mannikin and the Common Waxbill.
Season: From August to December in the winter-rainfall region, and from November to April elsewhere.
Clutch Size: 1-2 per host nest. Incubation Period: 11 days. Fledging Period: About 20 days.

The male Pintailed Whydah in breeding plumage is unmistakable with its tail which can measure up to 22 centimetres, but outside the breeding season it loses the long tail feathers and its plumage becomes duller, resembling that of the female.

The female bird is buff-coloured above and paler below with distinctive black and buff striping on the head. The breeding male is black above and white below.

IN THE GARDEN
Habitat: Seed-producing grasses planted in the open area will encourage this bird to visit the garden. Early in the breeding season, males often perch conspicuously on tall stems, such as bamboo.
Food Requirements: The dominant male of the species is very aggressive in the garden and will chase away other birds in an effort to claim the feeding table or seed-feeder for its females. Seed scattered on the grass should limit competition with other birds at the table.
Nesting: Any nests of host species in the garden will attract this bird to breed there.

DIRECTORY OF GARDEN BIRDS

Black Widowfinch
Vidua funerea (864) Length: 11 cm

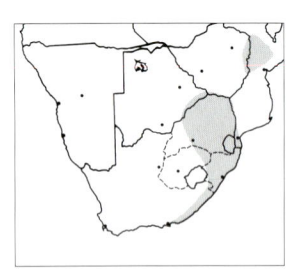

The Black Widowfinch is a common resident in the eastern and northern parts of the region but becomes nomadic in the winter. It is rather inconspicuous until the male appears in its breeding plumage, which is jet black with a white bill and orange-red legs and feet. The Black Widowfinch is a gregarious species in winter, and feeds in groups on the ground.

The Black Widowfinch parasitizes the Bluebilled Firefinch (above), and also imitates its song. The nestlings resemble those of its host in plumage and mouth markings.

DIET
Exclusively seeds, taken on the ground.

BREEDING
SITE: This species is a parasitic nester, and the Bluebilled Firefinch is its only host.
SEASON: January to April. CLUTCH SIZE: 1-3, usually 1 per host nest. INCUBATION PERIOD: Not known. FLEDGING PERIOD: Not known.

IN THE GARDEN
HABITAT: The Black Widowfinch is a common garden bird in the savanna and bushveld areas of its range. Seed-producing grasses planted in the open area will be an attraction to this bird.
FOOD REQUIREMENTS: These pretty little birds will be attracted to feeding tables and will consume any small seed that is offered there.
NESTING: Black Widowfinches, which are parasitic nesters, can breed in the garden only if the nests of Bluebilled Firefinches are built there.

The male of the species is black with a dull violet gloss. It has pale underwings, a whitish bill and reddish (in South Africa) or orange (further north) legs and feet.

DIRECTORY OF GARDEN BIRDS

Yelloweyed Canary
Serinus mozambicus (869) Length: 12 cm

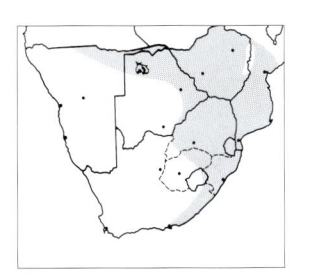

Although it has brown eyes, the Yelloweyed Canary is so named because of the yellow patches on the cheeks and the yellow eye-stripe. It is an attractive, common resident – one of the most common canaries – and is seen singly or in pairs during the breeding season, but otherwise in mixed flocks of up to 30 birds.

Above: *The sexes of this species look similar.*
Below: *Yelloweyed Canaries sometimes feed on flowers.*

The Yelloweyed Canary can be told from other canaries by its distinctive facial markings.

DIET
Seeds, insects including aphids, and small flowers.

BREEDING
Site: A deep, cup-shaped nest is constructed in a bush, tree or creeper and consists of grass, roots and tendrils, all bound together with spider web.
Season: Between September and April. **Clutch Size:** 2-5, usually 3 or 4. **Incubation Period:** About 14 days. **Fledging Period:** 16-24 days.

IN THE GARDEN
Habitat: This bird is not fussy about habitat and will forage on the ground, as well as in bushes and trees, throughout the garden.
Food Requirements: The Yelloweyed Canary will readily visit the feeding table and seed-feeders in the garden. It will consume most food on offer, but favours seed. This bird will also make use of any water in the garden for bathing. It is useful to the gardener because it eats insect pests such as aphids.
Nesting: This species will nest in a wide range of shrubs, bushes and trees, the nest usually being placed about two or three metres above the ground, and a favoured nest site being in a fork near the end of a branch partially covered by leaves.

DIRECTORY OF GARDEN BIRDS

Cape Canary

Serinus canicollis (872) Length: 13 cm

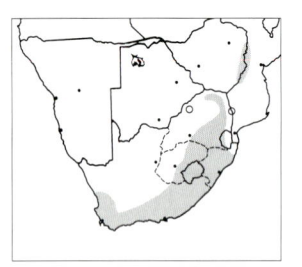

The Cape Canary has taken advantage of many exotic trees for nesting and roosting. Pine plantations in particular are a choice habitat. This bird is recognized as one of the best song birds in the region. It often visits gardens and may be seen in grassy and weedy areas or hopping around in fynbos vegetation.

Not only is Osteospermum ecklonis *an attractive flowering plant to cultivate, the seeds it produces will also be an attractant to the Cape Canary.*

SEASON: Between July and December. CLUTCH SIZE: 2-4, occasionally 5. INCUBATION PERIOD: 12-16 days. FLEDGING PERIOD: 15-18 days.

IN THE GARDEN

HABITAT: The Cape Canary will visit the open areas of the garden, particularly if wild grass, millet and other seed-producing crops have been planted. It may also spend time in any fynbos plants in the garden, but does not restrict itself to indigenous plant species.

FOOD REQUIREMENTS: This bird usually forages low down, often on the ground, looking for the small seeds of grasses and weeds. Mealworms and seeds offered on the feeding table or scattered on the ground in the open area will encourage this fine songster to enter the garden. Favoured food plants include *Ursinia*, *Osteospermum* and *Senecio* species. The Cape Canary will also sometimes eat fruit, and is especially partial to guavas and loquats.

NESTING: The nest is built mainly by the female, and indigenous vegetation is seldom used for breeding. The large trees favoured for nesting include exotics such as pines, poplars and oaks. The long tendrils of *Helichrysum* are favoured for nesting material.

This bird lacks the facial stripes of the Yelloweyed Canary, and has a yellow-olive face and greyish nape.

DIET

Almost exclusively small seeds, especially the soft green seeds of grasses and weeds; but also fruit and occasionally even insects.

BREEDING

SITE: A cup-shaped nest is made of thin sticks, roots and leaves and lined with plant down. It is situated from four to 20 metres off the ground in a tall tree.

DIRECTORY OF GARDEN BIRDS

Streakyheaded Canary

Serinus gularis (881) Length: 15 cm

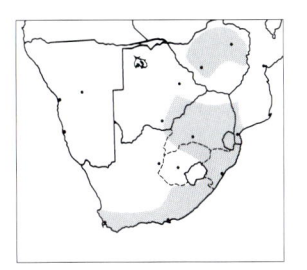

Although quite widespread, the Streakyheaded Canary is an inconspicuous bird, easily overlooked in the garden. It may be seen singly, in pairs or in small groups of up to eight birds, and occasionally as many as 50.

The white eyebrow stripe and streaked crown are the most distinctive features of the Streakyheaded Canary; the chin and throat are white, and the underparts greyish-brown.

DIET
Mostly seeds of weeds and grasses, as well as fruit, nectar and flowers. This bird will also feed on insects, taking termite alates from the air.

BREEDING
SITE: A cup-shaped structure of grass, twigs and leaves is built and is bound together with spider web. The nest is located in a bush or tree, and is usually well camouflaged and difficult to see. The lining includes bark strips, plant down and wool, if available.

Protea repens and other Protea species will be utilized by this bird for nectar. The Streakyheaded Canary also takes fruit, seeds, insects and flowers..

SEASON: Between September and March. CLUTCH SIZE: 2-4. INCUBATION PERIOD: 13-15 days. FLEDGING PERIOD: About 17 days.

IN THE GARDEN
HABITAT: This unobtrusive bird will favour weedy sections of the exclusion area, but will occur anywhere in the garden depending on the distribution of flowering shrubs. It is most often observed outside of the breeding season in gardens.

FOOD REQUIREMENTS: The Streakyheaded Canary has an extremely varied diet and is readily attracted to the feeding table, especially if fruit, mealie meal or seed are offered there. Since it has been known to take caterpillars, it might also be attracted to mealworms. The Cape Honeysuckle (*Tecomaria capensis*), aloes, and other nectar-producing plants will also encourage the birds into the garden.

NESTING: This canary prefers to nest near the top of a bush or small tree, about three to eight metres above the ground. A favoured nesting site is on top of clusters of pine cones. However, because of its shy nature, it does not breed regularly in gardens.

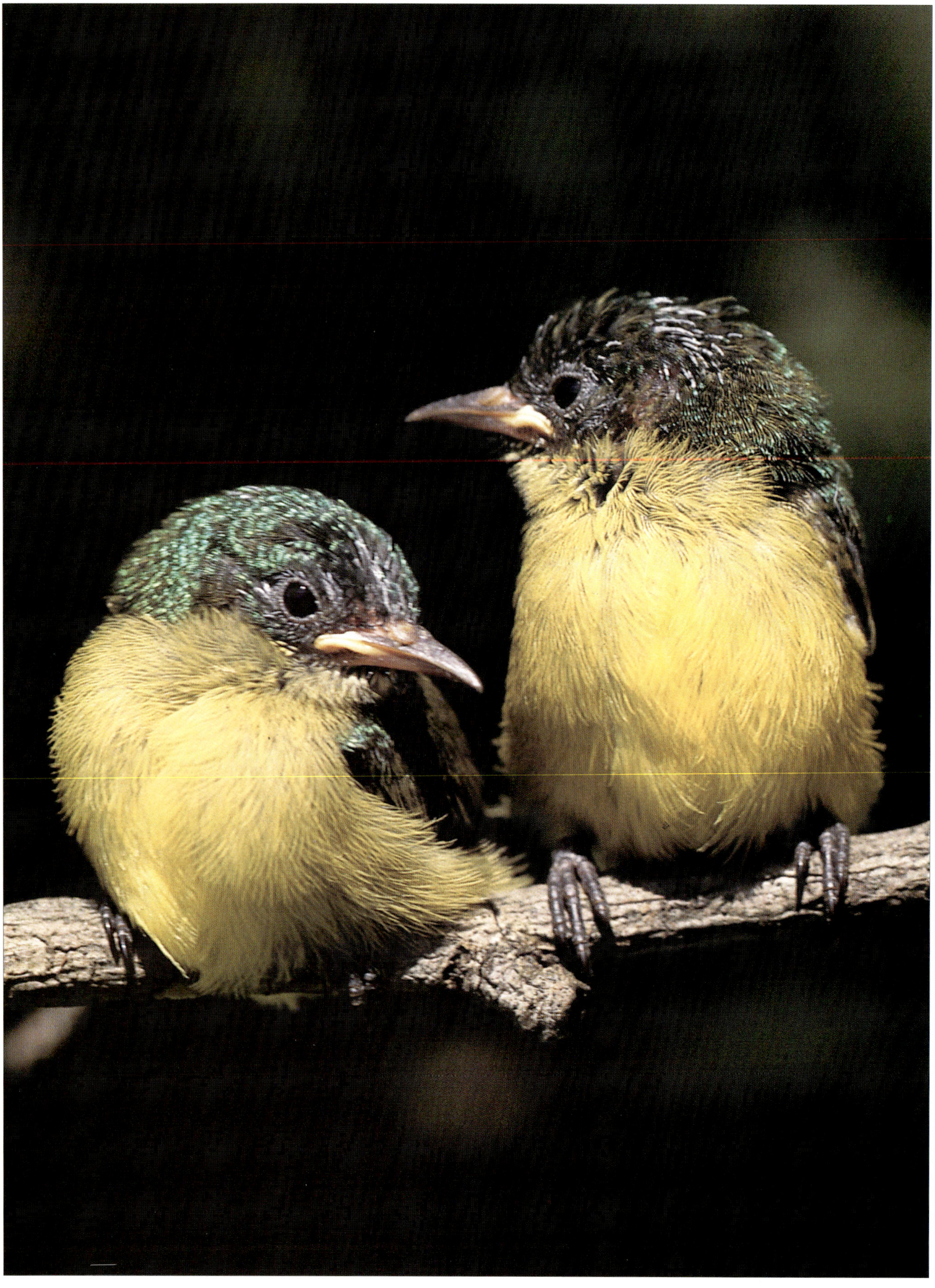

Other Garden Visitors

There are obviously other birds that will visit town and city gardens, some of them more common or conspicuous than others. Unfortunately, space limitations don't allow for a full discussion of each species. For information on distribution, habitat, breeding and other behaviour of the birds listed below, consult one of the relevant references suggested under 'Further Reading' (page 205).

Gymnogene *Polyboroides typus* (169)
Buffspotted Flufftail *Sarothrura elegans* (218)
Greenspotted Dove *Turtur chalcospilos* (358)
Fierynecked Nightjar *Caprimulgus pectoralis* (405)
Freckled Nightjar *Caprimulgus tristigma* (408)
Whiterumped Swift *Apus caffer* (415)
Whitebacked Mousebird *Colius colius* (425)
Malachite Kingfisher *Alcedo cristata* (431)
Trumpeter Hornbill *Bycanistes bucinator* (455)
Pied Barbet *Lybius leucomelas* (465)
Lesser Honeyguide *Indicator minor* (476)
Goldentailed Woodpecker *Campethera abingoni* (483)
Whitethroated Swallow *Hirundo albigularis* (520)
Wiretailed Swallow *Hirundo smithii* (522)
Redbreasted Swallow *Hirundo semirufa* (524)

House Crow *Corvus splendens* (549)
Southern Black Tit *Parus niger* (554)
Redeyed Bulbul *Pycnonotus nigricans* (567)
Whitethroated Robin *Cossypha humeralis* (602)
Garden Warbler *Sylvia borin* (619)
European Marsh Warbler *Acrocephalus palustris* (633)
Yellowbreasted Apalis *Apalis flavida* (648)
Greybacked Bleating Warbler
   Camaroptera brevicaudata (657b)
Neddicky *Cisticola fulvicapilla* (681)
Blackchested Prinia *Prinia flavicans* (685)
Spotted Flycatcher *Muscicapa striata* (689)
Dusky Flycatcher *Muscicapa adusta* (690)
Bluegrey Flycatcher *Muscicapa caerulescens* (691)
Black Flycatcher *Melaenornis pammelaina* (694)
African Pied Wagtail *Motacilla aguimp* (711)
Marico Sunbird *Nectarinia mariquensis* (779)
Olive Sunbird *Nectarinia olivacea* (790)
Spectacled Weaver *Ploceus ocularis* (810)
Blue Waxbill *Uraeginthus angolensis* (844)

Opposite: *Collared Sunbird chicks*

Bird Societies and Clubs

Southern African Ornithological Society,
P.O. Box 84394, Greenside 2034.
The Wildlife Society of Southern Africa,
P.O. Box 44189, Linden 2104

CAPE
Cape Bird Club, P.O. Box 5022, Cape Town 8000.
Eastern Cape Wild Bird Society, P.O. Box 27454,
Greenacres 6057.
Diaz Cross Bird Club, 39 African St, Grahamstown 6140.

ORANGE FREE STATE
Goldfields Bird Club, P.O. Box 580, Virginia 9430.
Orange Free State Ornithological Society,
P.O. Box 6614, Bloemfontein 9300.

NATAL
Natal Bird Club, P.O. Box 1218,
Durban 4000.
Natal Midlands Bird Club, P.O. Box 2772,
Pietermaritzburg 3200.

TRANSVAAL
Lowveld Bird Club, P.O. Box 4113, Nelspruit 1200.
North-eastern Bird Club, P.O. Box 6007,
Pietersburg Noord 0750.
Northern Transvaal Ornithological Society,
P.O. Box 4158, Pretoria 0001.
Rand Barbets Bird Club, 2 Flint Rd, Parkwood 2193.
Sandton Bird Club, P.O. Box 650890, Benmore 2010.
Vaal Reefs Bird Club, P.O. Box 5129, Vaal Reefs 2621.
Wesvaal Bird Club, P.O. Box 2413, Potchefstroom 2520.
Witwatersrand Bird Club, P.O. Box 72091, Parkview 2122.

ZIMBABWE
Ornithological Association of Zimbabwe,
P.O. Box 8382, Causeway, Zimbabwe.

BOTSWANA
Botswana Bird Club, P.O. Box 71, Gaborone, Botswana.

NAMIBIA
Namibian Bird Club, P.O. Box 67, Windhoek, Namibia.

TABLE OF INDIGENOUS PLANTS

The following table provides an extensive list of indigenous plants that are useful for planting in the bird garden. The botanical and common names of each species are given, as well as the height and spread, growing conditions for each plant, the climatic zone (summer or winter rainfall) to which it is suited, and information on where in the bird garden to plant it (see Chapter 1 for a discussion of garden habitats). The value of each plant in feeding birds is also given. Because almost any tree, shrub or creeper may be used as a nesting or roosting site, this information is not provided.

Botanical Name	Common Name	Height x Spread
Acacia albida	Ana Tree	15 m x 10 m
Acacia caffra	Hook-thorn	9 m x 6 m
Acacia erioloba	Camel Thorn	9 m x 7 m
Acacia galpinii	Monkey Thorn	18 m x 16 m
Acacia karroo	Sweet Thorn	8 m x 8 m
Acacia sieberiana var. *woodii*	Paperbark Thorn	12 m x 14 m
Acacia tortilis subsp. *heteracantha*	Umbrella Thorn	9 m x 7 m
Acacia xanthophloea	Fever Tree	12 m x 10 m
Agapanthus africanus	Dwarf Agapanthus	0,5 m x 0,5 m
Agapanthus praecox subsp. *orientalis*	Common Agapanthus	1 m x 0,75 m
Agathosma ovata	Oval-leaf Buchu	1,75 m x 1 m
Aloe arborescens	Krantz Aloe	3 m x 3 m
Aloe bainesii	Tree Aloe	8 m x 6 m
Aloe ferox	Bitter Aloe	3 m x 1 m
Aloe marlothii	Mountain Aloe	3 m x 1 m
Aloe striatula var. *caesia*	Basuto Kraal Aloe	1 m x 1 m
Aloe transvaalensis	Aloe	0,4 m x 0,4 m
Anisodontea scabrosa	Pink Mallow	1,8 m x 1,8 m
Apodytes dimidiata	White Pear	4 m x 3 m
Aponogeton distachyos	Cape Pondweed	spread 1 m
Aptenia cordifolia	Aptenia	0, 15 m x 0,6 m
Arctotheca calendula	Cape Weed	0,1 m x 0,4 m
Arctotis auriculata	Arctotis	0,3 m x 0,5 m
Arctotis fastuosa	Bittergousblom	0,6 m x 0,6 m
Arctotis 'Silver Lining'	Silver Arctotis	0,1 m x 0,3 m
Aristea major	Aristea	1,5 m x 1 m
Asystasia gangetica	Creeping Foxglove	0,3 m x 0,6 m
Athanasia crithmifolia	Klaas-louw Bush	1 m x 1 m
Barleria obtusa	Bush Violet	1 m x 1 m
Barleria repens	Small Bush Voilet	0,5 m x 0,5 m
Bauhinia galpinii	Pride-of-De Kaap	3 m x 4 m
Bauhinia natalensis	Natal Bauhinia	2 m x 1,5 m
Bauhinia tomentosa	Yellow Bauhinia	2 m x 3 m
Bolusanthus speciosus	Tree Wisteria	7 m x 4 m
Brachylaena discolor subsp. *discolor*	Coast Silver Oak	7 m x 10 m
Buddleja auriculata	Weeping Sage	4 m x 4 m
Buddleja saligna	False Olive	4 m x 3 m
Buddleja salviifolia	Sagewood	5 m x 4 m
Bulbine frutescens	Stalked Bulbine	0,3 m x 0,4 m
Burchellia bubalina	Wild Pomegranate	2,5 m x 1 m

Growing Conditions					Climatic Zone		Where in the Garden				Use for Birds				
Full sun	Dappled shade	Full shade	Frost hardy	Mod. frost hardy	Winter rainfall	Summer rainfall	Open area	Exclusion area	Canopy habitat	Wetland	Insects	Nectar	Fruit	Evergreen	Deciduous
●				●		●		●	●	●	●				●
●			●		●	●		●	●		●				●
●			●			●		●	●		●				●
●				●		●		●	●		●				●
●			●		●	●		●	●		●				●
●				●		●		●	●		●				●
●			●			●		●	●		●				●
●				●		●		●	●	●	●				●
●	●		●		●	●	●	●			●	●		●	
●	●		●		●	●	●	●			●	●		●	
●	●		●		●	●	●	●			●	●		●	
●				●		●		●	●		●	●		●	
●			●		●	●		●			●	●		●	
●			●			●		●			●	●		●	
●				●	●	●		●			●	●		●	
●						●		●			●	●		●	
●						●		●			●			●	
●			●		●	●		●			●			●	
●	●			●		●		●	●		●		●	●	
●			●		●	●				●	●			●	
●	●		●		●	●	●				●			●	
●	●		●		●	●	●			●	●			●	
●				●	●	●	●				●			●	
●				●	●	●	●				●			●	
●				●	●	●	●				●			●	
●	●		●		●	●				●	●			●	
	●	●			●	●	●	●			●			●	
●	●		●		●	●		●			●			●	
●	●			●	●	●		●			●			●	
●	●			●		●		●			●			●	
●				●		●		●			●				●
●				●		●		●			●				●
●	●			●		●		●			●				●
●				●		●		●	●		●				●
●			●			●		●	●		●			●	
●			●		●	●		●			●	●		●	
●			●		●	●		●			●			●	
●			●			●	●				●			●	
●	●			●		●	●				●			●	

193

TABLE OF INDIGENOUS PLANTS

Most plants will attract insects when flowering, even if the flowers are inconspicuous and lacking in copious amounts of nectar. The insects will provide food for a variety of birds and will also be taken to feed baby birds.

BOTANICAL NAME	COMMON NAME	HEIGHT X SPREAD
Calodendrum capense	Cape Chestnut	10 m x 4 m
Calpurnia aurea subsp. *aurea*	Natal Laburnum	4 m x 3 m
Carissa bispinosa	Num-num	2 m x 2 m
Carissa macrocarpa	Natal Plum	3 m x 2 m
Carpobrotus deliciosus	Purple Sour Fig	0,15 m x 1 m
Cassia abbreviata subsp. *beareana*	Sjambok Pod	6 m x 4 m
Cassine transvaalensis	Transvaal Saffron	5 m x 4 m
Cassinopsis ilicifolia	Orange Thorn	4 m x 4 m
Celtis africana	White Stinkwood	10 m x 4 m
Chlorophytum comosum	Hen-and-chickens	0,3 m x 0,3 m
Chondropetalum tectorum	Thatch Reed	1,5 m x 1,5 m
Chrysanthemoides monilifera	Bush-tick Berry	2 m x 2,5 m
Cineraria saxifraga	Wild Cineraria	0,15 m x 0,4 m
Clivia miniata	Bush Lily	0,75 m x 0,75 m
Coleonema album	White Confetti Bush	1 m x 0,75 m
Coleonema pulchellum	Confetti Bush	1,5 m x 1,5 m
Coleonema pulchrum	Pink Confetti Bush	1,5 m x 1,5 m
Combretum erythrophyllum	River Bushwillow	12 m x 10 m
Combretum microphyllum	Flame Combretum	4 m x 3 m
Combretum molle	Velvet Bushwillow	9 m x 4 m
Cordia caffra	Septee	6 m x 4 m
Crassula multicava	Fairy Crassula	0,2 m x 0,3 m
Crinum bulbispermum	Orange River Lily	1 m x 1 m
Crinum macowanii	River Crinum	1 m x 1 m
Crinum moorei	Moore's Crinum	1 m x 1 m
Crocosmia aurea	Valentine Flower	1 m x 0,3 m
Crotalaria capensis	Cape Rattlepod	3 m x 2 m
Croton sylvaticus	Forest Fever-berry	12 m x 10 m
Cussonia paniculata	Highveld Cabbage Tree	5 m x 2 m
Cussonia spicata	Common Cabbage Ttree	8 m x 4 m
Cyperus papyrus	Papyrus	2 m x 1 m
Dais cotinifolia	Pompon Tree	6 m x 4 m
Diascia integerrima	Twinspur	0,3 m x 0,45 m
Dierama pendulum	Harebell	1 m x 1 m
Dietes bicolor	Yellow Wild Iris	1 m x 1 m
Dietes grandiflora	Wild Iris	1 m x 1 m
Dimorphotheca cuneata	Bride's Bouquet	0,5 m x 0,6 m
Diospyros lycioides	Bluebush	5 m x 4 m
Diospyros whyteana	Bladder-nut	5 m x 3 m
Dodonaea angustifolia	Cape Sand Olive	4 m x 3 m

Full sun	Dappled shade	Full shade	Frost Hardy	Mod. frost hardy	Winter rainfall	Summer rainfall	Open area	Exclusion area	Canopy habitat	Wetland	Insects	Nectar	Fruit	Evergreen	Deciduous
●				●	●	●		●	●		●		●		●
●				●	●	●		●	●		●			●	
●	●			●	●	●		●			●		●	●	
●	●			●	●	●		●			●		●	●	
●	●		●			●	●				●			●	
●			●			●		●	●		●				●
●			●		●			●	●		●		●		
●	●		●		●	●		●			●		●	●	
●			●		●	●		●	●		●		●		●
●	●			●		●	●							●	
●			●		●	●				●				●	
	●			●	●	●	●	●			●			●	
	●	●	●		●	●		●			●		●	●	
●			●		●	●		●			●			●	
●			●		●	●		●			●			●	
●			●		●	●		●			●			●	
●			●		●	●		●	●		●				●
●				●				●	●		●				●
●			●					●	●		●				●
●				●	●	●		●	●		●		●		●
	●			●	●	●	●	●			●			●	
●			●			●				●	●				●
●	●				●	●				●	●				●
	●	●			●	●				●	●			●	
●	●		●		●	●				●	●			●	
●			●		●	●		●	●		●			●	
●				●		●		●	●		●		●		●
●			●		●	●		●	●		●		●		●
●				●	●	●		●	●		●		●	●	
●			●			●				●				●	
●			●			●		●			●				●
●				●	●	●	●				●			●	
●	●			●	●	●	●			●	●			●	
●	●		●		●	●	●			●	●			●	
●	●		●		●	●		●			●			●	
●			●		●	●					●			●	
●			●		●	●		●	●		●		●		●
●	●			●	●			●	●		●		●	●	
●			●		●	●		●	●		●			●	

TABLE OF INDIGENOUS PLANTS

Many indigenous plants do not produce large amounts of nectar or any fruit, but may provide a function in providing cover for birds. Some may be used purely for their decorative value.

BOTANICAL NAME	COMMON NAME	HEIGHT x SPREAD
Dombeya rotundifolia	Wild Pear	6 m x 3 m
Dovaylis caffra	Kei Apple	4 m x 3 m
Dracaena hookeriana	Dragon Tree	2 m x 1,5 m
Drosanthemum speciosum	Red Ice-plant	0,6 m x 0,6 m
Duvernoia aconitiflora	Lemon Pistol Bush	3 m x 3 m
Dymondia margaretae	Silver Carpet	0,1 m x 0,3 m
Dyschoriste rogersii	Blue Joy	0,5 m x 0,5 m
Ehretia rigida	Puzzle Bush	4 m x 4 m
Ekebergia capensis	Cape Ash	12 m x 12 m
Elegia capensis	Broom Reed	2,5 m x 1,5 m
Erica cerinthoides	Red Hairy Heath	0, 4 m x 0,4 m
Eriocephalus africanus	Wild Rosemary	1,75 m x 1,75 m
Erythrina lysistemon	Common Coral Tree	10 m x 6 m
Eucomis autumnalis	Pineapple Flower	0,75 m x 0,75 m
Eumorphia prostrata	Silver Cloud	0,5 m x 1 m
Euryops pectinatus	Grey Euryops	1 m x 1 m
Euryops virgineus	Honey Euryops	1,5 m x 1,5 m
Faurea saligna	Transvaal Beech	8 m x 6 m
Felicia amelloides	Blue Felicia	0,5 m x 0,5 m
Felicia bergerana	Kingfisher Daisy	0,2 m x 0,2 m
Felicia filifolia	Wild Aster	1 m x 1 m
Felicia heterophylla	True-blue Daisy	0,3 m x 0,3 m
Ficus ingens	Red-leaved Rock Fig	12 m x 12 m
Ficus sur	Cape Fig	12 m x 12 m
Ficus sycomorus	Sycamore Fig	12 m x 14 m
Galpinia transvaalica	Transvaal Privet	8 m x 8 m
Gardenia thunbergia	Starry Gardenia	5 m x 3 m
Gazania krebsiana	Gazania	0,25 m x 0,3 m
Geranium incanum subsp. *incanum*	Carpet Geranium	0,3 m x 0,3 m
Gerbera jamesonii	Barbeton Daisy	0,4 m x 0,3 m
Gloriosa superba	Flame Lily	1,5 m x 0,3 m
Grewia flava	Brandy Bush	2,5 m x 2,5 m
Grewia occidentalis	Cross-berry	5 m x 3 m
Halleria elliptica	Wild Fuchsia	2,5 m x 2,5 m
Halleria lucida	Tree Fuchsia	4 m x 2 m
Harpephyllum caffrum	Wild Plum	10 m x 8 m
Helichrysum argyrophyllum	Everlasting	0,1 m x 0,3 m
Helichrysum cymosum subsp. *cymosum*	Gold Carpet	0,1 m x 0,4 m
Helichrysum splendidum	Cape Gold	1 m x 0,5 m
Heteropyxis natalensis	Lavender Tree	6 m x 4 m

Full sun	Dappled shade	Full shade	Frost Hardy	Mod. frost hardy	Winter rainfall	Summer rainfall	Open area	Exclusion area	Canopy habitat	Wetland	Insects	Nectar	Fruit	Evergreen	Deciduous
●			●			●		●	●		●				●
●			●		●	●		●	●		●		●		●
	●	●		●	●	●		●			●		●	●	
●			●		●	●	●				●			●	
●	●			●		●		●	●		●	●	●	●	
●			●		●	●	●				●			●	
●				●		●		●			●			●	
●			●		●	●		●			●		●	●	
●				●	●	●		●	●		●		●	●	
●	●		●		●	●				●				●	
●			●			●	●				●	●		●	
●			●			●		●			●			●	
●				●		●		●	●		●	●			●
	●		●		●	●				●	●				●
●			●			●	●	●			●			●	
●			●			●		●			●			●	
●				●		●		●	●		●	●		●	●
●	●		●		●	●		●			●			●	
●			●		●	●		●			●			●	
●				●		●	●	●			●			●	
●			●		●	●		●	●		●	●	●		●
●				●		●		●	●		●	●	●		
●				●		●		●	●		●	●			●
●				●	●	●		●	●		●			●	
●				●	●	●		●	●		●			●	
●			●		●	●	●				●			●	
●			●		●	●	●				●			●	
●			●		●	●	●				●			●	
	●		●			●		●			●				●
●			●			●		●	●		●		●		●
●			●		●	●		●	●		●				●
●			●		●	●		●	●		●	●	●	●	
●				●	●	●		●	●		●	●	●	●	
●				●	●	●		●	●		●		●	●	
●			●			●	●				●			●	
●			●		●	●	●				●			●	
●			●			●		●			●			●	
●				●		●		●	●		●				●

TABLE OF INDIGENOUS PLANTS

Although there are plants that grow naturally only in the summer-rainfall or winter-rainfall region, many will thrive in both. A little extra care and attention will help plants survive outside of the areas where they naturally occur.

Botanical Name	Common Name	Height x Spread
Hypericum revolutum	Curry Bush	3 m x 3 m
Hypoestes aristata	Ribbon Bush	1,5 m x 1 m
Jasminum multipartitum	Starry Wild Jasmine	2 m x 2 m
Kiggelaria africana	Wild Peach	12 m x 11 m
Kirkia acuminata	White Syringa	12 m x 12 m
Kirkia wilmsii	Mountain Syringa	8 m x 8 m
Kniphofia praecox	Red-hot Poker	1,5 m x 1,5 m
Lampranthus aureus	Orange Vygie	0,45 m x 0,6 m
Leonotis leonurus	Wild Dagga	2 m x 1,5 m
Leucadendron argenteum	Silver Tree	7 m x 3 m
Leucospermum conocarpodendron	Tree Pincushion	4 m x 3 m
Loxostylis alata	Tigerwood	6 m x 4 m
Mackaya bella	Forest Bell Bush	3 m x 2 m
Melianthus comosus	Kruidtjie-roer-my-nie	1,5 m x 1 m
Melianthus major	Giant Honey Flower	2,5 m x 3,5 m
Monopsis lutea	Yellow Lobelia	0,2 m x 0,3 m
Mundulea sericea	Cork Bush	3 m x 2 m
Myrsine africana	Cape Myrtle	1,5 m x 2 m
Myrsiphyllum asparagoides	Cape Smilax	0,3 m x 0,8 m
Nemesia strumosa	Cape Jewels	0,3 m x 0,3 m
Nuxia floribunda	Forest Elder	8 m x 4 m
Nymania capensis	Chinese Lantern	4 m x 2 m
Nymphaea capensis	Blue Water Lily	0,4 m x 0,8 m
Ochna serrulata	Mickey Mouse Bush	2,5 m x 2,5 m
Olea europaea subsp. *africana*	Wild Olive	8 m x 6 m
Orphium frutescens	Orphium	0,6 m x 0,45 m
Orthosiphon labiatus	Pink Sage	1,5 m x 1,5 m
Osteospermum ecklonis	Blue-and-white Daisy Bush	0,75 m x 1,5 m
Othonna carnosa	Othonna	0,1 m x 0,6 m
Ozoroa paniculosa	Common Resin Tree	7 m x 5 m
Panicum maximum	Guinea Grass	1,5 m x 0,3 m
Pappea capensis	Jacket Plum	7 m x 6 m
Pavetta lanceolata	Forest Bride's Bush	5 m x 4 m
Pelargonium cucullatum	Wildemalva	1 m x 1 m
Pelargonium peltatum	Ivy-leaved Pelargonium	0,3 m x 2 m
Pelargonium reniforme	Kidney-leaved Pelargonium	0,15 m x 0,3 m
Peltophorum africanum	Weeping Wattle	9 m x 8 m
Phoenix reclinata	Wild Date Palm	5 m x 4 m
Phygelius capensis	Cape Fuchsia	1 m x 0,5 m
Phyla nodiflora	Daisy Lawn	0,1 m x 0,4 m

Full sun	Dappled shade	Full shade	Frost Hardy	Mod. frost hardy	Winter rainfall	Summer rainfall	Open area	Exclusion area	Canopy habitat	Wetland	Insects	Nectar	Fruit	Evergreen	Deciduous
●			●		●	●		●			●			●	
●	●			●	●	●		●			●			●	
●	●			●	●	●		●			●			●	
●			●		●	●		●	●		●		●	●	
●				●		●		●	●		●				●
●				●		●		●	●		●				●
●			●		●	●	●				●	●		●	
●			●		●	●	●	●			●			●	
●			●		●	●		●			●	●		●	
●				●	●	●		●			●			●	
●				●		●		●			●	●		●	
●				●		●		●	●		●			●	
	●	●		●		●		●			●			●	
●			●		●	●		●			●			●	
●			●		●	●		●			●			●	
●				●	●	●	●				●			●	
●			●			●		●			●				●
	●		●		●	●		●			●		●	●	
●	●			●	●	●		●			●			●	
●				●	●	●	●				●			●	
●				●		●		●	●		●			●	
●			●		●	●		●	●		●			●	
●			●		●	●				●	●				●
●				●	●	●		●	●		●		●		●
●			●		●	●		●			●		●	●	
●				●	●	●	●	●			●			●	
●			●			●	●				●			●	
●			●		●	●	●				●			●	
●			●			●	●				●			●	
●				●		●		●	●		●		●		●
●	●		●		●		●								●
●				●				●	●		●				●
●				●	●	●		●			●			●	
●				●	●	●		●			●			●	
●				●	●	●		●			●			●	
●			●			●	●				●			●	
●				●		●		●			●				●
●				●	●	●		●		●	●		●	●	
	●			●		●		●		●	●	●		●	
●	●			●	●		●							●	

TABLE OF INDIGENOUS PLANTS

Deciduous trees should be planted on the north-facing side of the house so as to ensure that the maximum amount of sunlight reaches the building during winter. The summer foliage will help to keep the house cool during the hot summer months.

Botanical Name	Common Name	Height x Spread
Pittosporum viridiflorum	Pittosporum	7 m x 5 m
Plectranthus ecklonii	Plectranthus	1,5 m x 1,5 m
Plectranthus fruticosus	Pink Fly Bush	1,25 m x 0,5 m
Plectranthus madagascariensis	Variagated Plectranthus	0,15 m x 0,45 m
Plectranthus saccatus	Stoep Jacaranda	0,5 m x 0,5 m
Plectranthus verticillatus	Gossip Plant	0,1 m x 0,5 m
Plumbago auriculata	Cape Leadwort	3 m x 3 m
Podalyria calyptrata	Sweetpea Bush	3 m x 3 m
Podocarpus falcatus	Outeniqua Yellowwood	12 m x 4 m
Podocarpus henkelii	Henkel's Yellowwood	10 m x 4 m
Polygala myrtifolia	Bloukappie	3 m x 3 m
Polygala virgata	Purple Broom	2 m x 1 m
Portulacaria afra	Spekboom	4 m x 3 m
Protasparagus densiflorus 'Mazeppa'	Emerald Carpet	0,3 m x 0,6 m
Protasparagus densiflorus 'Myers'	Cat's Tail Asparagus	0,5 m x 0,6 m
Protasparagus densiflorus 'Sprengeri'	Emerald Fern	0,4 m x 0,9 m
Protasparagus plumosus	Asparagus Fern	2 m x 1 m
Protea cynaroides	King Protea	1,8 m x 1 m
Protea repens	Sugarbush	3 m x 3 m
Rhamnus prinoides	Dogwood	4 m x 4 m
Rhigozum obovatum	Karoo Gold	3 m x 2 m
Rhoicissus digitata	Wild Grape	5 m x 3 m
Rhoicissus tomentosa	Common Forest Grape	5 m x 3 m
Rhus batophylla	Redberry Rhus	3 m x 4 m
Rhus chirindensis	Red Currant	6 m x 5 m
Rhus crenata	Dune Crow-berry	3 m x 2 m
Rhus dentata	Nana-berry	5 m x 4 m
Rhus lancea	Karee	7 m x 7 m
Rhus leptodictya	Mountain Karee	5 m x 5 m
Rhus lucida	Dune Taaibos	1,5 m x 1,5 m
Rhus nebulosa	Sand Taaibos	2 m x 3 m
Rhus pendulina	White Karee	8 m x 7 m
Rhus pyroides	Firethorn	5 m x 4 m
Rhus transvaalensis	Transvaal Taaibos	3 m x 3 m
Rhus undulata	Kuni Bush	5 m x 4 m
Rothmannia capensis	Wild Gardenia	6 m x 4 m
Rothmannia globosa	Bell Gardenia	4 m x 3 m
Ruttyruspolia x 'Phyllis van Heerden'	Ruttyruspolia	1,5 m x 1,5 m
Salvia africana-lutea	Beach Salvia	1,8 m x 1,8 m

Full sun	Dappled shade	Full shade	Frost Hardy	Mod. frost hardy	Winter rainfall	Summer rainfall	Open area	Exclusion area	Canopy habitat	Wetland	Insects	Nectar	Fruit	Evergreen	Deciduous
●	●			●	●	●		●	●		●		●	●	
	●			●	●	●		●			●			●	
	●	●		●	●	●		●			●			●	
	●			●	●	●		●						●	
●	●			●	●	●		●			●			●	
	●	●		●	●	●		●			●			●	
●	●			●	●	●		●			●			●	
●			●		●	●		●			●			●	
●			●		●	●		●	●				●	●	
●			●		●	●		●	●					●	
●			●		●	●		●			●			●	
●			●		●	●		●			●			●	
●				●	●	●		●			●			●	
●	●			●	●	●	●	●			●		●	●	
●	●			●	●	●	●	●			●		●	●	
●	●			●	●	●	●	●			●		●	●	
●	●		●		●	●		●			●			●	
●			●		●			●			●			●	
●			●		●			●			●	●		●	
●	●		●		●	●		●			●		●	●	
●			●			●		●			●				●
●				●	●	●		●			●		●	●	
●				●	●	●		●			●		●	●	
●				●	●	●		●			●			●	
●				●	●	●		●	●		●		●		●
●			●		●	●		●			●		●	●	
●			●		●	●		●	●		●		●		●
●			●		●	●		●	●		●		●	●	
●				●		●		●	●		●			●	
●				●	●	●		●	●		●			●	
●				●		●		●			●		●	●	
●			●		●	●		●	●		●		●	●	
●				●		●		●	●		●		●	●	●
●			●		●	●		●	●		●		●	●	
●			●		●	●		●			●			●	
●			●		●	●		●			●			●	
●				●	●	●		●			●			●	
●			●		●	●		●			●	●		●	

TABLE OF INDIGENOUS PLANTS

By planting a selection of fruit-producing species, you can ensure that food is available to birds at different times of the year. Take note of the fruiting periods of different plants with the aim to provide an almost constant supply of fruit for birds.

Botanical Name	Common Name	Height x Spread
Salvia chamelaeagnea	Blue Salvia	1 m x 1 m
Scabiosa africana	Pincushion	0,3 m x 0,3 m
Schotia brachypetala	Weeping Boer-bean	12 m x 8 m
Schrebera alata	Wild Jasmine	8 m x 7 m
Scilla natalensis	Blue Squill	1 m x 0,5 m
Senecio macroglossus	Flowering Ivy	3 m x 1,5 m
Senecio tamoides	Canary Creeper	5 m x 3 m
Senecio tanacetopsis	Lace-leaf Senecio	0,3 m x 0,5 m
Stachys aethiopica	Stachys	0,3 m x 0,5 m
Steirodiscus tagetes	Golden Edging Daisy	0,2 m x 0,2 m
Strelitzia nicolai	Natal Wild Banana	8 m x 4 m
Strelitzia reginae	Crane Flower	1,5 m x 1,5 m
Sutera grandiflora	Wild Phlox	1 m x 0,5 m
Sutera pauciflora	Trailing Phlox	0,1 m x 0,4 m
Syzygium cordatum	Water Berry	9 m x 7 m
Tecomaria capensis	Cape Honeysuckle	3 m x 3 m
Thamnochortus insignis	Thatch Reed	2 m x 1,5 m
Thunbergia alata	Black-eyed Susan	3 m x 1,5 m
Trema orientalis	Pigeonwood	13 m x 6 m
Trichilia emetica	Natal Mahogany	10 m x 10 m
Tulbaghia simmleri	Wild Garlic	0,4 m x 0,25 m
Tulbaghia violacea	Wild Garlic	0,4 m x 0,25 m
Turraea obtusifolia	Honeysuckle Tree	2,5 m x 2 m
Typha capensis	Bulrush	2 m x 0,5 m
Ursinia sericea	Magriet	0,4 m x 0,2 m
Vangueria infausta	Wild Medlar	5 m x 3 m
Veltheimia bracteata	Bush Lily	0,45 m x 0,45 m
Vepris lanceolata	White Ironwood	6 m x 5 m
Wachendorfia thyrsiflora	Bloodroot	2 m x 0,5 m
Warburgia salutaris	Pepper-bark Tree	10 m x 6 m
Watsonia borbonica subsp. *ardernei*	Witkanol	1,5 m x 0,5 m
Watsonia fourcadei	Suurkanol	1,2 m x 0,3 m
Widdringtonia cedarbergensis	Clanwilliam Cedar	10 m x 4 m
Widdringtonia nodiflora	Mountain Cypress	5 m x 4 m
Zantedeschia aethiopica	White Arum Lily	1,5 m x 1 m
Zantedeschia pentlandii	Yellow Arum Lily	0,6 m x 0,5 m
Ziziphus mucronata	Buffalo-thorn	9 m x 9 m
Ziziphus rivularis	False Buffalo-thorn	7 m x 3 m

Full sun	Dappled shade	Full shade	Frost Hardy	Mod. frost hardy	Winter rainfall	Summer rainfall	Open area	Exclusion area	Canopy habitat	Wetland	Insects	Nectar	Fruit	Evergreen	Deciduous
●			●		●	●		●			●	●		●	
●			●		●	●	●				●			●	
●				●		●		●	●		●		●		●
●				●		●		●	●		●			●	
●	●		●		●	●	●	●			●			●	●
●				●	●	●	●	●			●			●	
●				●	●	●		●			●			●	
●			●		●	●	●	●			●			●	
	●		●		●	●		●			●	●		●	
●			●		●	●	●				●			●	
●				●		●		●			●	●		●	
●				●		●		●			●	●		●	
●			●			●	●	●			●			●	
●	●			●	●	●	●	●			●			●	
●				●		●		●	●		●	●	●	●	
●				●		●		●			●	●		●	
●			●		●	●	●	●		●	●			●	
●				●	●	●		●			●			●	
●				●		●		●	●		●		●	●	
●				●		●		●	●		●	●			
●	●		●		●	●	●	●			●			●	
●	●		●		●	●	●	●			●			●	
●	●			●	●	●		●			●			●	
●			●		●	●				●				●	
●				●	●	●	●				●			●	
●			●		●	●		●			●		●		●
	●			●	●	●		●			●			●	
●			●					●	●		●		●	●	
●	●		●		●	●				●	●				●
●				●		●		●	●					●	
●			●		●					●	●			●	
●			●		●					●	●			●	
●			●		●	●		●	●		●			●	
●			●		●	●		●	●		●			●	
	●			●	●	●				●	●				●
	●			●	●	●				●	●				●
●			●		●	●		●	●		●	●	●		●
●			●		●	●		●	●		●	●	●		●

203

Useful Addresses

NATIONAL BOTANICAL GARDENS

Harold Porter National Botanical Garden
PO Box 35
Betty's Bay
7141
Phone (02823) 9711

Karoo National Botanical Garden
PO Box 152
Worcester
6850
Phone (0231) 7 0785

Kirstenbosch National Botanical Garden
Private Bag X7
Claremont
7725
Phone (021) 762 1166

Lowveld National Botanical Garden
PO Box 1024
Nelspruit
1200
Phone (01311) 2 5531

Natal National Botanical Garden (Pietermaritzburg)
PO Box 11448
Dorpspruit
3206
Phone (0331) 44 3858

Orange Free State National Botanical Garden (Bloemfontein)
PO Box 29036
Danhof
9310
Phone (051) 31 3530

Pretoria National Botanical Garden
Private Bag Z101
Pretoria 0001
Phone (012) 804 3200

Witwatersrand National Botanical Garden (Roodepoort)
PO Box 2194
Wilropark
1731
Phone (011) 958 1750/1

NURSERY ASSOCIATIONS

The associations listed below will offer general advice on plants and will be able to suggest reputable nurseries in your area to contact for purchasing plants.

South African Nurserymen's Association (Transvaal)
PO Box 514
Halfway House
1685
Phone (011) 315 1920

South African Nurserymen's Association (Natal)
PO Box 11636
Dorpspruit
3206
Phone (0331) 42 5779

South African Nurserymen's Association (OFS)
PO Box 28743
Danhof
9310
Phone (051) 51 1314

South African Nurserymen's Association (Eastern Cape)
PO Box 12760
Centrahill
6006
Phone (041) 332 458

South African Nurserymen's Association (Western Cape)
PO Box 109
Bergvliet
7945
Phone (021) 72 0203

SEED AND BULB SUPPLIERS

The following addresses will be useful if you want to purchase the seed of indigenous plants (in some cases plant bulbs too).

Department of Water Affairs and Forestry
Forestry Branch
Private Bag X93
Pretoria
0001

Cape Seeds & Bulbs
PO Box 4063
Idas Valley
Stellenbosch
7609
Phone (021) 887 9418

Feathers Wild Flower Seeds
PO Box 13
Constantia
7848
Phone (021) 794 6432

Silverhill Seeds
18 Silverhill Crescent
Kenilworth
7700
Phone (021) 762 4245

Sunburst Flower Bulbs
PO Box 183
Howard Place
7450
Phone (021) 531 9829

REHABILITATION CENTRES

The Animal Rehabilitation Centre (ARC)
PO Box 15121
Lynn East
0030
Phone (012) 808 1106

Useful Addresses

Centre for Rehabilitation of Wildlife (CROW)
PO Box 53007
Yellowwood Park
Durban
4011
Phone (031) 42 1127

Chipangali Wildlife Orphanage
PO Box 1057
Bulawayo
Zimbabwe
Phone (09263 9) 70764

South African National Council for the Conservation of Coastal Birds (SANCCOB)
PO Box 11116
Bloubergrant
7443
Phone (021) 557 6155

NATURE CONSERVATION DEPARTMENTS

These departments will offer advice on indigenous fish, where to obtain them and, if you intend netting them from dams in your area, whether a permit is required. They will also give advice on indigenous plants.

Cape Nature Conservation (Cape)
Private Bag X9086
Cape Town
8000
Phone (021) 483-3396

Chief Directorate Nature and Environmental Conservation (Transvaal)
Private Bag X209
Pretoria
0001
Phone (012) 323 3403

Natal Parks Board (Natal)
PO Box 662
Pietermaritzburg
3200
Phone (0331) 47 1961

Directorate of Nature and Environmental Conservation (OFS)
PO Box 517
Bloemfontein
9300
Phone (051) 405-5245

Department National Parks and Wildlife Management
PO Box 8365
Causeway
Zimbabwe

Fisheries Officer
Department of Animal Health & Production
Ministry of Agriculture
Private Bag 003
Gaborone
Botswana

Directorate Nature Conservation and Recreation Resorts
Private Bag 13306
Windhoek
Namibia
Phone (061) 63131

SUPPLIER OF FRESH-WATER FISH

(to all parts of South Africa):

Blyde River Aquaculture
PO Box 408
Hoedspruit
1380
Phone (01528) 35250

Further Reading

Ginn, P.J., McIlleron, W.G. & Milstein, P. le S. 1989. *The Complete Book of Southern African Birds*. Struik Winchester, Cape Town.
Joffe, P. 1993. *The Gardener's Guide to South African Plants*. Delos, Cape Town.
Johnson, D. & S. 1993. *Gardening with Indigenous Trees and Shrubs*. Southern Book Publishers, Johannesburg.
Le Roux, A. & Schelpe, T. 1988. *Namaqualand, South African Wildflower Guide 1*. Botanical Society of South Africa, Claremont.
Maclean, G.L. (6th ed) 1993. *Roberts' Birds of Southern Africa*. John Voelcker Bird Book Fund, Cape Town.
Newman, K. (4th ed) 1992. *Birds of Southern Africa*. Southern Book Publishers, Johannesburg.
Pienaar, K. 1991. *Gardening with Indigenous Plants*. Struik Timmins, Cape Town.
Onderstall, J. 1984. *South African Wild Flower Guide. Transvaal Lowveld and Escarpment*. Botanical Society of South Africa, Claremont.
Palgrave, K.C. (2nd ed) 1983. *Trees of Southern Africa*. Struik Publishers, Cape Town.
Sinclair, J.C. 1987. *Field Guide to the Birds of Southern Africa*. Struik Publishers, Cape Town.
Sinclair, J.C., Hockey, P.A.R. & Tarboton, W. 1993. *Sasol Birds of Southern Africa*. Struik Publishers, Cape Town.
Van Wyk, B. & Malan, S. 1988. *Field Guide to the Wild Flowers of the Witwatersrand and Pretoria Region*. Struik Publishers, Cape Town.
Van Wyk, P. (2nd ed) 1993. *Field Guide to the Trees of the Kruger National Park*. Struik Publishers, Cape Town.

INDEX

References to captions, photographs and illustrations are in italic; numbers in bold allude to a main reference.

A

Acacia caffra 24
Acacia karroo 24, 63
Acacia sieberiana 149, 166, 168, 169, 170, 171, 172
Acacia species 15, 21, 25, 51, 106, 110, 124, *149*, 168, *170*, 173
Acacia xanthophloea 63, 65, *83*, 85, 178, 179, 180, 181
Accipiter minullus 34, **95**
Accipiter ovampensis 81, **94**
Accipiter tachiro 83, **96**
Acridotheres tristis 50, **161**
Acrocephalus palustris 191
Agapanthus species 77, 165
Alcedo cristata 191
Aloe species *62*, *135*, 166, 167, 170, 171
Alopochen aegyptiacus 54, **93**
Amblyospiza albifrons 28, *45*, **177**
Andropadus importunus **139**
Anthreptes collaris **172**
ants *see* termites
Apalis
　Barthroated **149**
　Yellowbreasted 191
Apalis falvida 191
Apalis thoracica **149**
aphids 74, 75, 76, *78*, 79, *148*
Apus affinis **117**
Apus caffer 191
Arcea horta 113
Ardea cinerea 14, *80-1*
Arundo donax 46

B

babblers 15
Barbet
　Blackcollared *52*, **125**
　Crested **127**
　Pied 191
　Yellowfronted Barbet **126**
barbets 19, 25, 31, 32, 33, 50, 51, 53, 58, 162
bee-eating birds 84
bird-bath *12*, *40*, 184 *see also* water feature
bird-friendly
　small gardens 24
　smallholdings 82-3
　urban gardens 23
bird puddings 30, **35**
bird-unfriendly gardens 12, 22
Bishop, Red 24, *38-9*, *45*, *46*, 150, **182**
bishops 113, 184
bitterns 44
Bloodroot 21, 46
Bluegums 51, 72, *83*, 90, *94*, 95, 96, 105, 106, *136*, 170
Bokmakierie *48-9*, **157**
bone-apples 173
Bostrychia hagedash *70-1*, 77, 79, **92**
Bottlebrush 36, *169*

Boubou, Southern *12*, **155**
bracken 165
bramble 165
Brazilian Pepper 137
Breonudia species 96
Broom Reed 21, 66
Bubo africanus 18, 37, 52, 54, 58, 59, **116**
Bubulcus ibis **90**
Buddleja salviifolia 83
Buffalo-thorn 108
Bugweed 104, 109, 177
Bulbul
　Blackeyed *19*, 51, **138**
　Cape **137**, 138, 139
　Redeyed 191
　Sombre **139**
bulbuls 19, *25*, 33, 34, 182
Bulrushes 44, *46*, 178
Burchellia bubalina 172
Burhinus capensis **101**
Burkea africana 68
Buzzard, Lizard 34
buzzards 87
Bycanistes bucinator 191

C

Cabbage Tree, Highveld 65
Callistemon species 36
Callistemon viminalis 169
Camaroptera brevicaudata 191
Campethera abingoni 191
canaries 15, 31
Canary
　Cape **188**
　Streakyheaded **189**
　Yelloweyed **187**
canary creeper *25*
canopy habitat
　for nesting 51
　in urban gardens 18-21, 23
　on smallholdings 84
　plants for 18
Cape Ash 36, 109
Cape floral kingdom *see* fynbos
Cape Honeysuckle 24, 25, 36, *65*, 165, 167, 189
Cape Leadwort 17, 24, 65, 66, *68*, 168
Caprimulgus tristigma 191
Carissa bispinosa 36
Carissa macrocarpa 15, 24, 25, *51*, 52, 110
Carp, Japanese Koi 44
Cassine transvaalensis 108
Cassinopsis ilicifolia 15
caterpillars *73*, 74, 79, *149*
Celtis africana 66, 85, 104, 148, 177
Centropus burchelli 15, 21, 58, 77, **114**
Cercomela familiaris *26-7*, **143**
Ceryle rudis 40, **121**
Cestrum laevigatum 104
Cestrum species 36
chamaeleons 77
Chat
　Familiar *26-7*, **143**
　Mocking 132, **144**
chats 111
Chondropetalum tectorum 21

Chrysococcyx caprius **113**
Chrysococcyx klaas **112**
Cinnyricinclus leucogaster 29, **162**
Cisticola fulvicapilla 191
Colius colius **120**
Colius indicus 191
Colius striatus **119**
Columba arquatrix **104**
Columba guinea 31, **103**
Columba livia **102**
Combretum erythrophyllum 85
compost heaps **17**, 22, 23, 79
Coral Tree *124*, 171
　Common *171*
cormorants 86
Corvus albus **136**
Corvus splendens 191
Corythaixoides concolor 51, **110**
Cossypha caffra 52, **147**
Cossypha heuglini 32, **145**
Cossypha humeralis 191
Cossypha natalensis **146**
Coucal, Burchell's *15*, 21, 58, 77, **114**
coucals 21, 72, 87
Crane, Blue **86**
Crane Flower *36*
Crinum species 21, *46*
Crow
　House 191
　Pied **136**
crows 58
Cuckoo
　Diederik **113**, 153, 180, 182
　Emerald 156
　Klaas's **112**
　Redchested **111**, 145, 146, 147
Cuculus solitarius **111**
Cussonia paniculata 65
Cynodon grasses 14
Cypsiurus parvus **118**

D

dams 84-5
　fish for 86
　plants for 85
Darter 86
Dendropicos fuscescens **128**
Dicrurus adsimilis **134**
Dietes grandiflora 46
Dikkop, Spotted **101**
dikkops 37, 52, 79, 89
Diospyros mespiliformis 108, 109
Dogwood 36
Dove
　Cape Turtle *40*, **106**, 107
　Greenspotted 191
　Laughing *50*, **107**, 154
　Redeyed **105**, 107
doves 29, 31, 40, 52, 57
Dovyalis caffra 36, 52
dragonflies *47*
driftwood 30
Drongo, Forktailed **134**
drongos 37, 50
Dryoscopus cubla **156**
ducks 53, 77, 85
Dune Crow-berry 25, 35

E

Eagles
　African Fish 146
　African Hawk 83
　Wahlberg's 83
Ebony Diospyros 108, 109
Egret, Cattle **90**
egrets 55, 87
Ehretia rigida 36, 62, 66
Ekebergia capensis 36, 109
Elegia capensis 21, *66*
Eragrostis species 14
Eragrostis teff 52
ericas *62*, 165, *167*, 168
Erythrina species *124*, 168, 170, 172
Estrilda astrild **183**
Eucalyptus species 51, 72, 83, 90, *94*, 95, 96, 105, 106, *136*, 170
Euclea species 168
Euphorbia species 79
Euplectes orix 24, *38-9*, *45*, 46, **182**
exclusion area
　for nesting 51-2
　in urban gardens 15-18, 23, 40
　on smallholdings 83
　plants for **16**

F

feeders 29-30
　driftwood 30
　log 30
　natural 30
　pine cone 30
feeding
　artificial 31-4
　in small gardens 25
　natural 34-7
　nestlings 59
　sites 29
　shrubs **37**
　trees **36**
　what to feed 31
　where to feed 29
feeding log *30*, 34, 123, 124, 129, 134, 135, 138, 148, 152, 154-6, 158, 164
feeding-tables/platforms 25, *30*, 96, 102, 105, 106-8, *107*, 110, 111, 114, 120, 122-4, 127, 134, 137, 139, 140, 141, 143, 144, 147, 149, 150, 153-7, 159-61, 163, 164, 167, 173-5, 177-89
　building a 32-3
fertilizers 66-7
Fever Tree *63*, 65, *83*, 85, 178, 179, 180, 181
Ficus species 19, 96, 109, 110, 139
Ficus sur 108, *109*
Ficus sycomorus 108
figs, wild 108 , *109*, 139
Finch, Cuckoo 150
finches 15, 31
Firefinch, Bluebilled 186
fledgling period 89
Flufftail, Buffspotted 191
Flycatcher
　Black 191
　Bluegrey 191
　Dusky 191

206

INDEX

Fiscal **151**
Paradise *51*, **152**
Spotted 191
flycatchers 36
Forest Grape,
  Common *105*
Francolin
  Cape **97**
  Natal **98**
francolins 14, 15, 34, 52, 82, 89
Francolinus capensis **97**
Francolinus natalensis **98**
fruit beetles *17*, *73*, *79*
fruit-eating birds 19, 31, 33
fruit garden 37, 75-6
Fuchsia
  Tree 15, 36, 166, 168, 169, 170, 171, 172, 173
  Wild 25
fungicides 72
fynbos 36, **64**, *67*

G

garden habitats 14-23
Ginger Bush 173
go-away bird *see* Grey Lourie
Goose, Egyptian 54, **93**
Goshawk, African *83*, **96**
Grass
  Bayview 14
  Florida 14
  Guinea 14, 52, 85
  Kikuyu 14, 180
  Love 14
  Thatching *82*
  Weeping Love 52
grasses (wild) 14, 15
grebes 85
Grey Poplar 94, 95
groundcovers
  for exclusion areas 16, 17
  for open areas 14-15
guineafowl *13*, 14, 18, 34, 52, 77-8, 82
Guineafowl, Helmeted 18, **99**
Gymnogene 191

H

Hadeda *see* Ibis
Halcyon albiventris **122**
Halleria elliptica 25
Halleria species 15, 36, 165, 168, 169, 170, 171, 172, 173
Hamerkop 21, *41*, 44, *84*, **91**
hanging feeders 29-30, 33
Harvester Termite 77, *78*
Hawk, Bat 51
hawks 87
Helichrysum species 188
Heron, Grey 14, *80-1*
herons 44, 55, 86
Hibiscus species 172
high-traffic area 19-20
Hirundo abyssinica **132**
Hirundo albigularis 191
Hirundo cucullata **131**
Hirundo fuligula **133**
Hirundo rustica **130**
Hirundo semirufa 191
Hirundo smithii 191
Honeyguide, Lesser 191

Hook-thorn 24
Hoopoe 51, **123**
Hornbill, Trumpeter 191
hornbills 53

I

Ibis, Hadeda *14*, 55, *70-1*, 77, *79*, **92**
Iboza riparia 173
identification of birds 89
incubation period 89
Indicator minor 191
indigenous plants
  for feeding birds 35
  growing 68-9
  managing 63-7
  myths about 62-3
  when to plant 67-8
  where to find 68
Inkberry 104
insectivorous birds 19, 28, 31, 32, 34, 87

J

jacanas 44
Jacket Plum 108
Jynx ruficollis **129**

K

Karee *74*
Kei Apple 36, 52
kestrels 83
Kiggelaria africana *74*, *112*, 113
Kingfisher
  Brownhooded **122**
  Malachite *45*, *88*, 191
  Pied *40*, **121**
kingfishers 21, 44, 84
Kite, Blackshouldered *82*, *87*, 88
Kniphofia praecox 25
Kniphofia species 25, *28*, 165, 166

L

ladybirds 74, *75*, *77*
Lamprotornis nitens *60-1*, **163**
Laniarius ferrugineus *12*, **155**
Lanius collaris 50, *59*, **154**
Leonotis leonurus 36, 166
Leucospermum species 67
Lily, Blue Water *46*
  water 44
logs, *see also* feeding log
  for exclusion area 17-18, 83
  for water features *41*, 85
Lourie
  Grey 51, **110**
  Purplecrested 51, **109**
louries 19
low-traffic area 20-1
Lybius leucomelas 191
Lybius torquatus 52, **125**

M

Malaconotus blanchoti **159**
Mannikin, Bronze **184**, 185
Mantis Mixture **76**
Marigolds 78
Martin, Rock **133**
mealworms 31, **34**
Melaenornis pammelaina 191
Mesembryanthemaceae family 15

Metalasia muricata 173
moles 78-9
Motacilla aguimp 191
Motacilla capensis **153**
Mousebird
  Redfaced **120**
  Speckled **119**, 120
  Whitebacked 191
mousebirds 19, 31, 33
mulch layer 17, 34, 92, 97, *98*, 99, 111, 140, 142, 155, 157
Muscicapa adusta 191
Muscicapa caerulescens 191
Muscicapa striata 191
Myna, Indian 50, **161**
Myrsine africana 25

N

Natal Mahogany 36
Natal Plum 15, 24, 25, 51, 52, 110
natural feeders **30**
nectar-eating birds 33, 34, 36
Nectarinia afra **168**
Nectarinia amethystina 28, **171**
Nectarinia chalybea *62*, **167**
Nectarinia famosa **166**
Nectarinia mariquensis 191
Nectarinia olivacea 191
Nectarinia senegalensis **170**
Nectarinia talatala **169**
Neddicky 191
neighbours, enlisting help of 13-14, 24
nest-box 24-5, 54, 115, 125, 128, 143, 163, *174*, 176
  Barn Owl 57
  building a 56-7
  open 54, 57, *93*
nesting logs 25, 53-4, 124-9, 138, *143*, 145, 146, 160-3
  making your own **53**
nesting sites
  artificial 52-7, 123
  extraordinary 54-5
  ground-floor 30, 139, 189
  in small gardens 24-5
  materials for **55**, **58**
  natural 50-2
nestlings 31, 58-9
  rehabilitation of **59**
Nightjar
  Fierynecked 191
  Freckled 191
nightwatching **37**, 101, 116, 118, 130, 131, 132, 133, 134
Numida meleagris 18, **99**
Num-num 36
Nymphaea capensis 46

O

oak trees 188
Olea europaea
  subsp. *africana* 104
Olea species 19
Onychognathus morio *35*, **164**
open area 142
  in urban gardens 14-15
  on smallholdings 82-3
  plants for **14**
Orange Thorn 15
Oreochromis mossambicus 86

Oriole, Blackheaded 51, **135**
Oriolus larvatus 51, **135**
Osteospermum species 188
Owl
  Barn 34, **56**, *72*, 76, *87*, **115**
    nest-box for **57**, *115*
  Pearlspotted 88, 134
  Spotted Eagle 18, 37, 52, 58, *59*, **116**
    nest-box for **54**
owls 37, 54, 76, 87

P

Pachnoda sinuata 17
palm trees 118, 180
Panicum maximum 14, 52, 85
Papegaaiduif see Green Pigeon
Pappea capensis 108
parrot pigeon *see* Green Pigeon
Parthenocissus quinquefolia 173
Parus niger 191
Passer domesticus 50, 54, 58, **174**
Passer griseus **176**
Passer melanurus 54, **175**
pest management, *see also* pests
  by biological control 73
  integrated 73-4, 87
  in vegetable garden 75
  of common pests 77-9
  on smallholdings 87
  with chemicals 72-3, 87
pesticides 72-3
pests 74-7 *see also* pest management
  natural control of 76, 77
Phoeniculus purpureus 53, **124**
Phragmites Reed 46, *47*, 178
Phylloscopus trochilus **148**
Piet-my-vrou see Redchested Cuckoo
Pigeon
  Feral **102**, 103
  Green *28*, **108**
  Rameron **104**
  Rock 31, **103**
pigeons 31
Pigeonwood 104
Pin Oak 51, 180
pine trees 188
plant propagation
  from cuttings 69
  from seeds 68-9
Ploceus capensis 21, *45*, 46, **179**
Ploceus cucullatus **10-11**, **178**
Ploceus ocularis 191
Ploceus velatus *45*, **50**, **180**
Ploceus xanthops 24, **181**
Plover, Crowned 52, *79*, **100**
plovers 52, 79, 89
Plumbago auriculata 17, 24, 65, 66, 68, 168
Podocarpus species 104
Pogoniulus chrysoconus **126**
Polyboroides typus 191
pond 20, 24, *41*, 43, *see also* water feature
  an ecologically balanced **44**
  cleaning the 47
  constructing a cement 43
  fibre-crete **43**
  liners for 42-3

207

INDEX

plants and animals for 44
ready-made 42
Populus canescens 94, 95
praying mantises 74, 77
predator perches **87**
Prinia
  Blackchested 191
  Tawnyflanked **150**
Prinia flavicans 191
Prinia subflava **150**
Promerops cafer **165**
Protea repens **189**
proteas 165, 166, 168
pruning, indigenous plants 65-6
Puffback **156**
Puzzle Bush 36, 62, 66
Pycnonotus barbatus 19, 51, **138**
Pycnonotus capensis **137**
Pycnonotus nigricans 191

R

rats *see* rodents
Red-hot Poker *25*, *28*, 165, 166
Red Spider Mite *78*
Red Syringa 68
reeds 44, 177, 182
rehabilitating birds 59
rescue platforms **85**
Rhamnus prinoides 36
Rhoicissus tomentosa 105
Rhus crenata 25, 35
Rhus lancea 74
Rhus pendulina 19, 35
Rhus species 35, 165
River Bushwillow 85
Robin
  Cape *52*, 111, **147**
  Heuglin's 32, **145**, 147
  Natal **146**
  Whitethroated 191
robins 15, 29, 32, 34, 52, 54, 57
rodent-eating birds 87
rodenticides 72, 76
rodents 76, 87
roses *75*, 79

S

Sagewood 83
Salix babylonica 90
sand bath **13**, 97, 98
sand patch *see* sand bath
Sarothrura elegans 191
scale insect 74
Schinus terebinthifolius 137
Schotia species 168
Scopus umbretta 21, *41*, 44, *84*, **91**
seed bite test **69**
seed-eating birds 14, 15, 83, 87
  food for **31, 32**
seed-feeders *176*, 182, 185, 187
Senecio species 188
Senecio tamoides 25
Serinus canicollis **188**
Serinus gularis **189**
Serinus mozambicus **187**
Shrike
  Fiscal 50, *59*, **154**, 151, 155
  Greyheaded Bush **159**
  Orangebreasted Bush **158**
shrikes 19, 34, 36, 87

shrubs, *see also* indigenous plants
  for exclusion area 15-17, 83
  for feeding birds 36-7
  for nesting 52
  for open area 16
  for small gardens 24
Sigelus silens **151**
Silver Terminalia 68
Skiet-my-nou see Redchested Cuckoo
small gardens 24-5
  plants for **25**
smallholdings, birds on 81-7
snails 77
Solanum mauritianum 104, 109, 177
Spanish Reed 46
Sparrow
  Cape 54, 113, **175**, 176, 177
  Greyheaded **176**
  House 50, 54, 58, **174**, 175, 176
Sparrowhawk
  Black 51
  Little 34, **95**
  Ovambo *81*, **94**
sparrows 29, 31, 40, 52, 54
Spekvreter see Familiar Chat
Spermestes cucullatus **184**
Spookvoël see Greyheaded Bush Shrike
Starling
  European **160**
  Glossy *60-1*, **163**
  Greater Blue-eared 163
  Plumcoloured *29*, **162**
  Redwinged *35*, **164**
starlings 29, 51, 53
Strelitzia species *120*, *167*, 171
Strelitzia reginae 36
Streptopelia capicola 40, **106**
Streptopelia semitorquata **105**
Streptopelia senegalensis 50, **107**
Sturnus vulgaris **160**
sugar water 34, 165, 166, 167, 168, 169, 170, 171, 173
Sugarbird, Cape 34, **165**
summer-rainfall region 67
Sunbird
  Black *28*, **171**
  Collared **172**
  Greater Doublecollared 167, **168**
  Lesser Doublecollared *62*, **167**, 168
  Malachite **166**
  Marico 191
  Olive 191
  Scarletchested **170**
  Whitebellied **169**
sunbirds 34, 36, 58
Swallow
  European **130**
  Greater Striped **131**, 132
  Lesser Striped 131, **132**, 144
  Redbreasted 191
  Whitethroated 191
  Wiretailed 191
swallows 58
Sweet Thorn 24, 63
Swift
  Little **117**

Palm **118**
  Whiterumped 191
swifts 37
Sylvia borin 191
Syzygium cordatum 108, 109
Syzygium species 96

T

Tasselberry 173
Tauraco porphyreolophus 51, **109**
Tecomaria capensis 24, 25, 36, 65, 165, 167, 189
Telophorus sulfureopectus **158**
Telophorus zeylonus 48-9, **157**
Terminalia sericea 68
termites *34*, 77-8, *129*
Terpsiphone viridis 51, **152**
Thamnolaea cinnamomeiventris **144**
Thatch Reed 21
thorn trees 15, 21, 25, *51*, 63, 106, 110, 175
Thrush
  Groundscraper **142**
  Kurrichane **140**, 141
  Olive 15, 51, **141**
thrushes 19, 29, 34, 111
Tilapia
  Banded **44**, 47,86
  Mozambique 86
Tilapia sparrmanii **44**, 86
Tit, Southern Black 191
Trachyphonus vaillantii **127**
Transvaal Saffronwood 108
trees, *see also* indigenous plants
  for canopy habitat 18, 19-21, 84
  for exclusion area 15-17, 83
tree topiary 66
Trema orientalis 104
Treron calva *28*, **108**
Trichilia emetica 36
Tulbaghia species 78
Turdus libonyana **140**
Turdus litsitsirupa **142**
Turdus olivaceus 15, 51, **141**
Turtur chalcospilos 191
Tyto alba 34, 56, 57, *87*, **115**

U

Upupa epops 51, **123**
Uraeginthus angolensis 191
Ursinia species 188

V

Vanellus coronatus 52, *79*, **100**
vegetable garden 37, 75-6
veld management 86
Vidua funerea **186**
Vidua macroura **185**
Virginia Creeper 173
Vygie plants 15

W

Wachendorfia thyrsiflora 21, 46
Wagtail
  African Pied 191
  Cape 111, 113, **153**
wagtails 52, 72
Warbler
  European Marsh 191
  Garden 191

Greybacked Bleating 191
  Willow **148**
warblers 19
wasps 77
Water Berry 108, 109
water feature 47, 95, 105, 106, 109, 116, *117*, *121*, *130*, 132, *133*, 138, 150, 152, 153, 173, *184*, 187
  building a 41-3
  for small gardens 24
  modifying an existing 41
  sites for 40
Watsonia species 166
Waxbill
  Blue 191
  Common **183**, 185
waxbills 184
Weaver
  Cape *21*, *41*, *45*, 46, **179**
  Golden *24*, **181**
  Masked *45*, *50*, 178, **180**
  Spectacled 191
  Spottedbacked *10-11*, **178**
  Thickbilled *28*, *45*, **177**
weavers 15, 31, 51, 58, 113, 184
Weeping Bottlebrush 169
Weeping Willow 90
wetland area *181*, *182*
  creating a 45-6
  in urban gardens 21, 23, 40
  on smallholdings *84*, 84-6
  plants for 20, **46**
  value of **45**, *181*
White Bristle Bush 173
White-eye, Cape 36, *62*, **173**
white-eyes 33
White Karee 19, 35
White Stinkwood 66, 85, 104, 148, 177
Whydah, Pintailed 183, 184, **185**
Widowfinch, Black **186**
Wild Dagga 36, 166
Wild Garlic 78
Wild Iris *46*
Wild Olive 104
Wild Peach 74, *112*, 113
Wild Pomegranate 172
willows 105
winter-rainfall region 64, 67-8
  plants for **64**
woodborers *156*
Woodhoopoe, Redbilled 53, **124**
Woodpecker
  Cardinal **128**
  Goldentailed 191
woodpeckers 34, 51, 53
woolly plant lice 76
Wryneck, Redthroated **129**
wrynecks 34

X

Xeromphis species 173

Y

Yellowwoods 104

Z

Ziziphus mucronata 108
Zosterops pallidus 36, *62*, **173**